KANSAS GOVERNORS

KANSAS GOVERNORS

HOMER E. SOCOLOFSKY

UNIVERSITY PRESS OF KANSAS

All photographs courtesy of the Kansas State Historical Society except the following: photograph on p. 49, courtesy of the Historical Society of Pennsylvania; photograph on p. 63, courtesy of the National Archives; photograph on p. 69, courtesy of the National Archives; photograph on p. 112, from *Statue of George Washington Glick: U.S. 63rd Cong., 2d Sess., 1913–14* (Washington, D.C.: Government Printing Office, 1915).

Published by the University Press of Kansas (Lawrence, Kansas 66045), which was organized by the Kansas Board of Regents and is operated and funded by Emporia State University, Fort Hays State University, Kansas State University, Pittsburg State University, the University of Kansas, and Wichita State University

Library of Congress Cataloging-in-Publication Data

Socolofsky, Homer Edward, 1922–
    Kansas governors / Homer E. Socolofsky.
      p. cm.
    Includes bibliographical references.
    ISBN 0-7006-0421-9 (alk. paper)
      1. Kansas—Governors—Biography.   2. Kansas—Politics and
government.   I. Title.
F680.S63   1990
978.1′00992 – dc20
    [B]   89-29123
                                                            CIP

Printed in the United States of America
10 9 8 7 6 5 4 3 2 1

The paper used in this publication meets the minimum requirements of the American National Standard for Permanence of Paper for Printed Library Materials Z39.48-1984.

CONTENTS

List of Maps, Tables, and Figures   ix

Preface   xi

Governors and Acting Governors of Kansas: Who, When, and Where?   1

Biographical Sketches of the Governors and Acting Governors of the Territory of Kansas   31

    Andrew Horatio Reeder   33

    Daniel Woodson   40

    Wilson Shannon   43

    John White Geary   49

    Frederick Perry Stanton   55

    Robert John Walker   59

    James William Denver   65

    Hugh Sleight Walsh   70

    Samuel Medary   72

    George Monroe Beebe   75

Biographical Sketches of the Governors of the State of Kansas   79

    Charles Robinson   81

    Thomas Carney   86

    Samuel Johnson Crawford   89

    Nehemiah Green   94

    James Madison Harvey   96

    Thomas Andrew Osborn   99

    George Tobey Anthony   102

    John Pierce St. John   105

    George Washington Glick   109

John Alexander Martin   113

Lyman Underwood Humphrey   116

Lorenzo Dow Lewelling   119

Edmund Needham Morrill   123

John Whitnah Leedy   126

William Eugene Stanley   130

Willis Joshua Bailey   133

Edward Wallis Hoch   136

Walter Roscoe Stubbs   139

George Hartshorn Hodges   142

Arthur Capper   146

Henry Justin Allen   152

Jonathan McMillan Davis   156

Benjamin Sanford Paulen   158

Clyde Martin Reed   162

Harry Hines Woodring   165

Alfred Mossman Landon   172

Walter Augustus Huxman   180

Payne Harry Ratner   183

Andrew Frank Schoeppel   186

Frank Carlson   190

Frank Leslie Hagaman   194

Edward F. Arn   196

Frederick Lee Hall   200

John Berridge McCuish   204

George Docking   206

John Anderson, Jr. 209

William Henry Avery 212

Robert Blackwell Docking 215

Robert Frederick Bennett 219

John William Carlin 224

John Michael Hayden 227

Notes 231

Bibliography 235

Index 243

MAPS, TABLES, AND FIGURES

MAPS

1 Birthplaces of Kansas Territorial Governors and Acting Governors 3

2 Residences of Kansas Territorial Governors and Acting Governors When Appointed 4

3 Birthplaces of Governors of the State of Kansas 10

4 Residences of Governors of the State of Kansas When Elected 27

5 The Territory of Kansas 31

6 The State of Kansas 79

TABLES

1 Birthplaces of Territorial Kansas Population (1860) 4

2 Background of Kansas Territorial Governors and Acting Governors 6

3 Birthplaces of Population for the State of Kansas 11

4 Kansas Gubernatorial Elections 16

5 Background of Governors of the State of Kansas 24

FIGURES

1 Republican Percentage of the Gubernatorial Vote, 1859–1986 13

PREFACE

Kansas history has been an abiding interest for me and enters into almost all of my research. The integration of the political history of Kansas, through accounts of the governors, along with visual examples, has been a primary goal of this work. Designed as a basic reference tool for the state's history, it will be useful to all those interested in that subject. A strong sense of the flow of history pervades the general essays about territorial governors and state governors. These essays are followed by the biographical sketches of the ten men who served as governor or acting governor of the Territory of Kansas and the forty-one governors of the state of Kansas, complete with illustrations and autographs. Biographical sketches for each governor include genealogical data, together with brief materials on their pre- and post-gubernatorial lives. Voting data are provided, but most space is devoted to the governor's term in office. For a brief time, each of these fifty-one men served in a crucial executive position in the first one-and-one-third centuries that Kansas had identifiable political boundaries.

Work on this book began more than a decade ago when I did all but two of the Kansas governors for the four-volume *Biographical Directory of the Governors of the United States, 1789–1978*, edited by Robert Sobel and John Raimo (Westport, Conn., 1978). Later governors were added in an extension of this work, edited by John Raimo and published in 1984. In the same year *Biographical Directory of American Territorial Governors*, edited by Thomas A. McMullin and David Walker (Westport, Conn., 1984), did for territorial governors, but not acting governors, what had been done earlier for state governors. This book brings together in a single volume a far more complete treatment of both territorial and state governors as well as acting governors.

The research undertaken in this book required the same steps employed in other genealogical inquiries. Some of the family data needed for a complete record of the Kansas governors could be found only by examination of original census records or through family members. Since some governors have shielded their private lives from public view, historical inquiries necessarily have taken many forms. Publications such as all editions of the *Dictionary of American Biography*, the *National Cyclopedia of American Biography*, and *Who's Who in America* help provide crucial data. All Kansas history publications were also searched for contributions to this work.

The published accounts of the ten men who served as either governor or acting governor of the Territory of Kansas are fairly complete. Perhaps this is not surprising, since the territorial period continues to fascinate Kansans, and to many non-Kansans the "interesting" history of the area ends with attainment of statehood. Robert John Walker and James William Denver have been treated in full-scale biographies, and John White Geary's administration was promptly and fully reported by his private secretary. All territorial governors had much published about their particular administration in the earliest volumes of the *Kansas State Historical Collections*. As might be expected, the acting governors were less well-known, and their accounts were not as complete. Crucial data for various territorial governors or acting governors were provided by William Elsey Connelley in his *Kansas Territorial Governors* (Topeka, 1900).

The public life of governors of the state of Kansas has been examined in their official papers, through inaugural speeches and official reports to the legislature, in contemporary media, in historical articles, in masters' theses and doctoral dissertations, and in book-length published biographies. Only five Kansas governors—Charles Robinson, Samuel Johnson Crawford, Arthur Capper, Harry Hines Woodring, and Alfred Mossman Landon—have been the subject of full-scale biographies. Late in life Robinson and Crawford also prepared books about their own public career. Fifteen other governors—James Madison Harvey, George Tobey Anthony, John Pierce St. John, George Washington Glick, Lorenzo Dow Lewelling, John Whitnah Leedy, Edward Wallis Hoch, Walter Roscoe Stubbs, George Hartshorn Hodges, Jonathan McMillan Davis, Clyde Martin Reed, Walter Augustus Huxman, Andrew Frank Schoeppel, Frank Carlson, and Frederick Lee Hall—have had some portion or all of their careers spotlighted in either a master's thesis or a doctoral dissertation, and other such studies have examined a longer era that includes the roles of particular governors. The careers of other governors have been touched by publications in political science, such as

James W. Drury, *The Government of Kansas* (Lawrence, 1980); Marvin
Harder and Carolyn Rampey, *The Kansas Legislature: Procedures, Personalities and Problems* (Lawrence, 1972); *Selected Papers of Governor Robert F. Bennett: A Study in Good Government and "Civics Book" Politics*,
compiled and edited by H. Edward Flentje (Wichita, 1979); and
Marvin Harder, *Electoral Politics in Kansas: A Historical Perspective* (Topeka, 1981).

Voting data can be confusing. Statistics can be found in *American
Governors and Gubernatorial Elections, 1775–1978*, compiled by Roy R.
Glashan (Westport, Conn., 1979). However, if there is disagreement
about electoral statistics for Kansas governors, a more reliable source
is the official figures provided by the secretary of state and published
in convenient form as *Kansas Votes: Gubernatorial Elections, 1859–1956*,
compiled by Clarence J. Hein and Charles A. Sullivant (Lawrence,
1958); in *Kansas Votes: National and General Elections, 1956–1964* (Lawrence, 1965), compiled by Herman D. Lujan; and in the *Kansas Statistical Abstract*, edited by Thelma Helyar (Lawrence, various years).

Unless identified otherwise, photographs were obtained from the
collection of the Kansas State Historical Society, the source of all but
five of the pictures included. The oval-shaped official portraits of
Kansas governors (similar to those displayed in the outer office of the
governor in the Capitol—the frames are made in state prisons) are
from *Kansas!* magazine from Historical Society photos. Most of the
autographs come from "Autographs of the Governors of Kansas," a
collection presented to the Kansas State Historical Society in 1951 by
Edward Bumgardner of Lawrence, which includes signatures of all
but one of the territorial governors and acting governors. Other autographs come from official records on file at the Historical Society.

Research for this book has been supported by Kansas State University with a number of Faculty Research Grants, a Faculty Development Grant, and a College of Arts and Sciences award. In addition to
the resources of Farrell Library, Kansas State University, searches
have been made in the library, the archives, and the manuscript collection of the Kansas Research Center, Topeka; in the Watson Library, University of Kansas; the Newberry Library, Chicago; and the
Library of Congress, Washington, D.C. Research of this magnitude
has incurred many obligations. Credit must be extended to all those

who helped, but special thanks go to my wife, Penny, and son, Rob, who critiqued the manuscript; my daughter, Jennifer Sims, who did the maps; and three of the staff of the Kansas State Historical Society, Terry Harmon, Nancy Sherbert, and Bob Knecht.

Homer E. Socolofsky
Manhattan, Kansas

GOVERNORS AND ACTING GOVERNORS OF KANSAS

•—————————————————————•

WHO, WHEN, AND WHERE?

GOVERNORS AND ACTING GOVERNORS
OF THE TERRITORY OF KANSAS

All Kansas territorial governors and secretaries were appointed by one
of two presidents, Franklin Pierce (1853–57) and James Buchanan
(1857–61). Pierce, from New Hampshire, and Buchanan, from Pennsylvania, were both Democrats, so as one might expect each of the
ten men appointed to these posts in territorial Kansas were members
of that party. These appointees, at least initially, were supporters of
the objective of the national Democratic party to make Kansas a slave
state.[1]

   In the mid-nineteenth century territorial governors were only a
little less important than cabinet members. The job provided an annual salary of $4,000 (cabinet members got $5,000) in addition to
the opportunities to profit from new economic developments inherent in the settlement phase of any new area. Territorial secretaries
were paid $2,000 per year and, among other official duties, served as
acting governors during the absence of the governor from the territory. Either of these salaries—well above the average income for a federal employee—was attractive in the mid-nineteenth century.

   Neither the territorial governor nor the territorial secretary was under any obligation to the voters in the territory; their commitment
was to the president who had appointed them. Consequently, territorial governments were less responsive to voter opinion than were
state governments. Voters did have the opportunity to elect members of the territorial legislature, but none of the executives or judges
in the territory were elected.

   Nominally, territorial appointments were made for four years, but
the lengthiest tenure of any of the ten Kansas territorial governors or
acting governors was that of the last governor, Samuel Medary. Medary served only half that long (two years), Andrew Reeder slightly
more than thirteen months, Wilson Shannon eleven months, and
James William Denver, as both acting governor and governor, a com-

I

bined eight and one-half months. The terms of the others were even shorter. The secretaries served as acting governors for a total of more than five hundred days. Counting each change, there were twenty-six executive terms of governors and acting governors in the approximately six years and eight months of Kansas' existence as a territory.

The brevity of service for each of the territorial governors and secretaries suggests a lack of political competence, but the overall experience of these men proves otherwise. Except for Reeder and Daniel Woodson—the first governor and first secretary—and Hugh Sleight Walsh—the next to last secretary—all appointees had prior experience in a variety of elective legislative or executive positions. Short tenure was due to other factors, many of them resulting from the problems inherent in the national administration's efforts to make Kansas a slave state.

None of the Kansas territorial governors or acting governors was born any farther west than Ohio. Four were born in Pennsylvania, three in Virginia, two in New York, and one in the Ohio Territory. As might be expected for the nineteenth century, these men came from large families, in which the father was generally a farmer and the mother did not work outside the home. Also like other Americans in this era, most had no religious preference. Of those who did, Wilson Shannon was a Catholic, and Frederick Stanton, a Baptist; Daniel Woodson had a Baptist preference, and James Denver a Presbyterian, but neither was a church member. In keeping with nationwide occupational patterns for governors, six of the ten Kansas territorial governors and secretaries had been trained as lawyers, although one was serving as an editor when he received his appointment. Two others came into their Kansas position from careers in journalism; there were also one civil engineer and one merchant. Well educated for their era, five had graduated from college and another had attended college. Only two governors, John White Geary and James Denver, had prior military service; both served in the Mexican War.

Place of residence at the time these men were appointed to their Kansas positions was fairly diverse. Two each came from Pennsylvania, Ohio, and Kansas territory, and one each was living in Tennessee, Virginia, Washington, D.C., and California. All of the governors and secretaries were married, but, perhaps recognizing the temporary na-

Map 1. Birthplaces of Kansas Territorial Governors and Acting Governors

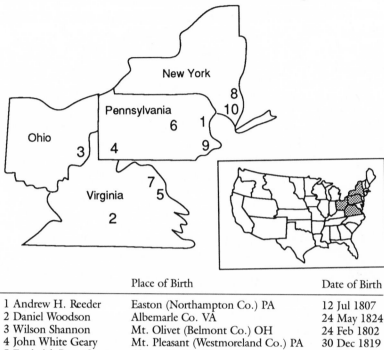

	Place of Birth	Date of Birth
1 Andrew H. Reeder	Easton (Northampton Co.) PA	12 Jul 1807
2 Daniel Woodson	Albemarle Co. VA	24 May 1824
3 Wilson Shannon	Mt. Olivet (Belmont Co.) OH	24 Feb 1802
4 John White Geary	Mt. Pleasant (Westmoreland Co.) PA	30 Dec 1819
5 Frederick Perry Stanton	Alexandria (Fairfax Co.) VA	22 Dec 1814
6 Robert John Walker	Northumberland (Northumberland Co.) PA	19 Jul 1801
7 James William Denver	Winchester (Frederick Co.) VA	23 Oct 1817
8 Hugh Sleight Walsh	Newburgh (Orange Co.) NY	10 Nov 1810
9 Samuel Medary	Montgomery Square (Montgomery Co.) PA	25 Feb 1801
10 George Monroe Beebe	New Vernon (Westchester Co.) NY	28 Oct 1836

ture of their appointments, few of them moved their families to Kansas territory. The families left behind ranged in size from three children to twelve, with an average of eight. As the official photographs capture, styles in personal appearance did differ in the territorial days; for example, only four of the governors—Shannon, Robert John Walker, Denver, and Walsh—were clean shaven, while the others retained their facial hair, even to full beards. Not revealed in the photographs is the overall physique of the territorial governors, which was as varied as today. The two extremes were represented by Walker,

Table 1. Birthplaces of Territorial Kansas Population (1860)

Place	Number	Percentage
Ohio	11,617	10.8
Missouri	11,356	10.6
Kansas	10,997	10.3
Indiana	9,945	9.3
Illinois	9,367	8.7
Kentucky	6,556	6.1
Pennsylvania	6,463	6.0
New York	6,331	5.9
Iowa	4,008	3.7
New England	4,208	3.9
All other free states	3,186	3.0
All other slave states	9,437	8.8
All foreign-born	12,690	11.8

Compiled from *People of Kansas: A Demographic and Sociological Study*, Carrol D. Clark and Roy L. Roberts (Topeka: Kansas State Planning Board, 1936), pp. 50–51, 208. The percentages are based on a territorial population of 107,206.

Map 2. Residences of Kansas Territorial Governors and Acting Governors When Appointed

1 Andrew H. Reeder
2 Daniel Woodson
3 Wilson Shannon
4 John White Geary
5 Frederick Perry Stanton
6 Robert John Walker
7 James William Denver
8 Hugh Sleight Walsh
9 Samuel Medary
10 George Monroe Beebe

who was five feet two inches and weighed only one hundred pounds, and Denver, who was six feet five and one-half inches tall and very heavy.

The average age for those assuming the governor's office was around forty-eight at the time of appointment, whereas the secretaries were much younger, averaging slightly over thirty-four. The average age for all ten was around forty-two years six months. In descending order, the governors' ages reveal Medary as the oldest, at age fifty-seven; Shannon and Walker in their fifties; Denver and Reeder in their forties; and Geary as the youngest, at thirty-six. Among the territorial secretaries, Walsh, at age forty-six, was the oldest; Woodson and Stanton were in their thirties; and George Monroe Beebe was only twenty-four when he became a short-term secretary.

Perhaps best prepared to assume the position of governor of territorial Kansas was Robert J. Walker, whose service included ten years as United States senator from Mississippi and four years as secretary of the treasury under Pres. James Polk. However, even he was driven by the rigors of the job to extreme behavior; frustrated by the position and the treatment he had received at the hands of the president and his cabinet in the closing days of his Kansas tenure, Walker challenged the United States attorney general to a duel, to which the attorney general declined. Walker's successor also resorted to dueling, although not while in office. James W. Denver, who had wide experience in appointive and elective positions in California and Washington, D.C., accepted a challenge to a duel while in California. Despite a bloodless exchange of fire on the first round, the challenger insisted on a second, and Denver killed him with his next shot.

The national Republican party came into being, in part, because of the passage of the Kansas-Nebraska Act, which created the territories of Kansas and Nebraska. Three of the ten Kansas territorial governors and secretaries—Reeder, Geary, and Stanton—defected to the Republican party in their post-Kansas years. Reeder actively campaigned in 1856 for John C. Fremont, the first Republican candidate for president, and he was a delegate to the Republican National Convention in 1860. Geary went on to serve for two terms as Republican governor of Pennsylvania, and Stanton, having previously served ten years

Table 2. Background of Kansas Territorial Governors and Acting Governors

Name	Dates of Service	Residence	Father's Occupation	Occupation	Number of Siblings	Number of Children	College Attendance	Veteran	Elective Office	Member of Congress	Other Federal Job	Age at Appointment	Age at Death	Church Membership*
1 Andrew H. Reeder (D)	7 Oct 1854–16 Aug 1855 (fired)	PA	farmer	law	–	8						47	56	–
2 Daniel Woodson (D)	17 Apr 1855–16 Apr 1857 (removed)	VA	–	printer	–	6					X	31	70	(Bapt.)
3 Wilson Shannon (D)	7 Sep 1855–18 Aug 1856 (fired)	OH	farmer	editor	8	8	Grad.		X	X	X	53	75	Cath.
4 John White Geary (D)	9 Sep 1856–20 Mar 1857 (fired)	PA	teacher & iron master	law & civ. eng.	4	3	Grad.	X	X			36	53	–
5 Frederick Perry Stanton (D)	15 Apr 1856–21 Dec 1857 (fired)	TN	bricklayer	law	–	6	Grad.		X	X	X	42	79	Bapt.
6 Robert John Walker (D)	27 May–16 Nov 1857 (resigned)	DC	law	law	7	8	Grad.		X	X	X	55	68	–
7 James William Denver (D)	acting 21 Dec 1857–12 May 1858, gov. 12 May 1858–10 Oct 1858 (resigned)	CA	farmer	law	10	4	Grad.	X	X	X	X	50	74	(Pres.)
8 Hugh Sleight Walsh (D)	3 Jul 1858–16 Jun 1860 (fired)	KT†	–	business	–	6			X			47	66	–
9 Samuel Medary (D)	18 Dec 1859–17 Dec 1860 (resigned)	OH	farmer	editor	–	12			X	X	X	57	63	–
10 George Monroe Beebe (D)	11 Sep 1860–9 Feb 1861 (job ended)	KT†	–	law	–	5	Grad.		X			24	90	–

*Parentheses indicate preference only   †KT = Kansas territory

in Congress as a Tennessee Democrat, became an ardent Republican after his term as secretary of Kansas territory.

Five of the ten governors and acting governors took up residence in Kansas following their removal from office, but two—Reeder and Stanton—moved elsewhere after about one year. Woodson, Shannon, and Walsh, however, lived the remainder of their lives in Kansas. Although George Beebe, the last acting governor, survived until 1924 when he died at age ninety, the average life span of all ten men was sixty-nine and a half.

The territorial period for Kansas was dominated by factional politics and violence. About fifty Kansans died violently, under circumstances that had political overtones. Nationally, the territory's identity was "Bleeding Kansas." Kansas was not an exception to the stereotype of an area under settlement; however, the nature of the political competition created an exaggerated image of unrest and violence in Kansas territory and the inability of the national administration to handle territorial affairs. "In each western territory the early years of organization were characterized by disruptive, confused, intensely combative, and highly personal politics that can best be described by the term *chaotic factionalism*."[2] The two states which came into existence just before Kansas, Oregon and Minnesota, were like Kansas in that one party dominated the early years of statehood, partly because of the conditions of the territorial period.[3]

GOVERNORS OF THE STATE OF KANSAS

A governor of Kansas, like the president of the United States, is the chief executive of his respective area. Certainly a Kansas governor has far less authority than a president, but on a lesser scale a Kansas governor occupies a position in the state's history analogous to that of a president in the nation's history. He serves as chief of his political party, as ceremonial head of the state, and as commander in chief of state troops.

Forty-one men served as governor of Kansas during the state's first 128 years. The Kansas constitution, silent on the qualifications of the state's chief executive official, provides only for a governor "chosen by the electors of the state." The sole restriction—that persons holding at the same time a seat in "congress, or officer of the state or of the United States" are ineligible—was removed in 1972. However, by their votes, Kansans have provided an informal profile of their governor: They have consistently elected male, white, native-born Americans of a dominant northwestern European stock, solidly middle-class and Protestant. There is no discrimination against foreign-born or alien persons in the formal qualifications for the office—or against women. However, few women have been candidates in Kansas, and those that have were put forward by minor parties. In fact, nationally, among more than twenty-five hundred state governors through over two hundred years, only nine women have become governor of a state.[4]

"Bleeding Kansas" gained notoriety in national annals during the territorial period, and those opposed to slavery eventually defeated the proslave faction. The antislave heritage of the state's founding leaders is apparent in their birthplaces. Only two of the state's governors through the nineteenth and early twentieth century were born in a slave state—James Madison Harvey in the West Virginia portion of Virginia and Edward Wallis Hoch in Kentucky—but even then they were from areas that remained loyal to the Union in the Civil War. Missouri, also a Union state, early contributed many people to the Kansas population but no governors until the twentieth century. Two of the last four governors were natives of that former slave state: Robert Blackwell Docking and Robert Frederick Bennett were both born in Kansas City, Missouri.

Thirteen of Kansas' forty-one governors were born in the state. Most governors born outside Kansas came from Illinois, Indiana, Ohio, and Pennsylvania; these states contributed eighteen of the first forty-one governors. These same Ohio River Valley states contributed heavily to Kansas population. Although there seems to be a strong identification of Kansas settlement days with New England, only two governors of Kansas, Charles Robinson and Edmund Needham Morrill, were born in New England, which closely approximates the direct contribution of these states to Kansas population numbers. Individual governors were born in New York, Wisconsin, and Iowa. No elected governor was born south or west of

Kansas, but a short-term governor who took over from the role of lieutenant governor was born in Colorado. The parents of most of the Kansas governors were also native-born Americans. Only four— Arthur Capper's father was born in England, Payne Harry Ratner's father was born in Russia, Andrew Frank Schoeppel's mother was born in Czechoslovakia, and George Docking's father was also born in England—are exceptions to the pattern.

The middle-class characteristics of Kansas governors are obvious. Nationally, almost two-thirds of all governors have been practicing lawyers. In Kansas more governors come from that profession than any other calling, but they total only thirteen. This is less than one in three—half the national proportion. Two governors trained in law were in other occupations when elected; one was a banker and another was an oilman. As occupations, farming, newspaper publishing, and banking were split evenly among twenty-one of the men who became governors. The political division among the farmers was Republican, four, Democrat, two, and Populist, one. The seven newspapermen who became governors were all Republicans. The first four bankers who served as governor were Republicans, and the last three were Democrats. The total number of merchants was three, evenly divided among the Republican, People's, and Democratic parties. Charles Robinson, usually referred to as "Doctor," was a non-practicing physician in Kansas and actually made his living as a farmer and real estate promoter. The profession of short-term governor Nehemiah Green was minister, even though he also farmed. There was one contractor who served as governor, Walter Roscoe Stubbs, and one independent insurance agent, John Michael Hayden.

More than half of the fathers of Kansas governors were farmers— twenty-three altogether. Eight fathers were small businessmen; two combined a ministerial career with another vocation; and two were bankers. Other occupations included a tanner, a full-time minister, an oil company superintendent, a clerk, and a railroad engineer. Three fathers were professionals, one each from law, medicine, and teaching. Most of the mothers of Kansas governors did not have employment outside the home.

Generally, Kansas governors have been men of above-average income or wealth. Some, such as Thomas Carney, Morrill, Capper, and

Map 3. Birthplaces of Governors of the State of Kansas

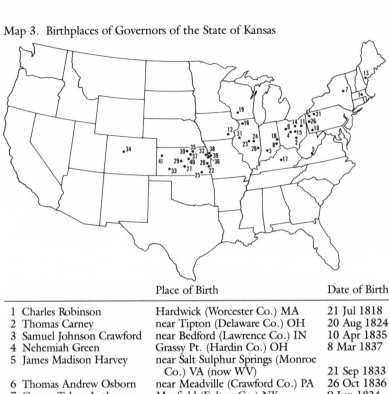

		Place of Birth	Date of Birth
1	Charles Robinson	Hardwick (Worcester Co.) MA	21 Jul 1818
2	Thomas Carney	near Tipton (Delaware Co.) OH	20 Aug 1824
3	Samuel Johnson Crawford	near Bedford (Lawrence Co.) IN	10 Apr 1835
4	Nehemiah Green	Grassy Pt. (Hardin Co.) OH	8 Mar 1837
5	James Madison Harvey	near Salt Sulphur Springs (Monroe Co.) VA (now WV)	21 Sep 1833
6	Thomas Andrew Osborn	near Meadville (Crawford Co.) PA	26 Oct 1836
7	George Tobey Anthony	Mayfield (Fulton Co.) NY	9 Jun 1824
8	John Pierce St. John	near Brookfield (Franklin Co.) IN	25 Feb 1833
9	George Washington Glick	near Greencastle (Fairfield Co.) OH	4 Jul 1827
10	John Alexander Martin	Brownsville (Fayette Co.) PA	10 Mar 1839
11	Lyman Underwood Humphrey	New Baltimore (Stark Co.) OH	25 Jul 1844
12	Lorenzo Dow Lewelling	Salem (Henry Co.) IA	21 Dec 1846
13	Edmund Needham Morrill	Westbrook (Cumberland Co.) ME	12 Feb 1834
14	John Whitnah Leedy	near Belleville (Richland Co.) OH	4 Mar 1849
15	William Eugene Stanley	(Knox Co.) OH	28 Dec 1844
16	Willis Joshua Bailey	near Mount Carroll (Carroll Co.) IL	12 Oct 1854
17	Edward Wallis Hoch	Danville (Boyle Co.) KY	17 Mar 1849
18	Walter Roscoe Stubbs	near Richmond (Wayne Co.) IN	7 Nov 1858
19	George Hartshorn Hodges	Orion (Richland Co.) WI	6 Feb 1866
20	Arthur Capper	Garnett (Anderson Co.) KS	14 Jul 1865
21	Henry Justin Allen	near Pittsfield (Warren Co.) PA	11 Sep 1868
22	Jonathan McMillan Davis	near Bronson (Bourbon Co.) KS	27 Apr 1871
23	Benjamin Sanford Paulen	near Clinton (DeWitt Co.) IL	14 Jul 1869
24	Clyde Martin Reed	near Champaign (Champaign Co.) IL	9 Oct 1871

(continued)

		Place of Birth	Date of Birth
25	Harry Hines Woodring	Elk City (Montgomery Co.) KS	31 May 1887
26	Alfred Mossman Landon	West Middlesex (Lawrence Co.) PA	9 Sep 1887
27	Walter Augustus Huxman	near Pretty Prairie (Reno Co.) KS	16 Feb 1887
28	Payne Harry Ratner	Casey (Clark Co.) IL	3 Oct 1896
29	Andrew Frank Schoeppel	near Claflin (Barton Co.) KS	23 Nov 1894
30	Frank Carlson	near Concordia (Cloud Co.) KS	23 Jan 1893
31	Frank Leslie Hagaman	Bushnell (McDonough Co.) IL	1 Jun 1894
32	Edward F. Arn	Kansas City (Wyandotte Co.) KS	19 May 1906
33	Frederick Lee Hall	Dodge City (Ford Co.) KS	24 Jul 1916
34	John Berridge McCuish	Leadville (Lake Co.) CO	22 Jun 1906
35	George Docking	Clay Center (Clay Co.) KS	23 Feb 1904
36	John Anderson, Jr.	near Olathe (Johnson Co.) KS	8 May 1917
37	William Henry Avery	near Wakefield (Clay Co.) KS	11 Aug 1911
38	Robert Blackwell Docking	Kansas City (Jackson Co.) MO	9 Oct 1925
39	Robert Frederick Bennett	Kansas City (Jackson Co.) MO	23 May 1927
40	John William Carlin	Salina (Saline Co.) KS	3 Aug 1940
41	John Michael Hayden	Colby (Thomas Co.) KS	15 Mar 1944

Henry Justin Allen, were regarded as wealthy. A noted exception was John Whitnah Leedy, Populist governor from 1897 to 1899, who lost his farm in the early 1890s. Leedy was the only governor to leave the state permanently and the only one to become a citizen of another country. An expatriate, he died in poverty in 1935.

Kansas governors have never sought the office because of its salary.

Table 3. Birthplaces of Population for the State of Kansas

Place	1890		1920	
	Number (in thousands)	Percentage	Number (in thousands)	Percentage
Kansas	487	34.0	968	55.0
Illinois	137	9.6	99	5.1
Ohio	116	8.0	54	3.0
Indiana	99	6.8	54	3.0
Missouri	84	5.8	139	7.9
Iowa	66	4.6	55	3.1
Pennsylvania	62	4.3	30	1.7
New York	40	2.8	16	.9
Virginia and West Virginia	23	1.6	14	.8
New England	17	1.2	6	.3
Foreign-born	147	10.3	111	6.3
All other states	250	17.2	229	13.0

Compiled from *People of Kansas: A Demographic and Sociological Study*, Carrol D. Clark and Roy L. Roberts (Topeka: Kansas State Planning Board, 1936), pp. 208–10.

In 1861 the annual salary of the Kansas governor was $2,000, half the amount paid by the federal government to a territorial governor. Subsequently this was raised to $3,000 in 1872; $5,000 in 1903; $8,000 in 1945; $10,000 in 1949; $15,000 in 1953; $20,000 in 1967; $45,000 in 1978; $56,000 in 1984; and $66,900 in 1987.[5] Perquisites of the office have increased even faster. The state budget, minimal at first, reached $1 million in 1869. It increased to $10 million by 1915; $100 million in 1948; $500 million in 1966; $1 billion in 1974; and, in the late 1980s, over $4 billion.

Samuel Crawford, taking office at age twenty-nine, was the youngest governor of Kansas, while Edmund Morrill, at sixty-one, was the oldest. Six governors were in their thirties when they took the oath of office, seventeen were in their forties, and sixteen in their fifties. Calculated by order of service, the first ten governors in the young state of Kansas averaged just over forty-one years of age, the next ten were close to fifty-one, the third group of ten were just under fifty, and the last eleven were just over forty-five. The average age for all Kansas governors is forty-seven years eight months at the time they entered office. Nationally, governors have been slightly older, just over forty-eight years of age.[6]

Educational attainments of Kansas governors have improved through the years, and governors have typically had more education than the general population. Of the first twenty governors, five graduated from college and seven others attended college. Of the last twenty-one governors, only one did not attend college; fifteen were college graduates. The string of such graduates elected as Kansas governor since 1932 is broken only by Frank Carlson, who attended a business college and took short courses for three years but did not earn a degree.

In the twentieth century, athletic ability has been honored more than in earlier times in Kansas. Most nineteenth-century Kansas governors were experienced horsemen, but that was on par with the times. More unusual were William Stanley, who was a noted archer, and George Hodges, who was a champion marksman with firearms. In the 1920s Andrew Schoeppel had an outstanding career on the University of Nebraska football team that defeated Notre Dame with its legendary "four horsemen." He received an honorable mention

Figure 1. Republican Percentage of the Gubernatorial Vote, 1859–1986

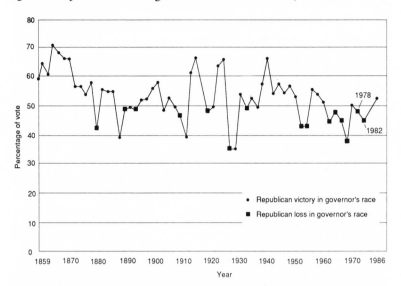

on one of Walter Camp's early All-American football teams, and later he had much experience as a sports official. George Docking was an avid tennis player who played in amateur competition for years and was a winner in city tournaments in Lawrence. On at least two occasions in the 1970s and 1980s, leading aspirants for the position of Kansas governor tried to use their statewide reputations as collegiate athletic stars as a springboard, but they were not elected.

Republican dominance is less apparent in the office of the Kansas governor than in either the state legislature or other statewide offices. In the nineteenth century, the Republican candidate for governor won all but three times: Glick, a Democrat, won in 1882, and Lewelling and Leedy, both Populists, won in 1892 and 1896, respectively. During the early years of statehood, there were many elections when the Democratic party did not field a candidate for governor under that party label, but there was always an opposition party facing the Republicans. In the twentieth century, Democratic party gains have paralleled growing urbanization in Kansas. Democratic candidates won in 1912, 1922, 1930, and 1936, but in each case they were unable to gain reelection. George Docking won the governorship in 1956 and was reelected in 1958, the first non-Republican to have a second term as governor. His son Robert Docking, also a Democrat, gained the seat in four successive elections, 1966 through 1972, and Democrat John Carlin was elected to four-year terms in both 1978 and 1982.

Control of the legislature has been held mostly by the Republican party in Kansas, although their margin in the early 1930s was very thin. Populists gained a majority from 1897–99, after having partial control in the early 1890s. Democrats gained control in the election of 1912, then lost a majority in the house (but not the senate) two years later. In 1976 the Democrats won a majority of the seats in the house of representatives. Interestingly, the party controlling the state legislature was the same as the governor's in only two years in the twenty years from 1967 to 1987, during the first two years of Robert Bennett's term. One wonders if Kansas voters produced these results to reduce prospective legislation. Historically, gubernatorial vetoes are more extensive when the governor and the legislative majority are from different parties.

Through the years Kansas gubernatorial elections with more than two major candidates have been unusual. However, more than twenty-five party labels have appeared in elections since 1859. The Republican party has fielded a candidate every time, under the same banner. The Democratic party, using that or another name, also was in every election. About a dozen other parties have put up candidates for governor under a variety of names. Most notable for its success as a third party was the People's Alliance, which came in second with 106,972 votes, or 36 percent, for John F. Willits in 1890. Renamed the People's party, it fused with the Democrats and won the governor's race in 1892 and 1896. In 1932 Dr. John R. Brinkley, an Independent candidate, polled 244,607, or almost 31 percent of the total, in his second of three attempts to gain the office. William Allen White, as an Independent candidate in 1924, received 22.7 percent of the vote. Henry J. Allen did not fare as well as a Progressive in 1914, when he got 84,060 votes, almost 16 percent of the total in a six-way race for governor.

Kansas gubernatorial elections have not experienced the violence recorded in Rhode Island in 1842 or in Kentucky in 1899 when those states teetered on the edge of internal civil war. Compared to those in many states, Kansas elections have been remarkably free of fraud. There were charges of election fraud leveled during the territorial period; otherwise, disputes historically have been restricted to county-seat elections. Nor have Kansas races been as close as the Massachusetts election in 1839 when Marcus Morton became governor by a single vote.[7] The closest statewide contest in Kansas history occurred when George Hartshorn Hodges won in 1912 over Arthur Capper by a mere twenty-nine votes.

The 1930 race for governor was another close one, when Harry Hines Woodring, Democrat, was declared the winner by 251 votes over Frank Haucke, Republican, fifteen days after the election. This race was complicated by the belated entry of Independent John R. Brinkley as a write-in candidate, since he had filed too late to get his name on the ballot. Reports that many Brinkley ballots were invalidated for improper marks or incorrect spelling add to the mystique of that election. Two years later Brinkley was again an Independent candidate but with his name on the ballot. Although he received a slightly larger percentage of the official vote, he again came in third in the race. His last try was in the Republican primary in 1934, when he was badly trounced by incumbent Alfred Mossman Landon.

The 1940 gubernatorial contest, when Payne Ratner was seeking re-election, was almost as close as the 1930 race. Ratner won over William Burke by 430 votes, with the outcome determined solely by absentee ballots, which at that time were counted after other ballots were totaled. Though there were no indications of an illegal count, this led to a procedural change in which absentee ballots were no longer segregated from the totals at individual voting places.

The persistence of some of the Kansas third parties in fielding candidates for governor, when there is slight chance of victory, is amazing. The Prohibition party has nominated a gubernatorial candidate in each election from 1886 to 1916 and from 1938 to 1982, rarely drawing more than 1 or 2 percent of the total vote. Socialists first placed a candidate for governor on the ballot in 1898. Their momentum peaked with the elections of 1912 and 1916 when they polled slightly more than 20,000 votes, about 4 percent of the total. Socialist opposition to United States participation in World War I weakened that

Table 4. Kansas Gubernatorial Elections

Date of Election	Estimated Eligible Vote	Total Vote Cast	% of Eligible Vote Cast	Republicans Candidate	Number of Votes	% of Vote	Democrats Candidate	Number of Votes	% of Vote	Minor Parties Candidate	Number of Votes	% of Vote
6 D 1859		13,249		CHARLES ROBINSON	7,848	59.2	Samuel Medary	5,401	40.8			
4 N 1862		15,450		THOMAS CARNEY	9,990	64.7	W. R. Wagstaff (U)	5,456	35.3			
8 N 1864		20,955		SAMUEL J. CRAWFORD	12,711	60.7	Solon O. Thacher (RU)	8,244	39.3			
6 N 1866		27,521		SAMUEL J. CRAWFORD	19,370	70.4	J. L. McDowell (NU)	8,151	29.6			
3 N 1868		43,676		JAMES M. HARVEY	29,795	68.2	George W. Glick	13,881	31.8			
8 N 1870		61,271		JAMES M. HARVEY	40,667	66.4	Isaac Sharp	20,496	33.5	W. R. Laughlin (W)	108	.1
5 N 1872		101,322		THOMAS A. OSBORN	66,854	66.0	Thaddeus H. Walker (LR)	34,468	34.0			
3 N 1874		86,372		THOMAS A. OSBORN	48,794	56.5	James C. Cusey (IR)	35,301	41.3	W. K. Marshall (T)	2,277	2.2
7 N 1876		121,827		GEORGE T. ANTHONY	69,176	56.8	John Martin	46,201	37.9	J. Paulson (T)	393	.3
										M. E. Hudson (IR)	6,020	5.0
5 N 1878		138,296		JOHN P. ST. JOHN	74,020	53.5	John R. Goodin	37,208	26.9	D. P. Mitchell (G)	27,068	19.6
2 N 1880		198,884		JOHN P. ST. JOHN	115,204	57.9	Edmund G. Ross	63,557	32.0	J. P. Culver (TM)	435	.2
										F. M. Stringfield (I)	219	.1
										H. P. Vroman (GL)	19,477	9.7
7 N 1882		179,379		John P. St. John	75,158	41.9	GEORGE W. GLICK	83,237	46.4	Charles Robinson (GL)	20,933	11.7
4 N 1884		265,239		JOHN A. MARTIN	146,777	55.3	George W. Glick	108,284	40.8	John Martin (I)	142	–
										H. L. Phillips (GL)	9,998	3.9
2 N 1886		273,487		JOHN A. MARTIN	149,615	54.7	Thomas Moonlight	115,697	42.3	C. H. Branscombe (Pro)	8,094	3.0
6 N 1888		330,714		LYMAN U. HUMPHREY	180,841	54.7	John Martin	107,408	32.5	Jeremiah D. Botkin (Pro)	6,439	2.0
										Peter P. Elder (UL)	35,837	10.8
4 N 1890		296,560		LYMAN U. HUMPHREY	115,025	39.0	Charles Robinson*	71,357	24.2	John F. Willits (PA)	106,972	36.0
										A. M. Richardson (Pro)	1,230	.4
8 N 1892		324,770		Abram W. Smith	158,075	48.7	(fused with People's party)			LORENZO D. LEWELLING (P)	163,507	50.0
										Isaac O. Pickering (Pro)	4,178	1.3
6 N 1894		300,135		EDMUND N. MORRILL	148,697	49.5	David Overmyer (SD)	26,709	8.9	Lorenzo D. Lewelling (P)	118,329	39.4
										Isaac O. Pickering (Pro)	5,496	1.8

Date	Total Vote	Candidate	Vote	%
3 N 1896	332,360	Edmund N. Morrill	160,530	48.3
		JOHN W. LEEDY (P)	167,041	50.5
		A. E. Kepford (I)	703	.2
		Horace Hurley (Pro)	2,347	.7
		Henry L. Douthart (N)	757	.2
8 N 1898	288,209	WILLIAM E. STANLEY	149,292	51.8
		John W. Leedy (P) (fused with People's party)	134,158	46.5
		William A. Peffer (Pro)	4,092	1.4
		Caleb Lipscomb (S)	635	.2
6 N 1900	350,611	WILLIAM E. STANLEY	181,893	51.9
		John W. Breidenthal (P) (fused with People's party)	164,793	47.0
		Frank Holsinger (Pro)	212	—
		G. C. Clemens (S)	1,258	.4
4 N 1902	287,169	WILLIS J. BAILEY	159,242	55.5
		W. R. Craddock	117,148	40.8
		J. H. Lathrop (P)	635	.2
		F. W. Emerson (Pro)	6,065	2.1
		A. S. McAllister (S)	4,078	1.4
8 N 1904	322,407	EDWARD W. HOCH	186,731	57.9
		David M. Dale	116,991	36.3
		James Kerr (Pro)	6,584	2.0
		Granville Lowther (S)	12,101	3.6
6 N 1906	315,379	EDWARD W. HOCH	152,147	48.2
		William A. Harris	150,024	47.6
		Horace Keefer (I)	1,131	.4
		J. B. Cook (Pro)	4,453	1.4
		Harry Gilham (S)	7,621	2.4
3 N 1908	374,773	WALTER R. STUBBS	196,692	52.5
		Jeremiah D. Borkin	162,385	43.3
		John W. Northrup (I)	68	—
		Alfred L. Hope (Pro)	3,886	1.0
		George Francis Hibner (S)	11,721	3.1
8 N 1910	325,954	WALTER R. STUBBS	162,181	49.8
		George H. Hodges	146,014	44.8
		William C. Cady (Pro)	2,372	.7
		S. M. Stallard (S)	15,384	4.7
5 N 1912	354,684	Arthur Capper	167,408	46.5
		GEORGE H. HODGES	167,437	46.6
		George W. Kleihege (S)	24,767	6.9
3 N 1914	528,207	ARTHUR CAPPER	209,543	39.7
		George H. Hodges	161,696	30.6
		Henry J. Allen (Pr)	84,060	15.9
		J. B. Billard (I)	47,201	8.8
		Silas W. Bond (Pro)	5,346	1.0
		Milo M. Mitchell (S)	20,360	3.8
7 N 1916	581,126	ARTHUR CAPPER	354,529	60.8
		W. C. Lansdon	192,037	33.0
		H. R. Ross (Pro)	13,366	2.3
		E. N. Richardson (S)	22,552	3.9
5 N 1918	433,743	HENRY J. ALLEN	287,957	66.4
		W. C. Lansdon	133,054	30.7
		George W. Kleihege (S)	12,731	2.9
2 N 1920	547,399	HENRY J. ALLEN	319,914	58.4
		Jonathan M. Davis	214,940	39.3
		Roy Stanton (S)	12,544	2.3
7 N 1922	532,803	W. Y. Morgan	252,602	47.4
		JONATHAN M. DAVIS	271,058	50.9
		M. L. Phillips (S)	9,138	1.7

982,878 55.7
1,007,398 52.9

Table 4 *(continued)*

	Total	%	Votes	Candidate	Votes	%	Candidate	Votes	%	Candidate	Votes	%	Candidate	Votes	%	Candidate	Votes	%
4 N 1924	1,031,934	63.9	659,680	BENJAMIN S. PAULEN	323,403	49.0	Jonathan M. Davis	182,861	27.7	William Allen White (I)	149,811	22.7	M. L. Phillips (S)	3,606	.5			
2 N 1926	1,056,079	48.1	507,901	BENJAMIN S. PAULEN	321,540	63.3	Jonathan M. Davis	179,308	35.3	H. Hilfrich (S)	7,046	1.4						
6 N 1928	1,081,039	61.1	660,646	CLYDE M. REED	433,391	65.5	Chauncey B. Little	219,327	33.2	Henry L. Peterson (S)	7,924	1.2						
4 N 1930	1,106,064	56.1	621,235	Frank Haucke	216,920	34.9	HARRY H. WOODRING	217,171	35.0	John R. Brinkley (I)	183,278	29.5	J. B. Shields (S)	3,866	.6			
8 N 1932	1,113,831	71.8	800,026	ALF M. LANDON	278,581	34.8	Harry H. Woodring	272,944	34.1	John R. Brinkley (I)	244,607	30.6	H. M. Perkins (S)	3,892	.5			
6 N 1934	1,121,579	70.3	788,651	ALF M. LANDON	422,030	53.5	Omar B. Ketchum	359,877	45.6	George M. Whiteside (S)	6,744	.9						
3 N 1936	1,129,325	75.1	848,084	Will G. West	411,446	48.5	WALTER A. HUXMAN	433,319	51.1	George M. Whiteside (S)	3,318	.4						
8 N 1938	1,137,077	66.5	756,698	PAYNE H. RATNER	393,989	52.1	Walter A. Huxman	341,271	45.1	Jonathan M. Davis (I)	15,605	2.0	C. Floyd Hester (Pro)	4,337	.6	Ida A. Beloof (S)	1,496	.2
5 N 1940	1,144,823	75.0	858,289	PAYNE H. RATNER	425,928	49.6	William H. Burke	425,498	49.6	David C. White (Pro)	5,227	.6	Ida A. Beloof (S)	1,636	.2			
3 N 1942	1,162,134	43.7	507,929	ANDREW F. SCHOEPPEL	287,895	56.7	William H. Burke	212,071	41.8	David C. White (Pro)	6,510	1.3	Ida A. Beloof (S)	1,453	.2			
7 N 1944	1,179,439	60.0	704,607	ANDREW F. SCHOEPPEL	463,110	65.7	Robert S. Lemon	231,410	32.8	David C. White (Pro)	7,794	1.1	W. W. Tamplin (S)	2,283	.3			
5 N 1946	1,196,740	48.3	577,694	FRANK CARLSON	309,064	53.5	Harry H. Woodring	254,283	44.0	David C. White (Pro)	12,517	2.2	Harry Graber (S)	1,830	.3			
2 N 1948	1,214,039	62.6	760,407	FRANK CARLSON	433,396	57.0	Randolph Carpenter	307,485	40.4	N. W. Nice (Pro)	17,035	2.2	W. W. Tamplin (S)	2,491	.4			
7 N 1950	1,231,331	50.3	619,310	EDWARD F. ARN	333,001	53.8	Kenneth T. Anderson	275,494	44.5	C. Floyd Hester (Pro)	9,431	1.5	W. W. Tamplin (S)	1,384	.2			

Election	Total Vote	%	Candidate	Vote	%
4 N 1952	1,280,774	68.1	EDWARD F. ARN	491,338	56.3
			Charles Rooney	363,483	41.7
			David C. White (Pro)	15,369	1.8
			W. W. Tamplin (S)	1,950	.1
2 N 1954	1,292,714	48.2	FRED L. HALL	329,868	53.0
			George Docking	286,218	46.0
			Chester A. Roberts (Pro)	5,531	.8
			W. W. Tamplin (S)	1,016	.2
6 N 1956	1,341,672	64.5	Warren W. Shaw	364,340	42.1
			GEORGE DOCKING	479,701	55.5
			Harry O. Lytle (Pro)	20,894	2.4
4 N 1958	1,311,444	56.1	Clyde M. Reed, Jr.	313,036	42.5
			GEORGE DOCKING	415,506	56.5
			Warren C. Martin (Pro)	7,397	1.0
8 N 1960	1,330,120	69.4	JOHN ANDERSON, JR.	511,534	55.4
			George Docking	402,261	43.6
			J. J. Steele (Pro)	8,727	.9
6 N 1962	1,351,614	47.3	JOHN ANDERSON, JR.	341,257	53.4
			Dale Saffels	291,285	45.6
			Vearl A. Bacon (Pro)	6,248	1.0
3 N 1964	1,361,306	62.5	WILLIAM H. AVERY	432,667	50.9
			Harry G. Wiles	400,264	47.1
			Kenneth L. Myers (C)	11,816	1.4
			Harry E. Livermore (Pro)	5,667	.7
8 N 1966	692,955		William H. Avery	304,325	43.9
			ROBERT DOCKING	380,030	54.8
			Carson E. Crawford (C)	3,858	.6
			Rolland E. Fisher (Pro)	4,742	.7
5 N 1968	1,346,000	64.0	Rick Harman	410,673	47.6
			ROBERT DOCKING	447,269	51.9
			Marshall Uncapher (Pro)	4,528	.5
3 N 1970	745,190		Kent Frizzell	333,227	44.7
			ROBERT DOCKING	404,611	54.3
			P. Everett Sperry (C)	4,312	.6
			Marshall Uncapher (Pro)	3,040	.4
7 N 1972	1,553,000	59.3	Morris Kay	341,440	37.0
			ROBERT DOCKING	571,256	62.0
			Rolland E. Fisher (Pro)	8,856	1.0
5 N 1974	783,875		ROBERT F. BENNETT	387,792	49.5
			Vern Miller	384,115	49.0
			Marshall Uncapher (Pro)	11,968	1.5
7 N 1978	736,792		Robert F. Bennett	348,403	47.3
			JOHN CARLIN	364,738	49.4
			Frank W. Shelton, Jr. (A)	16,619	2.0
			Barry Beets (Pro)	7,032	1.0
2 N 1982	763,263		Sam Hardage	339,356	44.4
			JOHN CARLIN	405,772	53.0
			James H. Ward (L)	7,595	1.0
			Frank W. Shelton, Jr. (A)	6,136	.8
			Warren C. Martin (Pro)	4,404	.6
4 N 1986	840,605		MIKE HAYDEN	436,267	51.9
			Tom Docking	404,338	48.1

A—American
C—Conservative
G—Greenback
GL—Greenback-Labor
I—Independent
IR—Independent Reform or National

LR—Liberal Republican
L—Libertarian
N—National
NU—National Union
P—People's
PA—People's Alliance

Pr—Progressive
Pro—Prohibition
RU—Republican Union
S—Socialist
SD—Stalwart Democratic
T—Temperance

TM—Traveling Men
U—Union
UL—Union Labor
W—Workingman
*Democratic & Resubmission

party in Kansas, though they continued to nominate candidates through 1954. Legislation in 1984 further handicapped minor parties and in effect eliminated them from the election of 1986. State law now requires that party candidates receive at least 1 percent of the total vote cast in a general election in order to be listed on the ballot in the next election. Otherwise, a place on the ballot requires valid petitions that carry signatures equal to at least 2 percent of the votes cast in the previous gubernatorial election.[8]

In the period before party primaries, a candidate had to appeal successfully to relatively few party leaders assembled in a state party convention. In those conventions, a candidate had to win a majority vote, necessitating sometimes numerous ballots. However, the party primary, first used in 1908, provided no opportunity for voting again, so a plurality—the person with the largest vote—determined the party's choice for the general election. This raises certain problems. In a primary election with a large field of candidates, the party runs a risk of selecting a winner who has a plurality far below half of the vote and who might not be the most attractive candidate to voters in a general election. Large numbers of candidates in a primary election also have a tendency to rupture party harmony.

Kansans expect their candidate for governor to be an interesting, tactful, good speaker, with a pleasing personality. Perhaps the ablest speaker among the nineteenth-century governors was John Pierce St. John, who gave an extraordinary number of speeches throughout his long life. Henry Allen and Frederick Lee Hall received high marks as platform orators in the twentieth century. The Chautauqua movement, offering summertime entertainment and serious discussion, was important in late-nineteenth- and early-twentieth-century Kansas. Some of the more able speakers among the Kansas governors spoke on the Chautauqua circuit as it moved from town to town. Others, such as Arthur Capper, were poor public speakers, but they compensated with other abilities. Campaigners in the nineteenth century appealed to voters without amplification of their natural voices, far different from the electronic enhancement available to later speakers. A pleasing television image also helps a candidate's chances.

Many campaign techniques changed greatly in the twentieth century. The nineteenth-century candidates for governor expended little effort in campaigning, leaving most tasks to their local supporters. The media, especially the newspaper press, was extremely partisan in their political views, and voters had a high degree of party loyalty that boosted voter turnout. The proportion of eligible voters who cast their ballot in an election decreased with the advent of the party primary (as party loyalty waned) and with the expansion of the electorate brought by women's suffrage. Consequently, a candidate had to tour the state to meet as many voters as possible. For some candidates, the campaign trail was a vacation and they enjoyed it; for others, it was a chore that had to be done. Radio first came into gubernatorial campaigns in a big way in 1930 when Independent candidate Dr. John R. Brinkley mounted his initial challenge to the major parties. Television first became part of the campaigns for governor in 1954 and 1956, during Fred Hall's two races.

Over the years, the importance of the party organization has diminished with regard to candidate selection. Candidates have their own campaign organization, and the image and issues presented by the candidates have had far more influence on the voter than party label. With the use of television and direct-mail campaigns, the costs of campaigns have gone up tremendously. Candidates in the 1980s, for instance, have spent more than $1 million in a losing primary election campaign. Special-interest groups have developed to support or oppose candidates, and "negative campaigning" has been employed when the prospect of victory could exploit an opponent's weakness, real or alleged. Marvin Harder finds many interrelated developments during the 1940s and 1950s that have modified politics in Kansas. These include atrophy of the party organizations, more split-ticket voting, greater educational level of voters, far greater work and professional options, accelerated population mobility including rural-to-urban migration, and expanded influence of the media.[9]

Candidates for the position of Kansas governor are traditionally expected to be God-fearing, and a member of some church. However, this characteristic was not noticeable among the earliest governors, who served during an era when church membership in the United States was not as widespread as in later years. Six of the first seven governors were not members of a church; the exception was Nehemiah Green, a Methodist minister, who was elevated to the governorship with the resignation of Samuel Crawford. James Harvey had no religious preference, while all of the other early governors had a church preference but not church membership. Among the remaining Kansas governors, only John Alexander Martin, with a Baptist preference, and John Leedy, with a Church of the Brethren (or Dunkard) preference, were not church members. Some governors changed denominations as adults. The list of church affiliations includes thirteen members of the Methodist church, four each of the Congregational and the Presbyterian churches, three of the Christian church, two each of the Christian Science, Lutheran, Quaker (Society of Friends), and Baptist churches, and one of the Episcopal church.

Military experience for the Kansas governor was important to voters in the nineteenth century and in the years following the two world wars. Kansas governors served in United States engagements from the Mexican War through Vietnam, the only exception being the short-duration Spanish-American War. Eight governors in the nineteenth century served in the Union army during the Civil War in various officer ranks: Crawford, Green, Harvey, George Tobey Anthony, St. John, Martin, Lyman Underwood Humphrey, and Morrill. Two other nineteenth-century Kansas governors emphasized their Civil War connections. Lorenzo Dow Lewelling enlisted as a drummer boy, until Quaker relatives bought his discharge; and Leedy unsuccessfully tried to enlist but was underage. No governor served in the Confederate army; a well-known former Confederate Kansan, William Alexander Harris, who served in both houses of Congress, did make a try for the governor's office, but he lost the race in 1906 by a narrow margin. Although Charles Robinson, the first Kansas governor, did not participate in any war, he had commanding officer status of free-state forces in the era of "Bleeding Kansas." There were six veterans of World War I, three in enlisted ranks and three officers, none ranking higher than first lieutenant. Woodring, Landon, Carlson, and Frank Leslie Hagaman were in the army; Ratner and Schoeppel in the navy. Four governors served in World War II: Edward F. Arn, the only officer, was in the navy; John

Berridge McCuish, in the army; Robert Docking, in the air corps; and Bennett, in the marines. Bennett was also in the Korean conflict, and Hayden was an army officer in Vietnam.

Kansans take an interest in the personal lives of their governors—whether they were married and what their family was like. Only three of the first forty-one Kansas governors—Crawford, Willis Joshua Bailey and Woodring—took the oath of office as single men; all of the others were married. Crawford married on November 27, 1866, after his reelection to a second term. Bailey married about five months after his inauguration and escorted the first bride into the newly acquired Kansas Executive Mansion, located at Eighth and Buchanan in Topeka. Woodring did not marry until mid-1933, after he was out of office; that marriage continued for twenty-seven years before ending in divorce. Governors who remarried after divorce were John P. St. John, who moved to Kansas with his second wife ten years after his divorce in 1859; Robert Bennett, who was divorced and remarried more than three years before his election; and John William Carlin, who was divorced and remarried half way through his first term, divorced again during his second term, and married for a third time after he left office. Six Kansas governors remarried after the death of their first wives, but none became widowers while in office. For Robinson, Lewelling, Morrill, and Landon, bereavement and remarriage had occurred prior to their terms; for others, such as Green and Arn, it was after their gubernatorial service.

Seven Kansas governors were childless: Robinson, Bailey, Capper, Benjamin Sanford Paulen, Schoeppel, Hagaman, and McCuish. For the remainder, family size ranged from one to ten children, with an average of three. Specifically, there were nine governors with two children, nine with four children, six with three children, five with one child, and five with five or more children.

The political route to the Kansas governorship has varied. Of course, three Kansas governors were not elected to that office but rather moved there from the post of lieutenant governor after the governor's resignation. However, the stand-in role of the Kansas lieutenant governor has always been minimal. No governor of Kansas has died in office; and although one—Robinson—was impeached, he was not convicted. The first eleven governors served in either the

Table 5. Background of Governors of the State of Kansas

Name	Dates of Service	Residence	Birthdate	Birthplace	Father's Occupation	Occupation	No. of Siblings	No. of Children	College Attendance	Veteran	KS Legislator	Member of Congress	No. of Unsuccessful Campaigns for Governor	Served as Lt. Gov.	Other Federal Job	Age at Inauguration	Years in Kansas at Election	Unsuccessful Candidate for Congress	Age at Death	Church Membership*
1 Charles Robinson (R)	9 Feb 1861–12 Jan 1863	Lawrence	21 Jul 18	MA	farmer	farmer	9	0	Grad.		X		2		X	43	7	X	76	(Univ.)
2 Thomas Carney (R)	12 Jan 1863–9 Jan 1865	Leavenworth	20 Aug 24	OH	farmer	merch.	–	5			X		0			39	5	X	63	(Pres.)
3 Samuel Johnson Crawford (R)	9 Jan 1865–4 Nov 1868	Garnett	10 Apr 35	IN	farmer	law	2	2	Grad.	X	X		0			29	6	X	78	(Epis.)
4 Nehemiah Green (R)	4 Nov 1868–11 Jan 1869	Manhattan	8 Mar 37	OH	farmer	min.	8	5	X	X	X		0	X		31	5		62	Meth.
5 James Madison Harvey (R)	11 Jan 1869–13 Jan 1873	Vinton	21 Sep 33	WV	farmer	farmer	4	6	X	X	X	X	0		X	35	10		60	–
6 Thomas Andrew Osborn (R)	13 Jan 1873–8 Jan 1877	Leavenworth	26 Oct 36	PA	farmer	law	–	1		X	X		0	X	X	36	16	X	61	(Meth.)
7 George Tobey Anthony (R)	8 Jan 1877–13 Jan 1879	Leavenworth	9 Jul 24	NY	farmer	news.	–	1	X	X	X		1			53	12	X	72	(Quaker)
8 John Pierce St. John (R)	13 Jan 1879–8 Jan 1883	Olathe	25 Feb 33	IN	farmer	law	–	3		X	X		1			46	10		83	Ch.Sci.
9 George Washington Glick (D)	8 Jan 1883–12 Jan 1885	Atchison	4 Jul 27	OH	farmer	law	–	2	X	X	X		2		X	56	25	X	83	Luth.
10 John Alexander Martin (R)	12 Jan 1885–14 Jan 1889	Atchison	10 Mar 39	PA	bus.	news.	4	8		X	X		1			46	28		50	(Bapt.)
11 Lyman Underwood Humphrey (R)	14 Jan 1889–9 Jan 1893	Independence	25 Jun 44	OH	law	banker	1	4	Grad.	X	X		0		X	45	18	X	71	Cong.
12 Lorenzo Dow Lewelling (P)	9 Jan 1893–14 Jan 1895	Wichita	21 Dec 46	IA	merch.	merch.	3	4	Grad.		X		1			47	6		53	Quaker
13 Edmund Needham Morrill (R)	14 Jan 1895–11 Jan 1897	Hiawatha	12 Feb 34	ME	tanner	banker	–	3	X	X	X	X	1			61	38		75	Cong.
14 John Whitnah Leedy (P)	11 Jan 1897–9 Jan 1899	LeRoy	4 Mar 49	OH	farmer	farmer	–	3			X		1		X	48	17		86	(Dunkard)
15 William Eugene Stanley (R)	9 Jan 1899–12 Jan 1903	Wichita	28 Dec 44	OH	MD	law	4	4	X		X		0		X	55	19	X	65	Meth.

No. & Name (party)	Term of office	Birth	St.	Occ.	Occ.			Ed.						Age		Rel.
16 Willis Joshua Bailey (R)	12 Jan 1903–9 Jan 1905	12 Oct 54	IL	farmer	banker	3	2	Grad.	X X		X X	1		X 49 24	77	Bapt.
17 Edward Wallis Hoch (R)	9 Jan 1905–11 Jan 1909	17 Mar 49	KY	baker	news.	–	4	X	X		X	0		56 34	76	Meth.
18 Walter Roscoe Stubbs (R)	11 Jan 1909–13 Jan 1913	7 Oct 58	IN	farmer	contr.	12	4	X	X		X	2		50 40 X	69	Meth.
19 George Hartshorn Hodges (D)	13 Jan 1913–11 Jan 1915	6 Feb 66	WI	teacher	merch.	2	2		X		X	2		47 44	81	Chris.
20 Arthur Capper (R)	11 Jan 1915–13 Jan 1919	14 Jul 65	KS	merch.	news.	4	0			X	X	1		50 50	86	Quaker
21 Henry Justin Allen (R)	13 Jan 1919–8 Jan 1923	11 Sep 68	PA	farmer	news.	6	4	X		X	X	0		X 51 49 X	81	Meth.
22 Jonathan McMillan Davis (D)	8 Jan 1923–12 Jan 1925	27 Apr 71	KS	farmer	farmer	1	3	X		X	X	5		51 51 X	82	Meth.
23 Benjamin Sanford Paulen (R)	12 Jan 1925–14 Jan 1929	21 Jul 69	IL	merch.	banker	5	0	X		X	X	0	X	56 55 X	91	Ch.Sci.
24 Clyde Martin Reed (R)	14 Jan 1929–12 Jan 1931	9 Oct 71	IL	farmer	news.	2	10			X		3		X 58 54	78	Meth.
25 Harry Hines Woodring (D)	12 Jan 1931–9 Jan 1933	31 May 87	KS	merch.	banker	5	3	X	X			3		X 44 44	80	Cong.
26 Alfred Mossman Landon (R)	9 Jan 1933–11 Jan 1937	9 Sep 87	PA	oil	oil	1	4	Grad.	X			0		45 29	100	Meth.
27 Walter Augustus Huxman (D)	11 Jan 1937–9 Jan 1939	16 Feb 87	KS	farmer	law	3	1	Grad.	X			1		X 50 50	85	Chris.
28 Payne Harry Ratner (R)	9 Jan 1939–11 Jan 1943	3 Oct 96	IL	merch.	law	2	3	Grad.	X X			0		40 24	78	Chris.
29 Andrew Frank Schoeppel (R)	11 Jan 1943–13 Jan 1947	23 Nov 94	KS	farmer	law	7	0	Grad.	X X	X		0		48 48	67	Meth.
30 Frank Carlson (R)	13 Jan 1947–28 Nov 1950	23 Jan 93	KS	farmer	farmer	1	1	X	X X	X		0		54 54	93	Bapt.
31 Frank Leslie Hagaman (R)	28 Nov 1950–8 Jan 1951	1 Jul 94	IL	clerk	law	1	0	Grad.	X			1		X 56 50	72	Epis.
32 Edward F. Arn (R)	8 Jan 1951–10 Jan 1955	19 May 06	KS	merch.	law	0	2	Grad.	X			0		44 44 X		Cong.
33 Frederick Lee Hall (R)	10 Jan 1955–3 Jan 1957	24 Jul 16	KS	law	law	1	1	Grad.				2		X X 39 35	53	Meth.
34 John Berridge McCuish (R)	3 Jan 1957–14 Jan 1957	22 Jul 06	CO	min.	news.	–	0	Grad.	X			0		X X 50 45	55	Pres.
35 George Docking (D)	14 Jan 1957–9 Jan 1961	23 Feb 04	KS	banker	banker	1	2	Grad.				2		X 53 52	59	Pres.
36 John Anderson, Jr. (R)	9 Jan 1961–11 Jan 1965	8 May 17	KS	farmer	law	2	3	Grad.	X			1		49 49		Meth.
37 William Henry Avery (R)	11 Jan 1965–9 Jan 1967	11 Aug 11	KS	farmer	farmer	2	4	Grad.	X X			1		X 53 53 X		Meth.
38 Robert Blackwell Docking (D)	9 Jan 1967–13 Jan 1975	9 Oct 27	MO	banker	banker	1	2	Grad.	X			0		42 41	57	Pres.
39 Robert Frederick Bennett (R)	13 Jan 1975–8 Jan 1979	23 May 27	MO	farmer	law	0	4	Grad.	X X			1		X 48 48		Pres.
40 John William Carlin (D)	8 Jan 1979–12 Jan 1987	3 Aug 40	KS	farmer	farmer	1	2	Grad.	X			0		38 38		Luth.
41 John Michael Hayden (R)	12 Jan 1987–	15 Mar 44	KS	farmer	ins.agt.	5	2	Grad.	X X			0		42 42		Meth.

Republican = (R); Democratic = (D); People's Party = (P)
*Parentheses indicate preference only

territorial or the state legislature before they became governor. In later years, sixteen others found service in the legislature to be an important route to the governorship, but its significance is less apparent during the twentieth century. Thirteen governors held local elective offices before reaching the state's highest office; their combined service totaled more than eighty years. Twelve men held state administrative positions before assuming the duties of governor. No governor came into the office after previous occupancy of any of the elective offices established by the constitution of 1859 other than lieutenant governor and attorney general. The four who held the position of lieutenant governor before election to governor were Thomas Andrew Osborn, Humphrey, Paulen, and Hall. In the post–World War II period, Arn and John Anderson, Jr., moved into the governor's office after gaining recognition as attorneys general. Although this prompted the impression that a new track to the governorship had been created, other attorneys general tried the same strategy without success. Arn and George Washington Glick were the only Kansas governors to have prior judicial experience. Clyde Reed was a judge on the Kansas Industrial Court, but this was actually a public service commission and not a judicial agency. Six governors had prior service with the federal government—four as members of Congress and two in appointive administrative positions.

It may come as a surprise that five of the better-known governors had no previous elective governmental experience, even at the local level. This list includes Lewelling, who was an employee in the Iowa reformatory system for at least eleven years prior to his move to Kansas; Capper, who served briefly on the appointive board of regents for Kansas State Agricultural College; and Woodring, Landon, and George Docking.

The older and more populous eastern portion of Kansas supplied most of the forty-one governors. Of the 105 counties in the state, ten counties produced twenty-six governors. The remaining fifteen governors came from fifteen different counties. The residences of most nineteenth century governors were in counties located one, two, or three tiers from the Missouri border. A total of five came from two counties, Leavenworth and Atchison, which have provided no twentieth-century governor. The premier counties for homesites

Map 4. Residences of Governors of the State of Kansas When Elected

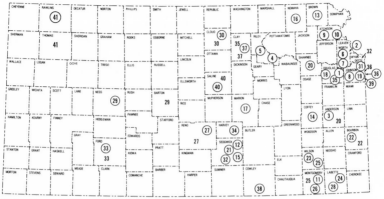

① Residences of Kansas governors when elected (see Table 5, pp. 24–25, for key)
ı Birthplaces of Kansas-born governors (see Map 3, pp. 10–11, for key)

among all forty-one governors are Johnson (with five) and Sedgwick (with four). An interesting trend occurred from 1922 through 1940, when six of the seven governors elected during that time came from four southeastern counties—counties that contributed only one other governor in Kansas history. Populous Shawnee County, although it has provided many candidates, was home to only one governor prior to election. It seems that Kansas voters are wary of gubernatorial candidates from such populated counties, since neither Wyandotte nor Shawnee have produced numbers of governors comparable to their large populations.

Likewise, western Kansas has trailed as a home for occupants of the governor's office. Only four governors come from counties west of U.S. Highway 81, often used as a dividing line between eastern and western Kansas: Walter Augustus Huxman—Reno County; Schoeppel—Ness County; Hall—Ford County; and Hayden—Rawlins County. Several others hail from counties intersected by that highway: Carlson—Cloud County; McCuish—Harvey County; Carlin—Saline County; and the four Sedgwick-based governors. The establishment of the "one-man, one-vote" rule in the 1960s necessitated reapportionment of the Kansas house and senate, and since then, gubernatorial hopefuls are less likely to come from the smaller, more rural counties because of the difficulty of gaining widespread political exposure before the Kansas voters. Four Kansas counties—Sedgwick, Johnson, Wyandotte, and Shawnee—contain more than 40 percent of the state's population, and the ten largest counties provide an urbanized population base which concentrates well over half of the state's population in less than 10 percent of the counties. Although chances are good that future governors will come from these larger counties, Hayden's election in 1986 certainly showed that a candidate from a rural county can beat the odds.

Persistence in seeking the office paid off for eight men who lost their first race for Kansas governor, but were elected on their second try. They were Glick (1868), Martin (1878), Hodges (1910), Capper (1912), Allen (1914), Jonathan McMillan Davis (1920), Clyde Martin Reed (1924), and George Docking (1954). However, eighteen Kansas governors, almost half of the total, left the governor's office in defeat. Robinson, Carney, Anthony, and Bailey were not renominated by the Republican party conventions for a traditional second term. Reed and Hall lost in the primaries in bids for reelection, and the other twelve lost in the general elections. Of those, John P. St. John and George Docking failed to win a third term; only Robert Docking, who also had a fourth term, was elected more than twice. None of the Democratic or Populist governors of the nineteenth century and the first half of the twentieth century were reelected. Nevertheless, the tenacity of many who run for the office of governor is apparent from the historical record. Robinson was denied a second term and lost attempts to regain the office in 1882 and in 1890; Stubbs was defeated in 1922 and 1924; Davis, a biennial candidate for some office, lost in races for governor in 1924, 1926, 1936, and 1938 (in all he was a candidate for governor six times). After losing his reelection bid in 1932, Woodring lost in 1946 and 1956. The 1958 Republican primary spelled the end of Hall's gubernatorial ambitions, and the same held true for Anderson in the 1972 primary.

In many other states, governors have had terms separated by duty in other roles, but not in Kansas. Once a Kansas governor has relinquished the office and its associated power—willingly or not—the voters have never given it back to him, although they might support election to another office. Indeed, Kansas governors have held a wide variety of public positions in their postgubernatorial years. Service in the Kansas house of representatives or senate attracted nineteenth-century governors Robinson, Green, Osborn, Anthony, and Lewelling. Six governors—Harvey, Capper, Allen, Reed, Schoeppel, and Carlson—held the position of United States senator; their collective service totaled almost one hundred years. Several were unsuccessful in seeking the United States Senate, namely, Crawford, Osborn, William Eugene Stanley, Stubbs, Davis, and Arn. Nevertheless, the move to the Senate from Kansas during the years 1918 to 1962 was more often from the governor's office than from all other positions.

Holding federal appointments after serving as a Kansas governor were Robinson, Harvey, Osborn, Leedy, Stanley, Bailey, Allen, Woodring, Huxman, George Docking, and William Henry Avery. Two governors were nominated for president—John P. St. John as the Prohibition candidate in 1884, and Alf M. Landon, who unsuccessfully sought the presidency in 1936 as the Republican nominee. After that defeat Landon retired from public office altogether. Crawford, Anthony, and Glick all failed to realize their hope of election to Congress. Perhaps the most unusual federal appointments were those of Osborn, who served for eight years as United States minister to Chile and later to Brazil; Woodring, who was assistant secretary of war and then secretary of war; Huxman, who became a federal judge; and George Docking, who was appointed director of the Import-Export Bank.

For more than two-thirds of the Kansas governors, the position was a brief interlude in their lives; twenty-six returned to their home community following their tenure in the governor's office, most to the same house and same job they held previously. The notable nineteenth-century exception was John W. Leedy, who lived briefly in Lawrence, and then in Seattle before moving to Alaska and eventually settling in the province of Alberta. Samuel Crawford moved to Emporia and then to Topeka, while maintaining a law office in Washington, D. C. Thomas Osborn established his home in Topeka, following eight years in foreign service with the Department of State. George Anthony spent several years in Mexico and later lived in Ottawa, Kansas.

The most peripatetic of twentieth-century Kansas governors was Fred Hall. After his term expired, he resided first in Topeka, then in several California cities, followed in quick succession by Dodge City, Wichita, and Shawnee. Topeka was the ultimate home for Alf Landon, for Harry Woodring following his Washington years, and for Walter Huxman in his capacity as federal judge. Ratner, Schoeppel, and Avery made their homes in Wichita after their gubernatorial years, although Avery later returned to his longtime home in Wakefield. Willis Bailey returned briefly to Baileyville, moved to Atchison, and later lived in Mission Hills.

The first forty-one men who served as Kansas governor were closely associated with majority groups within the state. All of them possessed the ability to gain statewide support for election as the state's chief executive. Some of the governors were outstanding communicators through the spoken word. Others demonstrated leadership and managerial abilities. Even though the average tenure of a governor has been short (slightly over three years), they have been more visible than any other Kansas public servant—with the possible exception of a United States senator for Kansas, and their average service has been about eight years. If something is wrong in state government, the governor is blamed. Similarly, he claims credit for the positive attributes of his term in office.[10] In the past writing of state history, the attention directed toward the governor has paralleled the manner in which national history places the president in the center of national politics. Just as citizens display interest in the nation's chief executive and what he says, on a lesser scale Kansans are attentive to what a governor does and says.

BIOGRAPHICAL SKETCHES OF THE GOVERNORS AND ACTING GOVERNORS OF THE TERRITORY OF KANSAS (1854–1861)

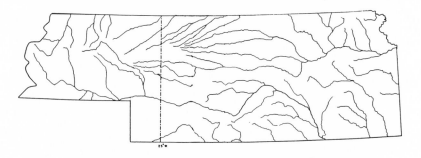

In 1861 the western Kansas border was set at 25° W.

ANDREW HORATIO REEDER

Pennsylvania (Democrat), commissioned 29 June 1854,
took oath 7 July, arrived in Kansas 7 October; served to 17 April 1855;
and 23 June–16 August 1855 (fired)

Born 12 July 1807, Easton (Northampton County) Pennsylvania; son of Absalom Reeder and Christiana Smith Reeder; educated at academy, Lawrenceville, New Jersey, and studied law; married Amelia Hutter, 3 sons and 5 daughters; died 5 July 1864, in Easton.

Andrew Horatio Reeder, from Pennsylvania, was an ardent supporter of Pres. Franklin Pierce, and was at his prime when he was appointed governor of the Territory of Kansas. At age forty-seven he was slightly corpulent, with an "erect form and determined aspect,"[11] of ruddy complexion, with full dark blue eyes and iron-gray hair. One source holds that a friend, Ely Moore, a former member of Congress, had recommended him to Pierce; another claims that local Democrats Asa Packer and John W. Forney had been responsible for the president's interest in him. Reeder was a committed Democrat but had never held public office. A northern "doughface" (because he was "soft" on the slavery issue), Reeder professed deep sympathy for the South. He favored the Kansas-Nebraska Act, which had repealed the Missouri Compromise of 1820. Before he left for Kansas, he consulted with President Pierce

33

in Washington and took his oath of office. The oath, administered by Peter V. Daniel, associate justice of the United States Supreme Court, stated, "I, Andrew Reeder, Governor of the Territory of Kansas, do solemnly swear upon the Holy Evangelists that as Governor of the Territory of Kansas aforesaid, I will support the Constitution of the United States, and will faithfully discharge the duties of the said office."[12] Opponents of slavery believed that Reeder had no more scruples about buying slaves than buying horses; in fact, he purportedly "expressed regret that he was unable to buy a number of slaves and carry them with him to Kansas Territory."[13]

The opening of the territories of Kansas and Nebraska to settlement stirred national interests. Both territories had been identified as areas without slavery in the Missouri Compromise of 1820. After California was admitted as a free state in 1850, there were thirty-two United States senators from free states and only thirty from slave states. For a generation, backers of the institution of slavery had defended it in the Senate. Potentially, the balance could be restored west of the slave state of Missouri in the new territory of Kansas if the region were admitted quickly as a slave state. The Kansas-Nebraska Act mandated the use of "popular sovereignty" on the determination of the future status of slavery in these territories. "Popular sovereignty" implied that all eligible voters would have a hand in deciding the status of slavery in these territories, but Nebraska Territory, with its location west of the free state of Iowa and farther from lines of communication, was not an immediate issue; all eyes were focused on Kansas. Thus, there was a rush to Kansas to produce a constitution for the new state declaring it either slave or free. The territorial governor had the authority to call elections and set voting places, and the first elections were for members of a territorial legislature and a congressional delegate.

Three months after he was commissioned as the first governor of the territory of Kansas, Andrew Reeder arrived on the riverboat *Polar Star* at Fort Leavenworth, where he was given a military salute. In response to an address of welcome, Reeder spoke in general terms of support for supremacy of the law. His unwillingness to call a prompt election for the territorial legislature antagonized proslavery advocates in the territory and in western Missouri. Reeder said he was interested first in electing a delegate to Congress. His friend Robert P. Flenniken had come with him to Kansas, hoping to be elected the congressional delegate, and a group of fellow Pennsylvanians had accompanied him to organize a colony.

In the meantime, citizens of Weston, Missouri, had invited Reeder to speak at a public gathering there. When Reeder refused due to the press of business, his action angered Missourians, who construed his response as unfriendly to slavery. Hence he was considered no better than an abolitionist. They were now sure that he was not "sound on the goose," a phrase used to indicate full sympathy and support for slavery. Reeder later testified that his life and person were threatened from that time. The election for the delegate to Congress was held on 29 November, and the proslave candidate, John W. Whitfield, won easily with 2,238 votes, compared to 305 for the Democrat, Flenniken, 348 for the free-state candidate, John A. Wakefield, and 22 votes scattered. In all likelihood there were 1,729 fraudulent as compared to 1,114 legal ballots in that election.[14] Obviously, Whitfield would have won without illegal support.

Supposedly, the well-known Kansas term "border ruffian" came from remarks Reeder made early in 1855 on a short visit to Pennsylvania and Washington, D.C. Reeder used the phrase to describe those proslave partisans engaged in unlawful action along the Missouri-Kansas border. Many militants gloried in that appellation and intentionally acted out the role they had been given. Reeder had also stated that Dr. John Stringfellow, speaker of the territorial house of representatives, "was responsible for the excitement along the border and that it would never have existed had it not been for the course pursued by him in agitating the public mind." At the territorial capital in Shawnee Mission, a displeased Stringfellow demanded an explanation from Reeder. Unable to satisfy Stringfellow with his response, Reeder was struck over the head with a chair and kicked while he was down. Two other proslavery officers kept Stringfellow from drawing his revolver and caused him to withdraw.[15]

James R. McClure, an early settler from Indiana who described himself as a "Douglas Democrat," fully endorsed Reeder's position.

He wrote later that Reeder was "very conservative in his political views. Although he was a free-state Democrat, he was disposed to act fairly towards the proslavery party, and was in favor of allowing the question to be settled by an honest vote of the people. He was surrounded by men who were very bitter towards the free-state sentiment, and who were determined by fair or foul means to make Kansas a slave state."[16]

As early as December 1854, Missouri's senator David Atchison had already urged President Pierce to remove Governor Reeder because he was not moving fast enough to make Kansas a slave state. Reeder authorized a census in early 1855 to determine the population for apportioning seats in the territorial legislature. Although the census showed 2,905 qualified voters, there were 6,307 ballots cast in the election on 30 March—by proslavery settlers, a few free staters, and many Missourians. Thirty-six proslavery candidates won overwhelmingly, to only three free-state candidates. Even though Reeder was threatened with assassination, he refused to provide election certificates for thirteen members of the house and four of the council because of ballot-box stuffing. He issued a proclamation for another election on 22 May to fill those vacancies. Again the proslavery candidates would have won a substantial majority without the additional bluster.

Reeder called the legislature to Pawnee, on the eastern edge of the Fort Riley reservation—a town that he had helped promote. Although touted as the head of navigation on the Kansas River, Pawnee was a poor choice as a new capital because of its raw frontier location. Most Kansans lived in counties only one or two tiers from the Missouri border, more than a hundred miles from Reeder's capital. The Pawnee townsite had few buildings to accommodate visiting legislators. The legislature occupied a recently constructed stone warehouse. One observer commented that "it was a novel sight, . . . to see grave Councilmen and brilliant orators of the House of Representatives cooking their food by the side of a log, or sleeping on a buffalo robe in the open air, with the broad canopy of heaven for covering."[17]

Convened on 2 July 1855, the territorial legislature calmly listened to Reeder's inaugural address. Then each house ousted all free staters seated by the second election and allocated those seats to pro-slavery candidates. Their second action was to adjourn the session to Shawnee Mission; Reeder vetoed the move, but it was passed over his veto. The Pawnee capital was occupied only four days. As soon as the legislature settled in at Shawnee Mission, they adopted Missouri's harsh slave code, with Reeder still questioning their authority to meet in a place not set by him.

On 27 July the members of the territorial legislature signed a memorial to President Pierce asking for Reeder's removal. Even before the arrival of the petition, Pierce had already taken action by offering Reeder another federal position. When he refused it, he was fired on 28 July on the tenuous charge of using his official position to further private speculative interests, including his alleged illegal speculation in Kansa Indian lands. The announcement was made in Washington three days later. Reeder departed his office on 16 August, but he stayed in Kansas for another year, endorsing the free-state cause.

After firing Reeder, President Pierce offered the territorial governorship to John L. Dawson, another Pennsylvanian, who declined. Wilson Shannon of Ohio wanted the job, and Pierce appointed him on 10 August 1855. In the meantime, Daniel Woodson, secretary of the territory, served as acting governor until Shannon arrived on the scene.

During Reeder's thirteen months as territorial governor, the Kansas capital, or the site of the governor's office, was moved frequently. The first location was Fort Leavenworth, where Reeder had a residence on the west side of the plaza and ate his meals with the post sutler. On 24 November 1854 his office was moved to Shawnee Mission; on 27 June 1855 he relocated to Pawnee, then returned to Shawnee Mission on 12 July. On 8 August 1855 the territorial legislature located the capital in Lecompton. Topeka and Minneola were unrecognized territorial capitals of the free-state government and were regarded as illegal by the federal administration.

In the year following his removal as governor of Kansas territory, Reeder gravitated to the unofficial government, comprised of the free-state Topeka movement. This group elected him and James H. Lane to the United States Senate, effective upon Kansas' achievement of statehood under the Topeka constitution. On 4 March 1856 their credentials were presented to the Senate, but that body refused to seat them because Kansas was not yet a state and had no senatorial seats. In March 1856 a three-man congressional committee, dominated by Free-Soilers, came to Kansas from Washington, D.C., and interviewed Reeder. He told them that he had gone to "the President, and gave him in the fullest manner, . . . and endeavored to impress upon him . . . that unless some decided course was taken, the actual settlers of the Territory would be subjected to most cruel persecution; that there was evidently a settled determination on the part of the border counties of Missouri—strong in men and means—to deprive them of the right of governing themselves, and regulating their own affairs." Reeder also stated that he was convinced "that there was a settled determination, by intimidation and force, to subjugate the Territory entirely to their will, in defiance of the right of the majority and the principle of the organic law."[18] Five months later on 4 August Reeder's credentials were presented to the United States House of Representatives as the delegate from Kansas. John W. Whitfield had held that position, but he was unseated after the 2 July report of the congressional investigation of Kansas troubles. However, Reeder's right to the seat was voted down 113 to 88, creating a vacancy for the position of Kansas delegate; it was subsequently filled in October by free-stater Marcus Parrott.

Back in Kansas, the territorial government convened a grand jury which brought charges of high treason, without hearing any evidence, against Reeder and other free-state leaders. Reeder refused to accept the arrest warrant and went into hiding, fearing that he would be assassinated. Later, disguised as a deckhand and woodchopper, he fled Kansas to what he described as "a freer atmosphere." His arrival in Illinois on 27 May 1856 generated excitement and enthusiasm there. Reeder returned to his law practice in Easton, Pennsylvania, where he made many speeches in the fall of 1856 on behalf of John C. Fremont, Republican candidate for president. In 1860 he was a delegate to the Republican National Convention, where the Pennsylvania contingent endorsed him as a vice presidential candidate. After war broke out in 1861, President Lincoln of-

After remaining in Kansas territory for a year following his firing as territorial governor, Reeder departed hurriedly because of threats on his life.

fered him a commission as brigadier general, which he declined on the grounds that he lacked military experience, although he indicated a willingness to accept another appointment.

Reeder was the name of post offices in Anderson County from 31 March to 21 November 1882; in Kiowa County from 16 January 1885 to 31 October 1891; and in Graham County from 9 September 1901 to 14 July 1903. There is still a Reeder township in Anderson County.

REFERENCES: Connelley, 1900; "Governor Andrew H. Reeder," 1875–81; Johnson, 1954; McClure, 1903–4; McMullin and Walker, 1984; Nichols, 1954; Rawley, 1969.

DANIEL WOODSON

Virginia (Democrat), acting governor, 17 April–23 June 1855;
16 August–7 September 1855; 24 June–7 July 1856;
18 August–9 September 1856;
12 March–16 April 1857 (removed as secretary)

Born 24 May 1824, Albemarle County, Virginia; orphaned at age 7; educated in local schools and for a short time at Lexington Academy; married Mrs. America Fuqua Christian Palmer, 14 October 1841, at Lynchburg, Virginia, 6 children with 2 sons and 1 daughter surviving to adulthood; religious preference Baptist but member of no church; died 5 October 1894, in Claremore, Indian Territory, although a resident of Coffeyville, Kansas.

A zealous Democrat, Daniel Woodson was appointed by President Franklin Pierce on 29 June 1854 as secretary of the Territory of Kansas, a position drawing $2,000 per year. Woodson took his oath of office in Washington, D.C. on 28 September. He was fully sympathetic with the southern designs for making Kansas a slave state, and he complied willingly with the wishes of the proslavery party. A contemporary account described him as a "tall, somewhat handsome young man."[19] Because he was acting governor while Gov. Andrew H. Reeder was out of the territory, Woodson became the executive who signed the first laws passed by the territorial legislature. Even though this legislature was accepted by the federal government as the only legitimate one in the territory, free staters called it bogus or fraudulent because of the voting irregularities involved in its election. They thus called the statutes it created the "bogus laws."

Woodson, born on a Virginia farm, had little opportunity for formal education. He was apprenticed in the printing trade where he gained a reputation for his skills. He served eight years as coeditor and publisher of the Democratic newspaper *Lynchburg Republican*, and in 1851 he became editor of another Democratic newspaper, the *Republican-Advocate* of Richmond. His leadership there triggered his appointment as the Kansas territorial secretary.

Woodson was again a key figure when he acted in Governor Shannon's stead. After Shannon was fired, Woodson issued an "extermination proclamation" on 25 August 1856, declaring the territory "to be in a state of open insurrection and rebellion,"[20] which inaugurated a three-week period of marches and countermarches of large-scale proslave and free-state armies. Acting Governor Woodson asked Col. P. St. George Cooke of Fort Riley to send troops to put down the insurrection. Cooke refused, saying that "civil war was not foreseen" in the Constitution and laws or in his orders. Woodson's official proclamation had urged all patriotic citizens to join in defense of the territorial law. Free staters believed that his action was designed to crush all free-state sentiment in the territory. Within his own framework, Woodson was a conscientious official, for he "believed in the righteousness of slavery, and was prepared to aid it in every way in his power."[21] This final episode of Woodson's control of the governor's office ended with the arrival of Governor Geary on 7 September.

Daniel Woodson was secretary during the all-too-brief administrations of governors Reeder, Shannon, and Geary, each of whom supposedly had four year appointments. However, their tenure was subject to the will of the president. Five times during the absence of these governors, Woodson served as acting governor of Kansas territory, for a total of slightly more than five months.

Later in his career Woodson became the receiver of public moneys at the federal land office in Kickapoo, beginning on 3 December 1857. He purchased a farm near Kickapoo in 1858. President Lincoln replaced him before the office was moved to Atchison on 6 September 1861, so Woodson returned to his farm where he lived until 1870. However, financial hardship plagued Woodson during these years. He relocated to Parker in Montgomery County, where he was editor of a newspaper. Parker, located on the southern Kansas border, had been established in 1869 and incorporated in 1871 with the expectation that it would be on a future railroad line. In a year's time, it had gained about fifty flourishing businesses, including the newspaper, and a population of nearly one thousand. But the railroad went instead to Coffeyville, a few miles north on the other side of the Verdigris River, and Parker's businesses began to relocate there. An early historical account of the area states that "the prosperous little city melted away like a mirage, only a few dwellings being left as landmarks."[22] Woodson followed the crowd and moved into Coffeyville, where he worked in the office of the *Coffeyville Journal*. Later he served for twelve years as the Coffeyville city clerk, relinquishing that post shortly before his death in 1894.

Woodson County, named for Daniel Woodson, was established in 1855. It was the only Kansas county named for a territorial official, until Davis County was changed to Geary in 1889.

REFERENCES: Andreas, 1883; Connelley, 1900; Johnson, 1954; Nichols, 1954.

WILSON SHANNON

Ohio (Democrat), commissioned 10 August 1855,
took oath 7 September 1855;
served to 24 June 1856 (sworn in a second time 13 June 1856);
7 July–18 August 1856 (fired)

Born 24 February 1802, near Mount Olivet (Belmont County), Ohio; son of George Shannon, a farmer, and Jane Milligan Shannon, 8 brothers and sisters; educated at Ohio University, Franklin College, and Transylvania University and studied law in the office of David Jennings and Charles Hammond; married Elizabeth Ellis and after her death Sarah Osbun, 8 children; religious preference Catholic; died 30 August 1877, in Lawrence, Kansas.

Wilson Shannon was appointed governor of the Territory of Kansas by Pres. Franklin Pierce on 10 August 1855. After all of his wanderings around North America, Shannon responded to the welcome provided by the first Kansans he met by saying that he came, not for adventure or to improve his fortune and leave, but to find a permanent home. He was a central figure in the most violent era in Kansas territorial history, known as "Bleeding Kansas."

After he was admitted to the Ohio bar in 1830, Wilson Shannon formed a partnership with a Judge Kennon in St. Clairsville. As a Democrat, he sought a seat in Congress in 1832 but lost by only thirty-seven votes. He was elected county attorney, serving from 1833 to 1835, and then state prosecuting attorney, from 1835 to 1838.

43

In 1838 he was nominated for governor of Ohio by the Democratic state convention; he defeated the Whig candidate Joseph Vance, 107,884 votes to 102,146. Two years later he lost to a Whig, Thomas Corwin, 129,312 votes to 145,442, but in 1842 Shannon regained the office in a rematch with Corwin, by a vote of 119,774 to 117,902.

Shannon was Ohio's first native governor, having been born there shortly before its admission to statehood. He pushed for strong Democratic party measures, such as limits on internal improvements and reform of state banks. In 1844 Shannon did not seek a third term; instead he backed Lewis Cass for the Democratic nomination for president, but James Polk was nominated. Before Polk was inaugurated Pres. John Tyler offered Shannon appointment as minister to Mexico, so he resigned as governor to accept. He was recalled in March 1845 because of his lack of tact in communicating with the Mexican government. The Mexican War began a short time later. Shannon returned home to set up a law practice in Cincinnati. In 1849 he organized a group from Ohio and neighboring Virginia to travel to the California mines. He returned to Ohio, empty-handed, in 1851. The next year he was elected to Congress, serving from 1853 to 1855, during which term he voted for the Kansas-Nebraska bill. He was not a candidate for reelection in 1854, perhaps because he realized that support for the act meant political suicide in most northern states.

Shannon was described as "an extreme Southern man in politics, of the border ruffian type."[23] His appointment as governor of the Territory of Kansas gave him complete authority to use federal troops to keep the peace, but sporadic violence of all types still broke out and drew national attention to Kansas. His widespread political experience far exceeded that of either Reeder or Woodson. However, the characteristics that had caused his dismissal as minister to Mexico were also evident in Kansas. Shannon blundered into one crisis after another, and his lack of diplomacy when dealing with opposing sides fueled the volatile situation. As a representative of the United States government, Shannon recognized the legality of the proslave territorial legislature. However, he responded too willingly to partisan requests—most notably, by giving control of the Kansas militia to a vengeful proslave sheriff, Samuel J. Jones, who broadly interpreted the mandate to restore order by planning the destruction of Lawrence. The resulting "Wakarusa War" of late 1855 was a tense, drawn-out situation with little bloodshed. Shannon was pressured to intervene, and he negotiated a "treaty" between the opposing forces, thereby giving the first official recognition of the free-state party. Shannon later told writer George Douglas Brewerton in an interview that he had to furnish Jones with "sufficient posse . . . or be forced into the disgraceful alternative of surrendering the Territorial government into the hands of an armed and lawless mob," which to him meant the free-state party. He also said that "it never occurred to me that the citizens of [Missouri] would cross into Kansas or volunteer their aid to carry out her laws."[24]

Shortly after the first territorial legislature adjourned, a convention assembled in Leavenworth to organize the "Law and Order party," generally referred to in Kansas history as the proslavery party. Governor Shannon, as a delegate to that meeting, was elected chairman, and resolutions were passed condemning the free staters and the Topeka constitutional movement. On 19 March 1856 the United States House of Representatives, dominated by northerners, appointed a three-man committee to investigate the Kansas situation. Two of the three were Free-Soilers, while the other was a proslave Democrat. Accompanied by four clerks, one reporter, and three sergeants-at-arms, they opened their investigation in Lecompton on 18 April, with subsequent hearings in Tecumseh, Lawrence, Leavenworth, and outside the territory. The Free-Soil congressmen received threatening letters while they were in Kansas. The 1,206-page congressional report—20,000 copies of which were published 2 July—provided a preordained free-state analysis of the Kansas troubles, along with a proslavery minority report. The house responded in August by unseating the Kansas delegate John W. Whitfield by a vote of 110 to 92, but it refused to seat Andrew Reeder by a vote of 113 to 88, thus creating a vacancy, and requiring a new election.

In May 1856 Shannon failed to intervene when a large proslave posse descended on Lawrence, destroying buildings and printing presses. In retaliation, a small party led by John Brown went along Pottawatomie Creek, forty miles south of Lawrence, and killed five proslave settlers in cold blood. This "Pottawatomie Massacre" brought renewed violence throughout the territory, even though supporters of both the proslave and free-state parties denounced the killings on Pottawatomie Creek as unwarranted and unprovoked. Shannon had lost control of the Kansas situation: His only response was a series of executive proclamations requiring all armed forces to disband. On 23 June 1856 Shannon headed for St. Louis on official business, and Daniel Woodson took over as acting governor. From St. Louis Shannon wrote President Pierce on 27 June about his great anxiety over "armed bodies of men entering the territory from the north, with views hostile to the peace of the country." However, he lacked similar concern when the state legislature of Alabama appropriated $25,000 to help establish slavery in Kansas. The presidential election of 1856 focused national attention on Kansas and on the inability of the Democratic party to handle the simple matter of organizing a territory for statehood.

Shannon had offered to resign in his June correspondence with the president, but apparently President Pierce had decided to fire him instead. Shannon sent a letter of resignation to the president on 18 August 1856; three days later, his notice of removal reached him at Lecompton, the Kansas territorial capital. In his resignation Shannon wrote that he had "received unofficial information of my removal from office, and finding myself here without the moral power which my official station confers, and being destitute of any adequate military force to preserve the peace of the country, I feel it due to myself, as well as to the government, to notify you that I am unwilling to perform the duties of government of this territory any longer. You will therefore consider my official connection as at an end." Shannon went east by riverboat, and on 7 September he met John Geary, the next governor, coming up river at Glasgow, Missouri. Because Shannon was still concerned about his personal safety, their discussions were brief.

Shannon served the longest continuous term of any territorial governor, more than nine and one-half months: his total time on the job was approximately eleven months. He was absent from his Kansas governorship twice, with Secretary Woodson serving as acting governor a total of thirty-three days.

Never again did Shannon seek public office. In spite of the hor-

Copy of a painting of an older Wilson Shannon, attributed to G. Shannon, 1884.

rendous treatment he had received as territorial governor, he was sincere about his statement when first reaching Kansas. A short time later Kansas became his home for the remainder of his life. He set up a law practice in Lecompton and later in Lawrence and Topeka. He argued some cases before the Kansas Supreme Court. By then he was commenting to visitors, "Govern Kansas in 1855 and '56! You might as well attempt to govern the devil in hell."[25] On many occasions he was a delegate to the state and the national Democratic conventions. Shannon, named for Wilson Shannon, was the first county seat in Anderson County, and it served as a post office from 30 April 1858 to 13 September 1860.

REFERENCES: Blackmar, 1912; Connelley, 1900; Johnson, 1954; McMullin and Walker, 1984; Nichols, 1954; Rawley, 1969; Robinson, 1898.

JOHN WHITE GEARY

Pennsylvania (Democrat), served 9 September 1856–12 March 1857 (fired, effective 20 March 1857)

Born 30 December 1819, near Mount Pleasant (Westmoreland County), Pennsylvania; son of Richard Geary, a school teacher and ironmaster, and Margaret White Geary, 4 brothers and sisters; educated in local schools and Jefferson College (graduated 1841); military experience, lieutenant colonel in Second Pennsylvania Infantry, Mexican War; brigadier general, Civil War; married (1) Margaret Ann Logan, 1843, 3 sons, (2) Mrs. Mary C. Henderson, 1858; died 8 February 1873, from a heart attack, in Harrisburg, Pennsylvania; buried there in the Mount Kalma Cemetery.

After turning down an offer to serve as territorial governor of Utah, John Geary accepted Pres. Franklin Pierce's appointment as territorial governor of Kansas on 31 July 1856. Proslavery Kansans were disappointed in Pierce's choice. They favored Acting Governor Woodson or Surveyor General John Calhoun, both of whom had demonstrated their affinity for the slavery cause. Geary spent a month arranging personal affairs, and then "armed with greater discretionary powers than had been given to either of his predecessors," he set out for Kansas.[26] Coming up the Missouri River, he had a brief encounter with departing governor Wilson Shannon as their riverboats docked at Glasgow, Missouri. He had also discussed the Kansas situation with Missouri's governor, Sterling Price, who agreed to let free-state settlers bound for Kansas travel unmolested.

Geary arrived at Fort Leavenworth on 9 September and headed the next day for Lecompton. Although he was the youngest governor of the Kansas territory, Geary believed that his administrative experience would enable him to bring quiet and order to "Bleeding Kansas."

Geary's career to that time had been varied. His father died while Geary was in college, and he had to take an assortment of jobs in the next few years to pay off his father's debts. These included teaching school, clerking in a store, serving as a civil engineer, studying law, surveying, and speculating in Kentucky land. Geary served as a captain in the Second Pennsylvania Infantry in the Mexican War and was with Gen. Winfield Scott on his march to Mexico City. A lieutenant colonel by the time of the last battles when Chapultepec was stormed, he was promoted to colonel because of his valor at Belen gate. Geary was a committed Democrat, and Pres. James Polk appointed him postmaster and mail agent for San Francisco on 22 January 1849. When the Whigs came into office several months later, Geary was replaced. He became the *alcalde* in San Francisco and in April 1850 its first mayor. As chairman of the California Democratic central committee, he supported California's request for statehood with free-state status. When his wife's health failed in 1852, he retired with his family to his Pennsylvania farm.

Geary had seen preparation for war on the approaches to the Territory of Kansas: Terror and chaos ruled in Kansas at the time of his arrival. In an endeavor to quiet conditions, Geary told his first Kansas audience: "I desire to know no party, no section, no North, no South, no East, no West; nothing but Kansas and my country."[27] His solution was to make use of federal troops, disband the existing militia, and create instead his own Kansas militia. On 17 October he began a twenty-day tour of the territory, gathering opinions wherever he went.

Geary soon clashed with the dominant proslavery legislature. He intercepted and turned back a large group of Missourians intending to destroy Lawrence. He vetoed a bill providing for an election of delegates to the Lecompton constitutional convention; the bill failed to allow for a referendum on any constitution prior to its submission to Congress, a vote which he believed was mandated by the "popular sovereignty" provision of the Kansas-Nebraska Act. The strongly proslave territorial legislature overrode his veto.

Geary sought to act with strict neutrality. For instance, on 7 January 1857 he responded to an appropriation of $20,000 by the Vermont legislature for relief of Kansas sufferers from a harsh winter by writing the Vermont governor that the money was not really needed. He said there was "doubtless some suffering . . . consequent upon the past disturbances and the present extremely cold weather; but probably no more than exists in other territories or in either of the states of the Union."[28]

Several days later Governor Geary gave a long speech to the assembled legislature in which he relayed his impressions of the territory. He recounted that he had "discovered great anxiety in relation to the damages sustained during the past civil disturbance." He recommended some sort of restitution for beleaguered settlers. Geary was also critical of territorial land laws that allowed bigger preemption claims and thus violated national laws; of improper accounting of public moneys; and of legislation which attacked "the theory of our territorial government; and destroys the freedom of speech, and the privileges of public discussion, so essential to uncloak public error, and enable the people properly to mould their institutions in their own way."[29] Dr. John H. Gihon, John Geary's private secretary, wrote the book *Geary and Kansas*, which was published in Philadelphia in 1857 and which revealed the frustrations of satisfying the divergent Kansas interests. At first Geary abhorred the proposals of Kansas abolitionists, and they in turn lacked confidence in him. However, by the time of the presidential election of 1856, he was on intimate terms with such free-state leaders as Charles Robinson and Samuel Pomeroy. Simultaneously he came to distrust the proslave party, and in communications to President Pierce, he blamed them for much of the violence and strife occurring within Kansas. He was offered and emphatically rejected the candidacy of United States senator from the national Democratic party of Kansas. Instead, Geary developed a plan with free staters that called for admission of Kansas as a state under the Topeka constitution with Geary, an administration Democrat, elected governor. However, congressional support for this scheme was lacking.[30]

Like his predecessors, Geary feared threats on his life, and he could not depend on federal troops for protection. His private secretary was even assaulted. Geary submitted his resignation to incoming president James Buchanan, expecting to be reappointed. Instead, after a tenure of only six months and three days, he was dismissed by Buchanan on 12 March with an effective date of 20 March. In a farewell message to Kansans, Geary noted that he had not sought the office and that it "was by no means desirable." As parting advice he noted that "most of the troubles which lately agitated the territory, were occasioned by men who had no especial interest in its welfare. . . . The great body of the actual citizens are conservative, law-abiding and peace-loving men, disposed rather to make sacrifices for conciliation and consequent peace, than to insist for their entire rights should the general good thereby be caused to suffer."[31]

Armed with two guns because of threats against him, Geary left the territory at night and reached Washington, D.C., on 21 March. He willingly spoke in public meetings and to the press about the dangers of the Kansas situation and the nature of its troubles. Gihon claimed in his book that the violence Geary had faced when taking over the governorship had been quieted. In truth, conditions were not as bad after his term as they had been before. On a personal level, Geary's earlier devotion to the Democratic party was slipping. By that time most northerners were incensed by the Dred Scott decision, handed down by the United States Supreme Court through Chief Justice Roger Taney, which held that Congress had no right to prohibit slavery anywhere. This sustained the angry debates over local regulation of the institution of slavery, as proposed in the "popular sovereignty" provision of the Kansas-Nebraska Act.

Geary returned to his farm in Pennsylvania and remarried. In April 1861 with the opening of the Civil War, he organized and commanded the Twenty-eighth Pennsylvania Infantry, which fought in many battles. Geary was wounded, recovered, and was promoted to brigadier general. He served in the Atlanta command, in Sherman's march to the sea, and as military governor of Savannah from December 1864 to April 1865.

With the return of peace, Geary was encouraged by the Pennsylva-

John W. Geary in his Civil War uniform.

nia Republican boss Simon Cameron to become the candidate for
governor in 1866. He won election to the three-year term against
Democrat Hiester Clymer, 307,274 votes to 290,096. In 1869 he defeated Democratic candidate Asa Packer for a second term, 290,552

votes to 285,956. During his administrations, industrial production expanded in Pennsylvania, and the state's large debt was reduced by $10 million. Geary strongly supported the Thirteenth, Fourteenth, and Fifteenth Amendments to the United States Constitution and exhibited a reform stance on labor union issues, on regulation of insurance and utility companies, and on the role of railroads in the economy. Less than a month after his second term ended, he died suddenly.

Geary Street in San Francisco, California, was named for John W. Geary, as was Geary City (later shortened to Geary) in Doniphan County, Kansas, which was a post office until 1905. Davis County, Kansas, was renamed Geary County by the state legislature in 1889. An effort to return to the original county name, honoring Jefferson Davis, was thwarted by Geary County voters in 1893.

REFERENCES: Blackmar, 1912; Connelley, 1900; Gihon, 1857; Johnson, 1954; McMullin and Walker, 1984; Nichols, 1954; Rawley, 1969; Robinson, 1898; Sobel and Raimo, 1978.

FREDERICK PERRY STANTON

Tennessee (Democrat), acting governor, 15 April–27 May 1857;
16 November–21 December 1857 (fired)

Born 22 December 1814, Alexandria, Virginia (then a part of D.C.); son of Richard Stanton, a bricklayer, and Harriet Perry Stanton; educated at Columbian University in Washington, D.C. (graduated 1833); married Jane Harriet Sommers Lamphier, 25 December 1835, 3 daughters and 1 son, with 5 other children dying in infancy; religious preference Baptist; died 4 June 1894, in Stanton, Florida.

Frederick P. Stanton was appointed secretary of the territory of Kansas by Pres. James Buchanan early in April 1857 and arrived for duty on 15 April. His appointment was part of a deal that brought Robert J. Walker to Kansas as territorial governor. He took over the duties of acting governor from Daniel Woodson and served for forty-one days prior to Governor Walker's arrival. During this period, he expressed the hopes of the new administration when he recited Longfellow's "Great Manitou" speech from *The Song of Hiawatha*, which urged all Indians to live together as brothers.[32] He also issued a proclamation apportioning delegates to the Lecompton constitutional convention on the basis of an incomplete census, which, according to some reports, did not count about half of the potential voters. For instance, only three delegates were allotted to nineteen counties located south of the Kansas River. The delegate election on

15 June merely decided which proslavery candidates would attend the constitutional convention. In the territorial legislative election of 5 October 1857, free staters won a majority of the seats in the legislature.

When Governor Walker was out of the territory on 1 December 1857, Stanton as acting governor issued a proclamation calling the legislature into special session on 7 December to submit a vote on the proposed Lecompton constitution. This action damaged the interests of the proslave party which sought to push the constitution through to congressional approval. Walker was forced out as governor, and Stanton was fired by President Buchanan, which drove him into the Kansas free-state party. Stanton served as acting governor just before and after Walker's tenure for a total of two months and twenty-six days.

Stanton had an illustrious career before he came to Kansas. Following his graduation from Columbian University (later renamed George Washington University), Stanton taught in a college in North Carolina where he also studied theology with the intention of becoming a Baptist minister. But he changed his mind and studied law; he was admitted to the bar, and in 1834 he set up his practice in Memphis, Tennessee. As a Democrat he was elected to the Twenty-third Congress in 1847. After his victory, his Whig opponent shot him in the neck, wounding him severely, then fled the country. Stanton served four subsequent terms in Congress; near the end of his congressional career, on 20 May 1854, Stanton gave a long speech in the House in support of the Kansas-Nebraska bill.

Shortly after his term as secretary of Kansas territory, Stanton wrote a long defense of his official career, published in the *National Intelligencer* (Washington) on 21 January 1858. He also spoke at the Chinese Assembly Rooms in New York City on 17 February 1858, where he said that the "effect of these proceedings [in Kansas] on the part of the minority, sustained by the Government of the United States, is to give influence and power to the individuals to whom the President alludes as dangerous and mischievous individuals." Stanton continued to reside in Kansas where he purchased a large estate two miles east of Lecompton. There he built one of the most spacious and costly residences in the area; for instance, the

Stanton gave this marble bust of himself to the Kansas State Historical Society in 1887.

third-floor ballroom was 50 feet square, and the whole house was finished in polished black walnut. (This house was later purchased by former Kansas governor Harry H. Woodring in the years just after World War II; he called it Rebel Hill.)

In 1861 Stanton was one of the candidates for the Kansas seats in the United States Senate, coming in fourth after winners James H. Lane and Samuel C. Pomeroy and third-place Marcus J. Parrott. Later that year he was appointed to the Senate by Gov. Charles Robinson on the assumption that Lane's acceptance of a federal appointment as brigadier general meant that he had resigned. But the Senate recognized no vacancy in the position, since Lane had not tendered an official resignation. At the beginning of the Civil War, Stanton joined the Republican party. Later he moved to Farmwell,

Virginia, and opened a law office in Washington, D.C., in partnership with his old friend Robert J. Walker. Their practice included cases reviewed by the United States Supreme Court.

Stanton was a member of the International Peace League and was its president in 1882. In 1886 he moved to Florida, near Ocala, to a town coincidentally named Stanton. He died there eight years later.

In Kansas, a town near Paola and townships in Miami, Linn, and Ottawa counties were all named for Frederick P. Stanton. In 1887, about the time he moved to Florida, Stanton gave the Kansas State Historical Society a marble bust of himself, executed by Horatio Stone, a Washington sculptor.[33]

REFERENCES: Andreas, 1883; Blackmar, 1912; Connelley, 1900.

ROBERT JOHN WALKER

Washington, D. C. (Democrat), took oath 9 May 1857;
served 27 May–16 November 1857 (resigned)

Born 19 July 1801, Northumberland, Pennsylvania; son of Jonathan Hoge Walker, a lawyer, and Lucretia Duncan Walker, 3 brothers and 4 sisters, 3 of whom died in infancy; educated at University of Pennsylvania (B.A. 1819, M.A. 1822), studied law in father's office in Pittsburgh, was court clerk; married Mary B. Bache, 4 April 1825, 8 children; died 11 November 1869, in Washington, D. C.; buried there.

During the James Buchanan presidential campaign, Robert John Walker wrote to that candidate privately saying that he did "not believe Kansas will become a slave state."[34] Ironically, the job President Buchanan had in mind for Walker was governor of the Territory of Kansas, which Walker had identified as a graveyard for governors. Buchanan believed that the Kansas issue could be settled if a man of Walker's prestige and national prominence were at the helm. The president and Stephen A. Douglas knew how to appeal to Walker and suggested that a successful resolution of the Kansas problem would open better career opportunities in the future. It was a highly visible spot and a challenge—three territorial governors had floundered before him. Walker's delicate health was a concern of his wife's, but he accepted the post, with Buchanan's assurance that he would guarantee all decisions that Walker would make in Kansas.

59

Robert J. Walker's professional career began with his practice of law in Pittsburgh in 1822. Following the death of his father, Walker moved his family to Natchez, Mississippi, where he joined his brother Duncan Walker in a law practice. He declined appointment as a judge and instead used his financial credit to purchase extensive plantations and slaves. He was elected judge of the state supreme court in 1828 but again declined to serve. By 1830 both Walker and his brother had become well known in the Mississippi bar. Walker was a strong supporter of Andrew Jackson, but he lost his first bid for public office—a seat in Congress—in 1832. He was elected to the United States Senate in 1835 as a Democrat and served for ten years. In the meantime, his brother Duncan had moved to Texas, where he had acquired much land before he died. Because of this association, Walker fully identified with the aspirations of Texans. He became the Texas spokesman in the Senate and began a nine-year campaign for its annexation.

Walker was a small man—5 feet 2 inches and weighing only about one hundred pounds. His health broke in the late 1830s so that he could not campaign for reelection. He won anyway, and still affected by his illness, he resumed his seat in the Senate. Walker had gone heavily into debt in Mississippi; although he reduced his liabilities considerably, he still owned slaves, even though he later said that he had manumitted his slaves in 1838.

Between 1844 and 1849 Walker reached the zenith of his political power. He was a delegate to the Democratic National Convention in 1844 in Baltimore, where he opposed Martin Van Buren and John C. Calhoun. When James Polk received the nomination for president, Walker became one of his chief campaign organizers. Polk's election was a victory for expansion of the United States and for Walker: The new vice president was George Mifflin Dallas, his uncle. Although Walker pushed for the position of secretary of state (given to James Buchanan), he accepted the post of secretary of the treasury. There he worked for a tariff reform that placed tax collections on an *ad valorem* base. The law passed by Congress is generally known as the Walker tariff. He also sought to restore an independent treasury, to keep government money outside the private banking system. Other major issues confronting the Polk administration were settlement of the Oregon question and the war with Mexico, and on both counts Walker ardently supported Polk's program. At the same time Walker was slowly moving away from his strong advocacy of slavery. In 1847, he privately arranged for a slave girl who served his wife to be freed. He was aligning himself with nationalists rather than sectionalists.

When Polk stepped down from the presidency in 1849, Walker set up a law practice in Washington, D.C. A visible though now private figure, he spoke out on the wisdom of the Compromise of 1850 and pushed for a transcontinental railroad to California. In succeeding administrations, Walker accepted, then resigned from, an appointment from President Pierce as minister to China. When James Buchanan became president, he formed his cabinet without his old friend Robert John Walker, which came as a surprise since there had been much support for Walker as secretary of state.

As a political figure, Walker had gained a reputation as a skillful manipulator, a highly effective senator, and one of the most successful secretaries of the treasury of all time. As a lawyer in Washington, D.C., he could earn more on a single case than he might expect annually as territorial governor.

Although he took his oath of office on 9 May 1857, Walker did not depart for Kansas until the middle of the month. His tangled finances—which included speculation on a grand scale—required much attention before he left for the west. Kansans were circumspect about their new governor: He pledged fair and free elections, but so had his predecessors. Once he arrived in Kansas, Walker reiterated his desire for full participation in elections to free staters and proslavery advocates alike. In his inaugural address Walker argued that free staters would need to use their right to vote to make Kansas a free state: "The law has performed its entire appropriate function when it extends to the people the right to suffrage, but it cannot compel the performance of that duty." He directed other comments to pro-slavery supporters: "What possible good has been accomplished by agitating in Congress and in presidential conflicts the slavery question?"[35] His speeches took a middle course, hence they were unsatisfactory to both sides. His role in Kansas became more precarious when dominant proslavery Democrats opposed him because he backed free elections—which to them meant a free state. Walker sought to unite free-state Democrats and pro-slave Democrats, to no avail. In the end he did not have the support from Washington that he had been led to expect. By July Buchanan was ill and the national administration was shifting its position on Kansas: Cabinet members from southern states were in control, and they denounced Walker. Buchanan had a talent for changing his mind under political stress; he faded beneath southern pressure.[36]

Elections for the territorial legislature in October brought a free-state majority, partly because Walker had thrown out more than twenty-eight hundred votes cast in two isolated, almost uninhabited regions along the Missouri border. This and other actions were not approved by the administration. By mid November, a depressed Walker returned to Washington. Although he talked amicably with Buchanan and addressed the cabinet on the Kansas situation, pleasantries turned sour when Walker told them that he intended to defeat the Lecompton constitution because Kansans were not permitted to decide whether or not they wanted that constitution. The choice instead was the constitution without slavery (effective only *after* statehood) or the constitution with slavery, both of which would make Kansas a slave state in spite of the language employed. Walker felt betrayed; he had been assured of support and it was not there. He resigned on 16 November 1857, after serving five months and nineteen days.

Although Walker turned his attention to his business interests, he continued to enter into discussions of the Kansas question. He held that "all free Government is based upon 'The Consent of the Governed.' " He sought to justify his position among southerners, without success, and he had dire warnings for the future of the Union. In March 1860, still angry over the way the president and his cabinet had treated him on the Kansas issue, he challenged Attorney General Jeremiah Black to a duel. Black refused to fight.

When the Civil War came, Walker cast his lot with the war Democrats, to restore the Union without slavery. With his old friend Frederick P. Stanton, he published the New York-based *Continental Monthly* from 1862 to 1864. Unlike many of his contemporaries, he believed the war concerned slavery, not states' rights. He became a

Walker in later years.

propagandist for the Union, describing secession as political suicide. Following the Emancipation Proclamation, Walker was approached by the secretary of the treasury Salmon P. Chase, to serve as the Union's financial agent in Europe. He accepted and carried out what he saw as his primary goals—to undermine Confederate credit abroad and to obtain loans for the Union. After the war, his old debts still dogged him. He again set up his law practice in Washington, D.C., with Frederick P. Stanton, although poor health required that his cases generally not take him into court. Walker also worked as a lobbyist: The Russian ambassador employed him over the purchase of Alaska, and Walker also lobbied for the purchase of Dutch New World possessions.

Greeley, in Anderson County, was originally known as Pottawatomie City, then Greeley, then Walker, then Mount Gilead, and finally Greeley again. The township surrounding that locale retains the Walker name.

REFERENCES: Brown, 1902; McMullin and Walker, 1984; Nichols, 1954; Rawley, 1969; Shenton, 1961; Smith, 1975.

JAMES WILLIAM DENVER

California (Democrat), acting governor 21 December 1857–12 May 1858;
appointed governor, served 12 May–3 July 1858;
30 July–10 October 1858 (resigned)

Born 23 October 1817, Winchester, Virginia; son of Patrick Denver, a farmer, and Jane Campbell Denver, 10 brothers and sisters; educated at Wilmington (Clinton County), Ohio, taught school in Missouri, studied law with Griffith Foos in Ohio, and attended Cincinnati College (graduated 4 March 1844); military experience, captain in Mexican War, brigadier general in Civil War; married Louise C. Rombach, 26 November 1856, 2 sons and 2 daughters; religious preference Presbyterian but member of no church; died 9 August 1892, in Washington, D.C.; buried Sugar Grove Cemetery, Wilmington, Ohio.

James W. Denver was on an inspection tour of Kansas as commissioner of Indian affairs when Buchanan determined to remove Acting Governor Frederick P. Stanton. Denver received a telegram on 10 December 1857, stating that he had been appointed secretary of the territory, and he became acting governor eleven days later. In an "Address to the People of Kansas," Denver stressed that "the great objects to be accomplished, in the opinion of the President, were to preserve the peace of the Territory and secure the freedom of the election."

Thirteen years earlier, Denver had graduated from law school and had settled in Xenia (Greene County), Ohio. He purchased the local Democratic newspaper, maintained a law office and a print shop, and enjoyed some slight success in this first business venture. After a year, he moved to Platte City, Missouri, where he combined law and newspaper work. His extraordinary size attracted attention wherever he went. He was six feet five-and-one-half inches tall, well built, with a militarylike carriage that made him seem even taller. Following the outbreak of the Mexican War in 1846, Denver accepted a captain's commission, as of 4 March 1847, to recruit a company of soldiers. In June, Denver's company joined Winfield Scott's army at Vera Cruz, and they participated in the march on and capture of Mexico City. When the war ended, Denver went back to Platte City, but in 1850 he headed for the California gold fields, reaching Sacramento in September. The following year he campaigned for state senator, won election, and served from 1851 to 1853. In August 1852 Denver was challenged to a duel by a leading politician; utilizing his right to pick the weapons, Denver selected Wesson rifles at forty paces. After the first bloodless exchange of fire, Denver's challenger insisted on a second shot, whereupon Denver killed him.

In March 1853 Denver was appointed California's secretary of state. The following year, he was elected to one of California's two seats in Congress as an anti-Broderick Democrat. He started for Washington on 4 October 1855, travelling via the Isthmus of Panama, a trip of two months. Because of the distance involved, he did not return to his California home at all during his congressional duty. In Congress Denver served on the Committee on Military Affairs and as chairman of the Select Committee on the Pacific Railroad. On 8 April 1857 he was appointed commissioner of Indian affairs by Pres. James Buchanan. He held this post for about nine months, until he became secretary and acting governor of the Territory of Kansas and later governor. When he resigned, he resumed his duties as commissioner of Indian affairs.

As governor of territorial Kansas, Denver indicated that he supported the action of the Lecompton constitutional convention and expected "the cooperation of all good citizens." Free staters had gained control of the legislature by the time Denver came to Kansas, and the vote on the Lecompton constitution, at first, merely let voters decide between two different types of slavery. Buchanan strongly supported this document, which provided for a slave state of Kansas, but another vote was required in the territory. The constitution was soundly defeated by the voters. In other actions Denver vetoed a bill to repeal the black laws, saying that this act "is a very stringent one, perhaps much more so than is necessary, but, so long as the territorial existence continues here, the owners of slaves have a right to claim protection for their property at the hands of the law-making power."[37] The legislature then passed a less extreme measure and Denver signed it. Denver also vetoed an attempt to move the territorial capital from Lecompton, a bank charter bill, and a bill commissioning officers in the militia that would have reduced the governor's power. Although the legislature passed these measures over his veto, they lacked administrative authority to carry out the new laws. Near the end of the legislative session, a bill was passed to elect delegates to another constitutional convention. Denver had three days, not counting Sunday, to sign the bill or permit it to become law, but the legislature adjourned before the time had passed. Thus, Denver had a "pocket veto" and held that the bill calling for a new constitutional convention at Leavenworth had not become law and thus the convention was out of order.

Denver seemed to be able to communicate to both sides in the Kansas argument, thereby serving as an effective mediator. When he resigned and prepared to leave the territory, a banquet honoring him was held in Leavenworth, and representatives of all political views were present. His biographer holds that he refused to aid either side but "took the position that his entire duty lay in enforcing the laws of the United States." A comparison between the time Denver arrived in the territory and when he resigned shows that "the change for the better was . . . noticeable."[38] His letters at that time show his enmity toward some free-state forces in the region. However, in 1884, when Denver returned to Bismarck Grove near Lawrence and spoke of his years as territorial governor, his remarks included the statement that "while I had my own views on the great question that agitated the country, as to whether it should be a slave State or a free State, it was not my put in, and I did not pro-

*James W. Denver in his
Civil War uniform.*

pose to mix with it. Had I been a citizen of this State, I never should have voted to introduce slavery into Kansas."

After a four-year absence, Denver finally returned to California in 1859. He sought nomination as senator that year but was defeated. When the Civil War began, he sided with the Union and tried to keep his California Democratic party united. On 14 August 1861 Pres. Abraham Lincoln commissioned Denver a brigadier general of volunteers and assigned him to the Department of the Pacific. For a short time he was assigned to Fort Leavenworth and later to Gen. R. S. Rosecrans's forces on the Ohio River. He also commanded a brigade under Gen. W. T. Sherman. In 1863 he resigned his commission to resume his practice of law in Washington, D.C., while maintaining his family home in Wilmington, Ohio. In 1870 and again in 1886, he was nominated as a Democratic candidate for Congress from Ohio, but both times he lost the general election. Denver was a delegate to the Democratic National Convention in 1876, 1880, and 1884. One of his sons followed in his footsteps and served as a Democratic member of Congress from Ohio from 1907 to 1913.

In 1858 gold was discovered on Cherry Creek, in western Kansas Territory. A month after Denver left the territory, a town company, made up of Lecompton men, named their new town Denver, located in Arapahoe County, Kansas Territory. It later became Colorado's capital. James W. Denver had served Kansas as acting governor for four months and twenty-one days and governor for four months.

REFERENCES: Barns, 1949; Connelley, 1900; McMullin and Walker, 1984; Nichols, 1954; Rawley, 1969; Robinson, 1898; Sobel and Raimo, 1978.

HUGH SLEIGHT WALSH

Kansas Territory (Democrat), acting governor 3–30 July 1858;
10 October–18 December 1858; 1 August–15 September 1859;
15 April–16 June 1860 (fired)

Born 10 November 1810, Newburgh, township of New Windsor (Orange County),
New York; son of John H. Walsh and Elizabeth DeWitt Walsh; educated in private
schools in Newburgh, New York; married Ellen Beekman, 18 August 1835, 6 children,
3 sons surviving to adulthood; died 23 April 1877, near Grantville (Jefferson County)
Kansas; buried first at Grantville, later in the Topeka Cemetery.

In 1857 Hugh Sleight Walsh moved to Kansas from Alabama. He
served as private secretary for acting governors Stanton and Denver
and on 12 May 1858 he took the oath as secretary of Kansas territory.
On four or five occasions (the official record is imprecise), Walsh
served as acting governor during the absences of governors Denver
and Medary. He fully conformed to the proslavery policy of President Buchanan. In the fall of 1858 his office was deluged with letters
of complaint from pro-slavers in southeastern Kansas, and he denounced the actions of James Montgomery and his supporters.
Walsh suggested to United States Secretary of State Lewis Cass that
a reward of $300 be offered for free-state partisan James Montgomery and $500 for John Brown. In 1862 members of the territorial
legislature, dominated by free staters, complained about the acting

governor's decisions and requested that he be fired. Walsh had had a dispute with legislators over their reimbursement for mileage from their residences, and he believed that his removal was the product of this disagreement.

When he was relieved of his job as secretary, he sought at first to retain his position, then he abruptly retired to his 480-acre farm operated by his son DeWitt in Kaw Township, five and one-half miles northeast of Grantville in Jefferson County. He became a prominent Democrat in the area with "pronounced opinions on all subjects, and was ready to speak of and defend them; but he never did so in an offensive manner, and always retained the friendship even of his political opponents."[39] Later he served as a county commissioner in Jefferson County.

Before his Kansas appointment, Walsh had lived in Mobile and Montgomery, Alabama, where his business was lost as a consequence of the Creek War. Following his marriage, he moved to Aberdeen, Mississippi, and operated a store and a tanyard (neither of which succeeded). Fellow Mississippian Jefferson Davis is credited with securing Walsh's appointment.

REFERENCES: Blackmar, 1912; Connelley, 1900; Nichols, 1954.

SAMUEL MEDARY

Ohio (Democrat), took oath 1 December 1858;
commissioned 22 December 1858;
served 18 December 1858–1 August 1859;
15 September 1859–15 April 1860; 16 June–11 September 1860;
26 November–17 December 1860 (resigned)

Born 25 February 1801, Montgomery Square (Montgomery County), Pennsylvania; son
of Jacob Medary, a farmer; educated at Norristown Academy; married Eliza Scott, 1
October 1823, 12 children; died 7 November 1864, in Columbus, Ohio; buried there in
Green Lawn Cemetery.

On 23 November 1858 President Buchanan appointed Samuel Medary governor of Kansas territory. At age fifty-seven Medary was the
oldest man to assume that post. He took his oath on 1 December
and arrived in Lecompton on 18 December, where he quickly talked
and belatedly acted upon the territory's sensitive issues. He objected to the assembling of the territorial legislature in Lawrence, a
ploy used by the free-state majority to protest the use of the proslave capital, Lecompton. Although supportive of the Lecompton
constitution, he followed President Buchanan's advice in suggesting
to Kansans that they submit a new constitution. He set the date for
election of delegates in June 1859. For the first time, delegates were
selected from the newly organized territorial Democratic and Republican parties, with the Republicans capturing thirty-five seats

and the Democrats seventeen. The convention met in Wyandotte in July and drafted a constitution which followed closely the Ohio document that Medary had supported in 1851. Kansans endorsed the new constitution in November 1859, by a two-to-one vote.

When Samuel Medary was sixteen years of age, he contributed to a local paper, the *Norristown Herald*, and it set for him the goal of becoming a newspaperman. His family (whose name was originally spelled and pronounced Maderia) moved to Montgomery County, Maryland, in 1820 and to Georgetown, D.C., in 1823. Two years later, he pushed westward to Batavia (Clermont County), Ohio. Within a few years Medary had served in many local positions, such as school trustee, county surveyor, and county auditor. He established the *Ohio Sun* at Bethel in 1828, in which he strongly supported Andrew Jackson's race for the presidency.

Medary broadened his political goals in 1834 with his election to the Ohio house of representatives as a Democrat; after one term, he went on to serve two terms in the Ohio senate. He was named supervisor of public printing in 1837, the same year that he purchased the *Ohio Statesman* at Columbus. He was editor of that Democratic paper for nearly twenty years. In 1844 Medary led the Ohio delegation to the Democratic National Convention in Baltimore. He strongly supported Polk and his expansionist program, and he endorsed the Mexican War in spite of his Quaker heritage. Medary continued to be active in many programs in Ohio—he was a promoter of the Ohio Horticultural Society, incorporator of four railroads, and supporter of the new constitution of 1851. In 1853, factionalism among Ohio Democrats kept him out of the Pierce cabinet, and he was offered the appointment of minister to Chile—which he declined. He then lost a bid for a seat in the United States Senate in 1854.

At the Democratic National Convention in Cincinnati in 1856, Medary served as temporary chairman. Although he had endorsed Stephen A. Douglas for president, Medary campaigned for James Buchanan after Buchanan's nomination. Buchanan appointed Medary as governor of Minnesota territory in March 1857; he served until it achieved statehood in May 1858, whereupon he returned to a postmaster position in Columbus.

Following acceptance of the Wyandotte constitution, an election for governor of the new state of Kansas was set for 6 December 1859. Medary was nominated by the Democrats, but his Republican opponent Charles Robinson won with 7,848 votes to 5,401. As territorial governor, Medary still retained local power. On 20 February 1860 he vetoed a law abolishing slavery; his message stated, "This bill appears to be more political than practical—more for the purpose of obtaining men's opinions than for any benefit or injury it can be to any one. . . . Two of the papers before me call upon you to pass the bill, to see what I may say, and compel me to act on the premises." He further stated that the law was premature because it merely enacted one of the provisions of the Wyandotte constitution.[40] Nevertheless, the legislature passed the bill over his veto. The territorial supreme court later endorsed Medary's position and found the law unconstitutional.

Expecting Kansas statehood to be approved soon, Medary resigned in late 1860 and returned to Columbus, Ohio. In January 1861 he established *Crisis*, a weekly eight-page national journal that was very critical of the Lincoln administration. As an "old wheelhorse of the Democracy," he reprinted Copperhead and anti-administration sentiment. Soldiers from a nearby camp mobbed and destroyed the *Crisis* office on 5 March 1863, undeterred by local police. On 20 May 1864 a federal grand jury in Cincinnati indicted Medary on charges of conspiracy against the national government. He was arrested, then released on bond, but never tried. In 1869, five years after his death, a monument was erected in Columbus in his memory. The legend, after recording Medary's birth and death, read:

In commemoration of his Public Services, Private Virtues,
Distinguished Ability and Devotion to Principle,
This monument is Erected by the
Democracy of Ohio.

REFERENCES: Blackmar, 1912; Connelley, 1900; McMullin and Walker, 1984; Robinson, 1898.

GEORGE MONROE BEEBE

*Kansas Territory (Democrat), acting governor 11 September–
26 November 1860; 17 December 1860–9 February 1861.
(Job ended when the governor of the state of Kansas took his oath.)*

George M. Beebe

*Born 28 October 1836, New Vernon (Westchester County), New York; son of Gilbert
Beebe and Phebe Ann Cunningham Beebe; educated in common schools, Middletown
Academy, and Albany Law University (graduated 1857); married (1) Cornelia Bennett, 12 June 1861, dec., and (2) Marie Louise Markey, 17 February 1910, 5 children;
died 1 March 1927, in Ellenville (Ulster County), New York; buried Woodlawn Cemetery, Newburgh, New York.*

Following his training in law, Beebe emigrated to Peoria, Illinois,
where he edited the *Central Illinois Democrat*, then to Troy (Doniphan County), Kansas, where he set up a law practice. In November 1859 he was elected as a Democrat to the territorial council with
a majority of fourteen votes. He served in the legislature from 2 January to 1 May 1860. He wrote the minority report against the bill
abolishing slavery, in which he stated, "Having found that there is
now invested in this territory between one-fourth and one-half million of dollars' worth of property in slaves, and believing that the
immediate prohibition of an existing right of property in any given
article is beyond either the legislative power of the states or terri-

tories, as contravening the letter and spirit of articles four and five of the amendments to the federal constitution, the minority recommends indefinite postponement of the bill."[41] Beebe was also one of the Kansas delegates to the Democratic National Convention in 1860, which met in Charleston, South Carolina.

Beebe was appointed secretary of the territory in May 1860, and he assumed his new duties on 1 July. He served as acting governor on two occasions: once in 1860, while Samuel Medary was out of the territory, for two months and fourteen days, and next, in late 1860, after Medary resigned, for one month and twenty-two days. During this time, a devastating drouth that lasted eighteen months destroyed crops and gardens and forced many settlers to emigrate from the territory. As acting governor, Beebe presented an annual message on 10 January 1861, just prior to the time the United States Senate took up Kansas statehood and following secession of four southern states. In it, Beebe still urged repeal of an act of the last legislature to prohibit slavery in Kansas which he said was clearly unconstitutional. He also spoke of premonitions about the future.

> For years have thick growing clouds been darkly gathering round the destiny of our country, until at length, with lurid lightning flashes and deep thunder detonations, the storm, wildly terrific, has burst upon us. So long as fraternal sentiments prevailed among the states, the Republic was prosperous–the people happy. But now, all is changed. Where Peace prevailed, now Discord reigns. The northern States, with one or two exceptions, have declared that 'a house divided against itself cannot stand'–that the Union, consisting of part free and part slave States, though now so divided, is not to fall, but is to be made harmonious, by the termination of an existing irrepressible conflict, in either rendering the States all free, or extending slavery over all; and on these propositions have triumphantly elected a President pledged to 'render the States all free.' What wonder, then, the South should feel alarmed for the safety of her institutions, and seek to strengthen herself for purposes of defense. . . . Intimately identified as her interests are with the perpetuity, progress and prosperity; of that Union

of States into which she has hoped soon to enter and take her equal place—while she could not witness a dissolution with feelings other than of deepest anguish—if God, in His wrath, shall tolerate the worst portent of this tempest of passion, now so fiercely raging, Kansas ought, and I trust will, decline identification with either branch of a contending family, tendering to each alike the olive offering—establish, under a constitution of her own creation, a government to be separate and independent among the nations.[42]

Beebe believed that the North should forego the crusade against the South, and he argued that Kansas must remain neutral. "But, if nothing can be done—if the worst must come, having been made the wand with which the magicians of Evil have aroused the elements, it may not be expected Kansas can stand an idle watcher of the storm." Beebe also commented on the Kansas "mania for town speculations." In a less serious vein Beebe commented on the 135,328 town lots, more than one per person, located in many towns in thirty-eight different counties. He said, "May not a reasonable apprehension be entertained, . . . that there will, ere long, be no lands left for farms in the territory?"

With his job in Kansas concluded, Beebe privately wrote the president that he wished to become secretary of the new territory farther west, composed of lands taken from Kansas at statehood. He did not get the appointment, and in 1862 Beebe moved to St. Joseph, Missouri, where he opened a law office. The following year he relocated to Virginia City, Nevada territory. He sought election to the state of Nevada's supreme court in 1865 as a Democrat but was defeated. Offered a position as collector of revenue in August 1866 by Pres. Andrew Johnson, he declined and returned to Monticello, New York, where for thirty years he edited the Democratic newspaper *Republican Watchman*. Beebe was elected to the New York state assembly in 1872 and 1873 and served as president of the New York Democratic state conventions in 1873 and 1874. He was elected to the Forty-fourth and Forty-fifth Congresses, serving from 1875 to 1879. Gov. Grover Cleveland appointed him as a member of the state court of claims in

1883, a position he held to 1900. Beebe also was a delegate to the Democratic National Conventions of 1876, 1880, and 1892.

REFERENCES: Blackmar, 1912; Connelley, 1900; *National Cyclopedia of American Biography*.

BIOGRAPHICAL SKETCHES
OF THE GOVERNORS
OF THE STATE OF KANSAS
(1861–1990)

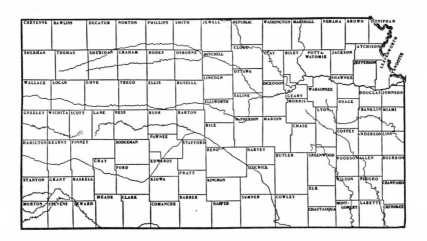

CHARLES ROBINSON

Lawrence (Republican), 9 February 1861–12 January 1863

Born 21 July 1818, Hardwick (Worcester County), Massachusetts; son of Jonathan Robinson, a farmer, and Huldah Woodward Robinson, 5 brothers and 4 sisters; educated at Hadley Academy, Amherst Academy, and Berkshire Medical School (graduated 1843); married (1) Sarah Adams, 1843 (died 17 January 1846), 2 children dying in infancy, (2) Sarah Tappan Doolittle Lawrence, 30 October 1851, no children; religious preference Universalist but member of no church; died 17 August 1894, of chronic bladder and stomach trouble, at his home Oakridge near Lawrence; buried Oak Hill Cemetery, Lawrence.

Following the admission of Kansas as a state on 29 January 1861, Charles Robinson was sworn in as governor on 9 February 1861. Robinson's message to the first state legislature provided his personal interpretation of the territorial history of Kansas, in which he had been an active and decisive participant.

In 1849, after teaching school and practicing medicine in Massachusetts, Robinson had joined an overland caravan to the California gold mines. His cross-country route portentously passed through Kansas, including the future townsite of Lawrence. In California, Robinson settled in Sacramento where he became a leader of the squatter association. He was wounded in a squatter battle, and he won election to the California house of representatives for the 1850–51 term. He returned to Massachusetts, where he edited the *Fitchburg News* from 1851 to 1854.

During late 1853 and early 1854, northern abolitionists became alarmed by the discussion of an eventual passage of the Kansas-Nebraska Act. Inspired by Massachusetts industrialist Eli Thayer's crusade for a free state of Kansas, Robinson came to Kansas Territory in July 1854 at the head of the first colony sent out by the Massachusetts Emigrant Aid Company. By September he had located the company headquarters in Lawrence, his home for the remainder of his long life. In Kansas Robinson was always known as "Doctor," but in reality he was a nonpracticing physician; he made his livelihood first as the agent of the emigrant company, later as a farmer (on his 1,600-acre farm just north of Lawrence), and finally as a real estate promoter. His cool, detached leadership provided a stabilizing influence for the Free-State party. A delegate to the Topeka constitutional convention in 1855, Robinson was elected governor for its active but illegal government. While traveling in Missouri, Robinson was arrested for professing to be the governor of Kansas territory; he was jailed and subsequently freed by antislave partisans. He later helped organize the Republican party. As that party's first candidate for governor, he opposed Democratic candidate Samuel Medary, the last territorial governor. Supporters of Medary sought to convince voters that the Republicans were abolitionists of the John Brown variety, while Republicans identified the Democrats as successors of the border ruffian mobs. In the election of 6 December 1859, Robinson won 7,848 votes to 5,401.[43]

When Robinson first spoke to the state legislature in 1861, he acknowledged the unprecedented drouth of the past year, which affected many trans-Mississippi areas. But his primary concern at that time was the threat secession had brought to an enduring federal union of all of the states. Contrary to his hope "that this issue will be withdrawn, and the nation advance in its career of prosperity and power, the just pride of every citizen and the envy of the world," civil war between the Union and the Confederacy erupted before three months of his term had passed.

Free staters had rejected Lecompton, the last territorial capital, as the state capital and Topeka was designated the new temporary site, with voters approving it as a permanent capital on 15 November 1861. At this time, both the governor's office and the senate were located in a rented downtown building at Sixth and Kansas Avenue called Museum Hall, while the house of representatives was convened in the Congregational Church. Robinson lived at the Tefft House, located at Seventh and Kansas Avenue, while he was governor.

The new state had a sizable debt, no money in its treasury, and immense problems due to the outbreak of the Civil War. As a Union war governor, Robinson was responsible for recruiting troops for federal service, but throughout the war the number of Kansas volunteers far surpassed the quotas assigned to the state. Despite these pressures, Robinson's executive decisions were usually sound: His administration set important precedents for Kansas, created state agencies and a state agricultural society, established the earliest state institutions, and organized the judicial system.

However, a primary obstacle to Governor Robinson was his ongoing feud with Sen. James H. Lane for control of the Republican party. In fact, Robinson had delayed convening the legislature after his swearing-in until 26 March 1861, in an attempt to reduce the influence of his powerful rival. Late in 1861, Lane promoted the idea of a gubernatorial election held at the same time as fall congressional elections; despite the fact that Robinson had just assumed office in 1861, he claimed that Robinson's term was expiring because he had been elected two years earlier. Robinson in turn appointed a replacement for Lane in the Senate on the assumption that the senator had resigned when he accepted a commission as general in the Union army. Lane retaliated by instigating impeachment proceedings against Robinson and two other state executives for selling Kansas bonds below rates established by the legislature. The other state officers were convicted on one of the charges and removed from office, while Robinson was acquitted of all charges. Robinson believed that the convicted officials were victims of an attack directed at him, so as compensation he appointed them as junior officers in Kansas regiments: Neither survived the war.

Even though he was vindicated, the impeachment trial came so close to the meeting of the Republican state convention on 17 September 1862 that Robinson failed to gain renomination. He had many supporters, but he was never popular with the voters. Supporters of Jim Lane drove Robinson from the Republican party, and in later years he was a political maverick. He was a strong believer in temperance but he did not favor prohibition. He backed most other reforms that stirred Kansas voters in that era, such as women's suffrage, blacks' rights, antimonopoly action, and financial reform. Perhaps he might have had more influence had he remained in the Republican party, but his political loyalty in 1862 was for the Union party ticket that was backed by anti-Lane Republicans and Democrats. Robinson served eight years as state senator, beginning in 1873, elected either as an Independent, Independent Reform, or Independent Greenback candidate. He did not garner the nomination for governor in the Independent Reform convention of 1874, but as a National Labor Greenback party candidate for governor in 1882, he won 20,933 votes out of 179,379 cast. His participation in this election helped divide the vote, enabling George Washington Glick, the first Democratic governor of Kansas, to be elected. Robinson ran unsuccessfully as a Democrat for the state senate in 1884, for Congress in 1886, and for governor in 1890 (when he came in third, receiving 71,357 votes out of 296,560 cast). In the 1890 race, Robinson's support for fusion between the Farmers Alliance and Democrats may have influenced such joint ventures in later elections.

Following his term as governor, Robinson lived out his years in Lawrence. For two years in the early 1870s, Robinson served on the board of directors of the Quindaro State Normal School, an institution for blacks near Kansas City. He was almost seventy years old when Pres. Grover Cleveland appointed him superintendent of Haskell Indian Institute on 1 January 1887. During the two years he held that position, the number of students at Haskell more than doubled. He was also president of the Kansas State Historical Society. His service as a regent for the University of Kansas totaled twelve years, and in recognition, he received an honorary Doctor of Laws degree from the University of Kansas in 1887. Robinson, in Brown County, was named for him.

In 1879 at the quartercentennial celebration of the creation of the Kansas territory, Robinson still echoed his moderate and reasonable demeanor when he recalled the "Bleeding Kansas" era: "The old contentions, bitterness, and irrepressible conflict between the North and South have given place to mutual respect, love and good-will. The United States now constitute, in reality as well as in name, like institutions, like aspirations and a common destiny."[44]

REFERENCES: Blackmar, 1902; Carlin and Richmond, 1982; Castel, 1958; Crawford, 1911; Robinson, 1898; Wilson, 1975.

THOMAS CARNEY

Leavenworth (Republican), 12 January 1863–9 January 1865

Born 20 August 1824, near Tipton (Delaware County), Ohio; son of James Carney, a farmer, and Sarah Carney, 3 brothers, 1 half brother, and 2 half sisters; educated in nearby Berkshire; married Rebecca Ann Canaday, 13 November 1851, 5 sons; religious preference Presbyterian but member of no church; died 28 July 1888, in Leavenworth, from apoplexy; buried in Mount Muncie Cemetery, Leavenworth.

On the evening of 12 January 1862, Thomas Carney took the oath of office as governor of Kansas from a Topeka newspaper editor, who also happened to be a notary public. When he assumed office, Carney was reputedly the wealthiest man in Kansas.[45] His successful business in Leavenworth was the source of his prosperity, but his administration was dominated by the effects of the Civil War.

Carney had gained his early business experience in Ohio as a hauler of freight. He also had trained for many years in the dry-goods wholesale business in Cincinnati before he moved to Leavenworth in 1858. There he established the first exclusively wholesale concern in the territory, selling groceries and shoes. His business, Thomas Carney and Company, prospered. His political career began with his election as a Republican to the first state house of representatives during 1861–62. He was nominated for governor by the Republican state convention because he was regarded as a supporter of Jim Lane. Carney won election on 4 November 1862 over Union party candidate W. R. Wagstaff, 9,990 votes to 5,456. Wagstaff was backed by Democrats and anti-Lane Republicans.

As governor, Carney sought every means to improve the financial health of the state. He journeyed to New York City to sell state bonds, and he pledged his personal wealth as collateral for repayment. He ordered recruitment of the last six regiments organized for Civil War duty. He personally paid the expenses of having 150 men patrol the Kansas-Missouri border (which totaled $10,000), but he unfortunately disbanded this force three days before William Quantrill's infamous raid on Lawrence. Carney donated $1,000 of his own money to Lawrence to help the survivors of Quantrill's massacre. When Maj. Gen. Sterling Price's Confederate force pushed west from central Missouri in October 1864, Carney called out the 12,622-man militia. By that time it was obvious that Carney would not have a second term. He had permitted an anti-Lane faction in the Kansas legislature to elect him United States senator in February 1864 in an election called illegally since Lane's seat would not be vacant until 4 March 1865.

Carney's administration was a stormy one, but he laid the basis for financial solvency for the state. State institutions were created in Manhattan, Emporia, Osawatomie, Leavenworth, and Lawrence during his term, and he made substantial gifts to some of them. Newspapers commented favorably on his ninety-minute speeches as governor, and those speeches published show the self-educated Carney as a polished orator. During his last year as governor (after 10 December 1863), Carney's office was located in temporary quarters in a leased brick building on Kansas Avenue in Topeka, which served as the capitol.

In subsequent years Carney continued his wholesale business, while serving as mayor of Leavenworth (1865–66), as director of the Lawrence and Fort Gibson Railway, and as an organizer and president of the first national bank in Kansas, the First National Bank of Leavenworth. During financial crises of the 1870s, he suffered business reversals. The *Dodge City Times* reported on 24 March 1877 that Carney was in Dodge City buying buffalo hides and bones. He had gotten into a poker game, and believing that he had an unbeatable hand, he put everything into the pot and lost. The newspaper commented that "the next eastward bound freight train carried an old man, without shirt studs or other ornament, apparently bowed down by overwhelming grief, and the conductor hadn't the heart to throw him overboard."[46] Nevertheless, by the time of his death in 1888, he possessed much property in Leavenworth.

REFERENCES: Blackmar, 1902; Carlin and Richmond, 1982; Castel, 1958; Connelley, 1918; Crawford, 1911; Miller and Snell, 1963; Plummer, 1971.

SAMUEL JOHNSON CRAWFORD

Garnett (Republican), 9 January 1865–4 November 1868

Born 10 April 1835, near Bedford (Lawrence County), Indiana; son of William Craw-
ford, a farmer, and Jane Morrow Crawford, 2 brothers and 1 sister; educated at country
schools, read law in Bedford, and attended law school of Cincinnati College (graduated
1858); military experience in Civil War, 1861–64, captain to colonel (brevetted briga-
dier general) and in an Indian campaign, 1868–69, colonel; married Isabel Marshall
Chase, 27 November 1866, 1 son and 1 daughter; religious preference Episcopalian but
member of no church; died 21 October 1913 in Topeka; buried in Topeka Cemetery.

At the age of twenty-nine, Crawford became the state's youngest
governor—and one of the tallest at six feet one inch. He was the
first to have both peacetime service and election to a second term.
Crawford had moved to Kansas territory in 1859, locating his law office in Garnett, the county seat of Anderson County. He attended
the first Republican convention and was later nominated representative after a territorial residency of only nine months. Crawford was
elected to the first Kansas house of representatives on 6 December
1859, but he served only from 26 March to 10 May 1861 because he

was given a commission and granted leave to recruit troops in Anderson and Franklin counties. He was a captain in the Second Kansas Infantry, which fought at the Battle of Wilson's Creek on 10 August 1861.

In September 1864, although he had been out of the state for more than three years, Crawford was nominated for governor by the Lane faction of the Republican party. He formally accepted his nomination on 30 September and left his position as commanding officer[47] of the Second Kansas Colored Infantry regiment (also known as the Eighty-third U. S. Colored Infantry) in Arkansas. His return to Kansas came shortly before Confederate forces under Sterling Price reached the state's border. Crawford joined Kansas troops to defend eastern Kansas from Price's army. No doubt his participation in the Battle of Mine Creek, the biggest battle ever fought on Kansas soil, was of more value politically than personal campaigning: Crawford was elected over the Republican-Union (anti-Lane Republican and Democratic) candidate Solon O. Thacher by a vote of 12,711 to 8,244.[48] James McGrew of Wyandotte became his lieutenant governor.[49]

Crawford's long absence from the state and lack of civilian administrative experience appeared to be a liability. But he enjoyed unusual popularity, especially during his first year, from both the citizenry and the press because of his outstanding war record. Rapid developments took place during his four years: The war ended, the state's population almost doubled, and thirty-six counties were created (one named Crawford, with Crawfordville as temporary county seat). Of national interest was Crawford's appointment of a successor to reelected Senator James H. Lane, who had committed suicide as a result of melancholia. Passing over prominent political figures, he named Edmund G. Ross, whom he had known as a fearless soldier. Ross was to later cast one of the crucial votes for acquittal in the impeachment trial of Pres. Andrew Johnson—to Crawford's surprise.[50]

In 1866 Crawford was reelected 19,370 votes to 8,151 over National Union candidate J. L. McDowell. For his second term Crawford picked as his lieutenant governor Nehemiah Green, whom he had first met at the Republican party convention in September 1866. At

Crawford's behest Green received 366 out of 392 delegate votes, and he proved to be a productive running mate.[51]

Crawford's lame-duck term was more difficult for him, yet he looked upon it as coming under "auspicious circumstances." In his long official message to the legislators he said, "Ours is a government of the people, and when their wishes are made known through the medium of the ballot-box it is our imperative duty to comply therewith." He showed his partisan loyalty by declaring that the result "of recent elections in all the loyal States, clearly and unmistakably declares that this Government was intended to be, and *must* and *shall* be, established upon the eternal principles of freedom and impartial justice, that all their blessings and privileges may be secured." An important event in this term was the legislature's election of two United States senators. There was also considerable debate over eliminating references to sex and race in election eligibility during Crawford's second legislative session. Despite the lack of widespread public opposition to expanding the vote to women or blacks, white male voters would not approve a change.

Governor Crawford was generally anti-Indian, and he opposed the treaty-making procedure for buying the Cherokee Neutral Tract and the Osage lands. His protests, combined with the hostility in the lower house of Congress, led to an end of treaty making with Indians. With increased settlement and the extension of the railroads, more Kansas settlers were killed by Indians during Crawford's last two years as governor than in all other years of state or territorial history.[52] Consequently, he vehemently urged removal of all Indians from Kansas reservations. As protection for settlers, he ordered the recruitment of the Eighteenth Kansas Cavalry and the Frontier Battalion: These troops marched about 2,200 miles in their four months of service, without achieving their goal of tracking down Indians. Laws to permit counties to vote bonds for railroad construction, to provide state taxes to build state buildings, to support forestation in Kansas, and to establish a state geological survey were passed during this administration. Crawford also supported unanimous approval of the Thirteenth and Fourteenth Amendments to the United States Constitution by the state legislature.

After an unsuccessful effort to gain the Republican nomination for

PROCLAMATION.

STATE OF KANSAS,
Executive Office,

Topeka, Sept. 14, 1868.

The recent acts of atrocity perpetrated by hostile Indians upon citizens of Kansas, with other accumulating circumstances, indicate with unerring certainty that a general Indian war is inevitable. The United States forces in this Department are too few in number to answer the emergency, and the appeals of our frontier settlers for protection and redress cannot with honor be disregarded.

The undersigned, therefore, hereby calls into active service, for a period of three months, unless sooner discharged,

FIVE COMPANIES OF CAVALRY,

To be organized from the Militia of the State, for service upon the border. Each man will be required to furnish his own horse ; but arms, accoutrements and rations will be furnished by Major General Sheridan.

One Company, to be recruited in the Republican Valley, will rendezvous at Lake Sibley ; one Company in the Solomon Valley will rendezvous at Ayersburg, one Company will rendezvous at Salina, one Company at Topeka, and the remaining Company at Marion Center.

Recruiting Officers will be designated for each Company, and when notice of the organization of a Company shall have been received, the men will be mustered and Company officers appointed. Each Company will consist of not less than eighty (80) nor more than one hundred (100 enlisted men.

As the State has no fund at present from which the men hereby called into service can be paid, it is expressly understood that all claims for service must await the action of the next Legislature.

S. J. CRAWFORD,
Governor.

Proclamation activating the 19th Kansas Cavalry, with which Crawford served as the commanding officer.

Congress in 1868, Governor Crawford received federal permission to recruit the Nineteenth Kansas Volunteer Cavalry for service under Gen. George Armstrong Custer against Indians in a winter campaign.[53] Thirteen hundred men were recruited in three weeks. Crawford resigned as governor on 4 November 1868—the day after the general election—to take command of the Kansas regiment as its colonel, a post he held until 2 March 1869. Since he was leaving at home a twenty-year-old wife and a four-month-old daughter,[54] the timing of his resignation may have come as a surprise to some citizens. But his action was consistent with his attitude and record concerning Indians throughout his years in the governor's office. Moreover, his entry into statewide politics had come from his military role: He may have been trying to revive his political fortunes. The Nineteenth Kansas Cavalry's objective was never realized because Custer wanted his own troops to engage the Indians.[55]

When Crawford returned from the winter campaign of 1868–69, he moved his family to Emporia, where he practiced law and was a real estate promoter. In an era when corruption and scandal permeated state and national politics, Crawford joined a Republican reform faction known as the "purifiers." As a candidate of the purifiers in 1871, he was defeated in his try for the United States Senate by Alexander Caldwell of Leavenworth. As a leader of the purifiers in 1872, he won the presidency of the state Liberal Republican convention. This splinter party fused with the Democrats in 1872 but lost. Crawford was politically inactive until 1876 when he became the Independent Greenback candidate for Congress. By the time of that election much of his law practice had moved to Topeka, and he also maintained a branch office in Washington, D. C. In 1878 he was an unsuccessful Independent candidate for a nonexistent at-large seat in Congress, running on the assumption that Kansas deserved an additional seat because of its population explosion.

On 5 March 1877 Crawford was appointed by Gov. George Anthony to the highly remunerative position of Kansas state agent, in which he prosecuted the state's claims against the federal government for a percentage of the amount received. The fact that he held that position for fourteen years, under five governors and seven legislative sessions, is an indication of his political abilities. All told, he received more than $200,000 from the state for his services. Although Topeka continued to be his home (he erected a business block and built a fine mansion there), he spent much time in Washington, D.C., at his farm near Baxter Springs, and on summer vacations on Nantucket Island. His memories of his glory years in the 1860s were published shortly before his death.

REFERENCES: Castel, 1958; Crawford, 1911; Moore, 1897–1900; Plummer, 1962; Plummer, 1971.

NEHEMIAH GREEN

Manhattan (Republican), 4 November 1868–11 January 1869

Born 8 March 1837, Grassy Point Township (Hardin County), Ohio; son of Shepard Green, a farmer, and Mary A. Fisher Green, 4 brothers and 4 sisters; educated at subscription schools and Ohio Wesleyan; military experience in Civil War, 1861–63, first lieutenant, 1864, sergeant major in Ohio National Guard; married (1) Ida K. Leffingwell, 1860 (died 1870), 3 children, (2) Mary Sturdevant, 1873, 2 children; religious preference Methodist; died 12 January 1890 of long illness brought on by war service, in Manhattan; buried in Sunset Cemetery, Manhattan.

When Gov. Samuel J. Crawford resigned on 4 November 1868 to take command of a Kansas regiment, Nehemiah Green became governor for the final sixty-nine days of Crawford's term. A "caretaker governor" during a period when the legislature was not in session, there was little business for Green to attend to.

Green first arrived in Kansas territory in 1855 with several of his brothers, when he staked a claim at Palmyra (Baldwin City). He returned to Ohio in 1857 to enter the Methodist ministry. After service in the Civil War, he was sent to Manhattan, Kansas, as minister of the Methodist Episcopal church. The 1866 Republican party convention nominated him for lieutenant governor, and he was elected and assumed his post for Governor Crawford's second term.

After his gubernatorial stint, Green became presiding elder (dis-

The Winchester Model 1866 Presentation Rifle given by Samuel Crawford to Nehemiah Green in 1871, now in the possession of the Kansas State Historical Society. The engraving reads "To Nehemiah Green from S.J.C." Behind the breech appears "Wichita, Oct. 21st, 1871."

trict superintendent) of the Methodist church for the Manhattan district. For a while he taught close-order drill to military tactics students at Kansas State Agricultural College. In 1873 he retired to his farm in the Blue Valley, north of Manhattan, which he acquired after selling a farm in Pottawatomie County. He was a regent of the Kansas State Agricultural College from 1873 to 1874 and was elected to the Kansas house of representatives in 1880, serving as speaker *pro tem* during 1881–82. Green, in Clay County, was named for him, and he provided a church bell to the first church built there.[56]

REFERENCES: Crawford, 1911; Plummer, 1971; Riley County Genealogical Society, 1976.

JAMES MADISON HARVEY

Vinton (Republican), 11 January 1869–13 January 1873

Born 21 September 1833, near Salt Sulphur Springs (Monroe County), Virginia, now part of West Virginia; son of Thomas Harvey, a farmer, and Mary Walker Harvey, 4 brothers; educated at common and select schools in Indiana, Illinois, and Iowa and trained as a surveyor and civil engineer; military experience in Civil War, captain, also brigadier general in state militia; married Charlotte Richardson Cutter, 1854, 4 sons and 5 daughters, all born in Riley County; died 15 April 1894, of Bright's disease, at his farm home near Vinton; buried in Highland Cemetery, Junction City.

James Madison Harvey was the first Kansas governor to serve two full terms and the first to serve in the United States Senate. He was also the first to occupy the capitol, moving into the newly completed east wing early in his first term. During all four years as governor, Harvey lived at the Tefft House at Seventh and Kansas Avenue, while his wife, Charlotte, stayed at the Harvey farm near Vinton most of the time.

When living in Adams County, Illinois, Harvey had joined a party heading west, lured by the stories of the Pike's Peak gold strike. His caravan met so many disappointed miners that near Fort Kearney, Nebraska, he turned back to Riley County, Kansas, where he got a preemption claim near Vinton, now within the borders of the Fort Riley military reservation. He earned money to pay for his claim by teaching school, quarrying rock, and driving freight wagons. He added to his land after he became a full-time farmer-rancher.

Originally a Whig, Harvey was a Republican by the time he settled in Kansas. He was elected to the state house of representatives (1865–66) and to the senate (1867–69). In 1868 he was nominated for governor by the Republican state convention, and he won with 29,795 votes against the 13,881 received by George Washington Glick, the Democratic candidate. He was reelected in 1870 with 40,667 votes; his opponents were Isaac Sharp, Democrat, who garnered 20,496 votes, and the Workingman candidate W. R. Laughlin, who won 108 votes from two southeastern counties.

The Republican party worked harmoniously during Harvey's two administrations. Two early issues involved claims filed as a result of Indian raids and land conflicts in southeastern Kansas. Additional business included settling the claims from the Civil War raid of Sterling Price; replenishing the military and contingency funds; strengthening bribery laws; creating new judicial districts; and establishing new counties, one of which was named Harvey. Although Kansas voters failed to approve suffrage for black males in 1867, the state legislature in 1869 made Kansas the first state to ratify the Fifteenth Amendment to the United States Constitution. New state institutions and a reorganized State Board of Agriculture were other accomplishments of Harvey's administrations.

"Old Honesty" Harvey—a nickname he carefully guarded—did not seek a third term but retired instead to his Riley County farm in Vinton. When Alexander Caldwell resigned as United States senator, Harvey was elected to fill that post by the state legislature on 2 February 1874 to serve until 3 March 1877. He spent three years in the early 1880s in New Mexico, Arizona, Utah, and Nevada as a government surveyor. Then, seeking a milder climate, he moved his family back to Virginia for six years but returned in 1890 to his Vinton farm. Although he did leave again the following year to work as a government surveyor in the Oklahoma panhandle, the Vinton site remained his home until his death.

REFERENCES: Carlin and Richmond, 1982; Crawford, 1911; Knauer, 1953; Riley County Genealogical Society, 1976.

THOMAS ANDREW OSBORN

Leavenworth (Republican), 13 January 1873–8 January 1877

Born 26 October 1836, near Meadville (Crawford County), Pennsylvania; son of Carpenter Osborn, a carpenter, and Elizabeth Morris Osborn; educated at common school and Allegheny College (preparatory department), 1855–57, apprenticed to Meadville printer and studied law; married Julia Delahay, 1870, 1 son; religious preference Methodist but member of no church; died on 4 February 1898 of a severe hemorrhage while on a trip to his birthplace, Meadville, Pennsylvania; buried in Topeka Cemetery.

In 1872 the Republican state convention nominated Thomas Andrew Osborn for governor. He defeated the Liberal Republican candidate Thaddeus H. Walker by 66,854 votes to 34,468, and times looked good for Osborn and for Kansas. There were many new miles of railroad track under construction, and settlers in large numbers were moving to Kansas. But the Panic of 1873, when several large eastern banks failed, turned the national economy sour and Kansas was affected along with the rest of the country. In addition to problems brought on by the panic, three crises faced Osborn during his first term—the threat of an Indian uprising, the grasshopper plague of 1874, and embezzlement by the state treasurer.

In 1873, Governor Osborn received news from southern Kansas that Indians were about to attack new settlements. He requested

the protection of federal troops, to little avail. Actually, since the
Indians did not attack, it seemed to substantiate the belief of the
army officers that these fallacious reports of Indian aggression were
made to get federal troops and federal money into a frontier region.
Another stress on Kansas settlers was a prolonged drouth in the
1870s which brought tremendous invasions of Rocky Mountain lo-
custs (grasshoppers) into Kansas and other Great Plains states. Grasshoppers were destructive throughout the decade, but 1874 was the
worst, especially for areas of recent settlement. Newly arrived settlers expected to produce sufficient bounty from their gardens to
enable them to survive, but grasshoppers literally ate them out of
house and home. Osborn convened a special session of the legislature to provide public relief for those in need. Laws were passed enabling counties to vote taxes or to sell bonds for relief purposes—a
role considered appropriate for counties but not for the state. A
third difficulty for Osborn was caused by another elected state official, the treasurer, who was involved in a variety of illegal deals using
state money. To avoid formal impeachment charges and likely conviction, the treasurer resigned.

Renominated in 1874, Osborn defeated the Independent Reform
candidate James C. Cusey, 48,794 votes to 35,301, with 2,277 votes
cast for the Temperance candidate W. K. Marshall. During his second term another state treasurer was found defrauding the state
through forgery, counterfeiting, and embezzlement. The governor
responded quickly to protect the state with stricter laws for receiving and handling money. The state constitution was amended to
provide for biennial legislative sessions, with two-year terms for representatives and four-year terms for senators. (As a matter of interest, each house of the state legislature reached its present size during
Osborn's four years—40 in the senate and 125 in the house.) Osborn
sought a constitutional convention for substantial alterations in the
state constitution, but he was unsuccessful—further evidence of
Kansans' historic resistance to additional conventions.

Osborn's prior career in Kansas had been politically oriented, although he had had business experience in banking, journalism, real
estate, and mining while still in Pennsylvania and Michigan. Following his admittance to the bar in Pontiac, Michigan, in 1857, Osborn

departed for Kansas, settling in Elwood and later moving to Leavenworth. In Doniphan County, Kansas, he was elected to the first state senate as a Republican, serving from 1861 to 1863, during which time he held a key position as presiding officer of Governor Robinson's impeachment trial. He was lieutenant governor (1863–65) and United States marshal for Kansas (1864–67). His forced removal from the office of marshal by Pres. Andrew Johnson added to his popularity in Kansas.

In 1877, following his four years as governor, Osborn was a leading candidate for the United States Senate, but he lost to Preston B. Plumb. Pres. Rutherford B. Hayes appointed Osborn minister to Chile in 1877, and in 1880 he presided over a peace conference involving Peru, Chile, and Bolivia. He also helped settle the Patagonian boundary dispute between Argentina and Chile. President Garfield made him minister to Brazil in 1881. He returned to Kansas in 1885 and established his residence and law practice in Topeka. Osborn headed the Kansas delegation to the Republican National Convention in 1888, and he served two terms (1889–97) as Shawnee County's state senator. From 1894 to 1898 he was a director of the Atchison, Topeka and Santa Fe Railroad.

REFERENCES: Malin, 1964; Socolofsky, 1977.

GEORGE TOBEY ANTHONY

Leavenworth (Republican), 8 January 1877–13 January 1879

Geo, T. Anthony

Born 9 June 1824, Mayfield (Fulton County), New York; son of Benjamin Anthony, a farmer, and Anna Odell Anthony, 4 sisters and brothers; educated during winter months annually at county school, apprenticed in tin and coppersmithing; military experience in Civil War, captain (brevetted major) in Seventeenth New York Independent Battery; married Rosa A. Lyon, 1 son; religious preference Quaker but member of no church; a diabetic, died 5 August 1896, of pneumonia, in Topeka; buried in the Topeka Cemetery.

In 1876 George Tobey Anthony won nomination for governor from the Republican state convention, where he gained a majority vote on the seventh ballot in a highly competitive contest against six other candidates. He won election with 69,176 votes against John Martin, Democratic candidate, with 46,201. M. E. Hudson, Independent-Reform candidate, and J. Paulson, Temperance, received a total of 6,020 votes. Although Anthony's visibility with the public was no doubt enhanced by his famous cousin—suffragette Susan B. Anthony, sister of Leavenworth publisher Daniel R. Anthony—the new governor was an able speaker and debater in his own right. He was the first Kansas governor to present his message to the state legislature orally; in addition, he addressed the legislature just before he retired as governor.

Shortly after the patent on the telephone by Alexander Graham Bell in 1876, the first telephones were installed in Kansas. During his administration, problems associated with the Panic of 1873 still handicapped the economy. Anthony therefore supported only those programs that required little state funding—a state reformatory for younger criminals, a state commission of fisheries, and a stronger temperance movement. A major crisis for him was the railroad strike in 1877, as Kansans emulated workers in the East. Anthony sent state militia to Emporia to protect private property. When a soldier accidentally killed a Congregational minister, Anthony promptly recalled the militia; however, this debacle gave ammunition to his opponents. Anthony had the upper hand in the 1878 Republican state convention, but his votes peaked at 106 after seventeen ballots. Opposed by future governors John P. St. John and John A. Martin, each of whom had substantial support, Anthony broke the impasse by throwing his votes to St. John, thus giving him the nomination.

As a young man, Anthony had opened his own tinshop in Medina, New York, immediately after his apprenticeship in the trade. Later he had a commission business in New York City. From 1861 to 1864 he was loan commissioner for Orleans County, New York. He moved to Leavenworth, Kansas, in 1865 to become editor of the *Daily Bulletin*, owned by a cousin, Dan Anthony. A Republican, he was appointed assistant assessor of internal revenue in 1867 and collector of internal revenue in 1868. In 1867 he purchased the *Kansas Farmer*, using it to back diversified farming in Kansas during the six years of his ownership. He was president of the State Board of Agriculture (1873–76), which had been created in 1872. Anthony not only had an impact on its development but also was at the helm in the days when this agency both catered to the needs of Kansas farmers and served as the official immigration bureau for the state.

Similarly influential was Anthony's presidency of the State Board of Centennial Managers (1874–76), an agency created to organize the participation of Kansas in the Centennial Exposition in Philadelphia. This board, motivated by a desire to change the Kansas image from a "bleeding," starving, drouth-stricken, and grasshopper-infested state to a land of bountiful crops, had many ideas for a Kansas exhibit. They convinced the state legislature to expend almost 4 percent of the annual state budget to erect the Kansas building at the Philadelphia fair and to display in elaborate fashion the abundance of Kansas agriculture.

Following his two years as governor, Anthony managed a Pottawatomie County farm and invested in railroads, including the Mexican Central for which he was general superintendent from 1881 to 1883. He spoke throughout Kansas on behalf of temperance when the constitutional amendment on prohibition came up in 1880. He was elected to the state house of representatives in 1885 from Leavenworth County. At that time he was president of the Wyandotte and Northwestern Railway Company. He was a member of the Board of Railroad Commissioners (1889–93), a delegate to the Trans-Mississippi Congress in New Orleans (1892), and the appointed state superintendent of insurance (1895). Throughout, his family home remained in Ottawa where he served a number of years as editor of the weekly and daily *Republican*. In 1892 the Republican State Convention nominated him for congressman-at-large, but he lost to William A. Harris, the Democratic-Populist candidate. Anthony, county seat of Harper County, was founded while he was governor and was named for him.

REFERENCES: Snell, 1974; Socolofsky, 1977; Socolofsky, 1987; Tripp, 1964; Williams, 1972.

JOHN PIERCE ST. JOHN

Olathe (Republican), 13 January 1879–8 January 1883

Born 25 February 1833, near Brookfield (Franklin County), Indiana; son of Samuel St. John, a farmer, and Sophia Snell St. John, 1 brother and 1 half brother; educated at common county school and studied law; military experience in Civil War, lieutenant colonel; married (1) Mary Jane Brewer, 1852, 1 son, divorced 1859, (2) Susan J. Parker, 28 March 1860, 2 children surviving infancy; religious preference Congregational then later Christian Science; died 31 August 1916 after suffering heat prostration in Olathe; buried in Olathe Cemetery.

In 1878, the Republican state convention gave John P. St. John the nomination for governor over the incumbent George T. Anthony and rival John A. Martin. He defeated the Democratic candidate John R. Goodin by 74,020 votes to 37,208, with the Greenback candidate D. P. Mitchell receiving 27,068 votes. St. John was the first governor to have formal inauguration ceremonies. Held on the steps of the newly completed east wing of the State Capitol, it was described in the nationally distributed *Harper's Weekly*. St. John's official residence was at the Tefft House at Seventh and Kansas Avenue. In 1880, in his second race, St. John defeated United States

Sen. Edmund G. Ross—a former Republican now running as a Democrat—115,204 votes to 63,557. Three minor party candidates polled 20,183 votes in that election.

In 1847 John St. John's family moved from Indiana to Illinois. St. John married his first wife there in 1852, but three months after the wedding, he hastily departed without his wife for California. There he mined, cut wood, worked in a store, worked on a steamboat, fought against Indians (when he was twice wounded), and began the study of law. After traveling to Mexico, Central and South America, and Hawaii, he returned to Illinois around 1859 and was admitted to the Illinois bar in 1860. After service in the Civil War, St. John moved to Independence, Missouri, and then in 1869 to Olathe, Kansas. As a Republican he was elected to the state senate in 1872 from Johnson County but declined renomination four years later. He also refused the Prohibition party's nomination for governor in 1876.

A major development in St. John's first term was the legislative initiative to place a constitutional amendment for prohibition before the voters in 1880. With strong support from the governor, constitutional prohibition was approved, and the legislature wrote an enforcement law. As an ardent prohibitionist, St. John started the first of many gubernatorial "water banquets," where no beverage stronger than water was served. Governor St. John was the official host for the visit of Pres. Rutherford B. Hayes, for whom a water banquet was appropriate. However, it was less appreciated by the nonteetotaler former president, Gen. Ulysses S. Grant, during his visit.

Two other important issues faced St. John as governor. Kansans near the southern border feared another Indian uprising in their area, and they voiced their frustrations in letters to the governor. A mounted guard was created to protect settlers along that boundary. A second crisis stemmed from the fact that Kansas had become the "promised land" for thousands of blacks emigrating from southern states. St. John organized assistance for these "Exodusters," many of whom came to Kansas without resources. On a different front, St. John opened a coal mine at the penitentiary in Lansing to provide jobs for the prisoners, due to a dominant belief of the era that such institutions should be self-supporting.

Henry Worrall's sketch of the inauguration of John P. St. John on 13 January 1879, published in the 8 February issue of Harper's Weekly.

In 1882 Governor St. John controlled 80 percent of the delegates in the Republican state convention, enabling him to receive an unprecedented nomination for a third term. However, he was defeated by Democrat George Washington Glick, 83,237 votes to 75,158. Of significance in this election was the candidacy of Charles Robinson, the first governor of Kansas, on the National or Greenback-Labor ticket; he received 20,933 votes. The campaign issues were the third-term issue and St. John's ardent support for both prohibition and women's suffrage. The sizable third party vote and a belief that St. John was in league with the railroads led to his defeat in the election and virtually forced him out of the Republican party.

St. John's fervor for prohibition had brought him many backers and many antagonists. In fact, the first town named for him had a name change within fourteen months, and the county with his name was redesignated by the legislature after he was out of office.

However, St. John, seat of Stafford County, still commemorates him.

The Prohibition party nominated St. John for president in 1884, and he attracted much attention in his campaign, receiving fifteen times more votes than previous Prohibition candidates. The votes he received in New York alone were decisive, for he probably reduced the Republican tally and thereby cost James G. Blaine the state—and the presidency, making Grover Cleveland the first Democratic president since the Civil War.

The loss of the election did not dampen St. John's enthusiasm for prohibition; he traveled more than 350,000 miles and made 4,500 speeches in support of it. Reform-minded, he also backed free silver, direct election of United States senators, women's suffrage, and government ownership of railroads. He severed his Prohibition party connections in 1896 and rallied to the Democratic candidacy of William Jennings Bryan in 1900. St. John remained active until the summer of his death in 1916.

REFERENCES: Bader, 1986; Carlin and Richmond, 1982; Davis, 1976; Frederickson, 1930; Pickett, 1968.

GEORGE WASHINGTON GLICK

Atchison (Democrat), 8 January 1883–12 January 1885

Born 4 July 1827, near Greencastle (Fairfield County), Ohio; son of Isaac Glick, a farmer-stockman, and Mary Vickers Sanders Glick, 1 sister and 3 brothers; educated at Central College and studied law in office of R. P. Buckland and Rutherford B. Hayes; military experience in Mexican War (enlisted but saw no action), judge advocate general (colonel) in Ohio State Militia, officer in the Second Kansas Regt., Civil War, wounded; married Elizabeth Ryder, 17 September 1857, 1 daughter and 1 son; religious preference Lutheran; died 13 April 1911, in Atchison; buried in Mount Vernon Cemetery, Atchison.

On his second race as a Democratic candidate for governor, George Washington Glick won in 1882 over incumbent John P. St. John by a vote of 83,237 to 75,158, with 20,933 going to the Greenback-Labor nominee and Kansas' first governor, Charles Robinson. Glick's victory was a personal, rather than a party, triumph since no other Democrat had ever won a statewide race in Kansas before. Earlier he was the Democratic party nominee for governor in 1868, when he lost to James Harvey, 13,881 votes to 29,795. When Glick sought reelection in 1884, he lost to a fellow Atchisonian, Republican John A. Martin, by a vote of 146,777 to 108,284, with the Greenback-Labor candidate H. L. Phillips picking up 9,998 votes.

As a Democratic governor, Glick's program during his two years was not much different from that of his Republican predecessors. He emphasized creation of a railroad commission, rural road improvement, tax assessment equalization, and a civil service law. His son, Frederick H. Glick, served as his private secretary. While governor, Glick resided at the Copeland Hotel located at Ninth and Kansas Avenue. During this administration the legislature set new congressional districts, based on the 1880 census. Glick called a special session of the legislature in March 1884 to deal with an outbreak of hoof-and-mouth disease among cattle. That session established a Livestock Sanitary Commission, which employed a state veterinarian. Kansans also began to assume responsibilities for national events. In 1884 they responded to devastation in flood-ravaged areas in Ohio by sending sixty-one carloads of corn for relief.

George Washington Glick had a long political career in a variety of public positions. He was admitted to the Ohio bar in 1850, and he practiced law in Fremont. He was nominated for Congress by the Democrats in 1858. He declined, accepting instead a state senate nomination, but he lost that election. Perhaps this loss explains why he moved that year to Atchison County, Kansas, where he avidly combined his Democratic party allegiance with the free-state movement. He bought the large Shannon Hill farm, located just west of Atchison, and established a law partnership with Alfred G. Otis.[57] On his land Glick raised white, purebred Shorthorn cattle, a coloration not preferred by most Shorthorn breeders. Later he was the first master of the Shannon Hill Grange of the Patrons of Husbandry. As a Democrat, Glick was a delegate to the Wyandotte constitutional convention and was elected to the state house of representatives in 1863, 1864, 1865, and 1868; from 1873 to 1879 he served in the senate. He was also judge of the Second Judicial District from 1877 to 1881 and was four times a delegate to the Democratic National Convention, both before and after his stint as governor.

Glick was an organizer and member of the State Board of Agriculture for thirty-four years and its president during 1902–3. Pres. Grover Cleveland appointed him state pension agent from 1885–1889. He was one of the Kansas commissioners of the Centennial Exposition of 1876 and served on the State Boards of Managers for

George Washington Glick's statue, originally in Statuary Hall of the United States Capitol, is now on the House side of the Capitol.

the Chicago Columbian Exposition (1893), the Trans-Mississippi International Exposition in Omaha (1898), and the Louisiana Purchase Exposition in St. Louis (1904). He lost a race in 1897 as a candidate for state senate, and another in 1900 (to Charles Curtis) as a candidate for Congress. He was also a director of both the Union Pacific and the Atchison, Topeka and Santa Fe and president of the Atchison and Nebraska Railroad. Glick served as president of the state Historical Society in 1909. In the early twentieth century he spent part of each year in Florida where he had an orange grove.

In 1913, two years after his death, the first Democratic-controlled legislature in Kansas appropriated $6,000 for a statue of Glick to be sculpted by Charles Henry Niehaus, which was accepted in 1915 by Congress for placement in the United States Capitol. Glick was the name of a post office in Kiowa County from 16 March 1883 to 26 April 1890, when it was renamed Belvidere.

REFERENCES: Carlin and Richmond, 1982; McIlvain, 1931; U.S. Congress, 1915; Williams, 1972.

JOHN ALEXANDER MARTIN

Atchison (Republican), 12 January 1885–14 January 1889

Born 10 March 1839, Brownsville (Fayette County), Pennsylvania; son of James Martin, a boardinghouse keeper, justice of peace, and postmaster, and Jane Montgomery Crawford Martin, 2 sisters and 2 brothers; educated at common school and apprenticed to a printer at age 15; military experience in Civil War, colonel (brevetted brigadier general) of Eighth Kansas Infantry; married Ida Challis, 1 June 1871, 8 children, 1 dying in infancy; religious preference Baptist but a member of no church; died 2 October 1889, of pleuro-pneumonia, in Atchison; buried in Mount Vernon Cemetery, Atchison.

After narrowly missing the Republican nomination for governor in 1878, John A. Martin's time came in 1884 when the rules of the Republican state convention were suspended and he was nominated by acclamation. In a race against the incumbent governor George Washington Glick, he was elected by 146,777 votes to 108,284, with H. P. Phillips, Greenback-Labor candidate receiving 9,998. Two years later he was unanimously renominated for a second term and reelected, receiving 149,615 votes against 115,667 for Democrat Thomas Moonlight and 8,094 for the Prohibition candidate C. H. Branscombe.

Martin's career had always been tied up in Kansas. He moved to the Kansas Territory in 1857, at age nineteen, and settled in Atchison. In 1858 he purchased the *Squatter Sovereign*, a proslavery newspaper, and changed its name to *Freedom's Champion* (later the *Daily Champion*). After the Civil War, he served as commander in chief of a state encampment of the Grand Army of the Republic, a veterans' organization; as an incorporator and a president of the state Historical Society; as an incorporator of the *Kansas Magazine*; and as a Kansas representative on the United States Centennial Commission. An ardent Republican, Martin was chairman of the Atchison County Republican Central Committee during most years from 1859 to 1884. He attended the Republican National Conventions of 1860, 1868, 1872, and 1880 and was a member of the Republican National Committee from 1864 to 1884, with a term as its secretary (1880–84). Before he was old enough to vote, he was secretary of the Wyandotte constitutional convention, and he was elected to the first session of the state senate, serving until 27 October 1861 when he became an officer in the Eighth Kansas Infantry. He was also mayor of Atchison in 1865 and from 1878 to 1880.

In the first three years of his tenure, Martin was governor during boom times: Land put into cultivation exceeded two million acres, railroads added two thousand miles of track, taxable property expanded, and many new towns were created. However, during his last year in office, the boom conditions of the mid-1880s collapsed, and drouth and recession affected general economic conditions in Kansas. As governor, Martin's dominant interests were the well-being of old soldiers from the Union army and their families, the state of Kansas, and the Republican party. New in this administration were the State Board of Health, a school for feebleminded persons, and a soldiers' orphans home. Women won the right to vote in city elections. The state militia became the Kansas National Guard, and a Bureau of Labor Statistics was created. In 1886 Martin helped negotiate a settlement in the Missouri Pacific strike. Real estate speculation was rampant during this time, and Martin became alarmed by community rivalries for a county seat. In these so-called county seat wars, when disputes turned violent the governor was forced several times to send in state troops to restore order. Although there had been some question about his stance toward pro-

Governor John A. Martin on the steps of the State Capitol with state employees.

hibition at the time of his election, his support for the movement strengthened during his governorship. Martin resided at the Copeland Hotel, located at Ninth and Kansas Avenue, during his four years as governor, while his large family stayed at the home in Atchison.

Martin did not seek a third term but went back to the *Daily Champion* in Atchison, worn out by his efforts to restore the economic optimism that Kansans had enjoyed when he first became governor. He died less than a year later, and more than five thousand people attended his funeral. Shortly after his death, his fourth child and eldest son, Evan Challis, was renamed John Alexander Martin, Jr.

REFERENCES: Carlin and Richmond, 1982; Liebengood, 1936; Malin, 1931; Walker, 1936.

LYMAN UNDERWOOD HUMPHREY

Independence (Republican), 14 January 1889–9 January 1893.

Born 25 July 1844, New Baltimore (Stark County), Ohio; son of Lyman Humphrey, a lawyer and district judge, and Elizabeth A. Everhart Humphrey, 1 brother; educated at Massilon High School, Mount Union College, and University of Michigan, graduated 1867; military experience in Civil War, 1861–65, first lieutenant, in twenty-seven battles, wounded twice; married Amanda Leonard, 25 December 1872, 2 sons and 2 other children dying in infancy; religious preference Congregational; died 12 September 1915 in Independence; buried in Mount Hope Cemetery, Independence.

In 1888 Lyman Underwood Humphrey won nomination for governor from the Republican state convention, as the candidate of a conservative faction. More than a dozen hopefuls, some reformist-agrarian, had surfaced in that convention. The election was an outstanding victory for Humphrey (the first governor from southeast Kansas), since he carried all but two counties and registered the largest plurality to that date. He won 180,841 votes, while Democrat John Martin received 107,480, followed by Union Labor candidate

Peter P. Elder, with 35,837, and the Prohibition candidate J. D. Botkin with 6,439. In contrast, the 1890 election for Humphrey was a squeaker; he was reelected with 39 percent of the vote cast, by a very slim margin over the new farmers' party. He received 115,025 votes; John F. Willits, People's Alliance, 106,972; Charles Robinson, Democratic and Resubmission, 71,357; and A. M. Richardson, Prohibition, 1,230.

Prohibition and the metropolitan police commissioners were two critical issues during Humphrey's first term. The United States Supreme Court ruled in April 1890 that states could not restrict the importation and sale of liquors in "original [unopened] packages," hence many original package outlets opened in Kansas. Congress in August 1890 enacted a law nullifying the court decision, but further litigation ensued before Kansas prohibition laws were upheld. To put teeth into its prohibition, Kansas law had provided for the gubernatorial appointment of police commissioners in all first-class cities. Humphrey's many appointments incurred the wrath of home-rule supporters. The opening of Oklahoma to white settlement in 1889, large corn crops, the subsidization of a sorghum-sugar industry, Humphrey's appointment of Bishop W. Perkins to the United States Senate after the death of Preston B. Plumb, and a new flourishing salt industry, were some of the events of these years.

During Humphrey's second term, the legislature was dominated by Farmers Alliance representatives who elected William A. Peffer to the United States Senate seat vacated by John James Ingalls after eighteen years.[58] Humphrey refused to bill the state for his official travel, and at the conclusion of his term, he returned to the state treasury the bulk of his contingent fund. During his gubernatorial years, Humphrey's residence was the Copeland Hotel. A Kansas City newspaperman called the hotel "Copeland County," because so much important political activity affecting the state took place there. In 1892 Humphrey did not seek a third term but was a candidate instead for the third district seat in Congress. He was defeated by the candidate of the fused Democratic and People's parties. He returned to the practice of law in Independence and did not seek further political office.

During his pre-Kansas career, Lyman U. Humphrey was admitted to the Ohio bar in 1868. He moved a short time later to Shelby County, Missouri, where he was a teacher and newspaperman. In 1871, with his mother and brother, he moved to Independence, Kansas, and helped establish the *South Kansas Tribune*. A Republican, Humphrey lost a race for the state house of representatives in 1871. In 1873 he formed a law partnership with Alexander M. York.[59] Humphrey was elected to the state senate in 1876. When Melville J. Salter[60] resigned as lieutenant governor in 1877 to accept a federal appointment as register of the Independence land office, Humphrey was his replacement. He was reelected as lieutenant governor in 1878 and served on the state Republican committee. He became a district judge and had another term in the senate, from 1885 to 1889.

REFERENCES: Argersinger, 1967; Argersinger, 1974; Carlin and Richmond, 1982.

LORENZO DOW LEWELLING

Wichita (People's), 9 January 1893–14 January 1895

Born 21 December 1846, Salem (Henry County), Iowa; son of William Lewelling, a nurseryman and Quaker minister, and Cyrena Wilson Lewelling, 3 brothers and sisters; educated at Knox College, Eastman's Business College of Poughkeepsie, New York and Whittier College of Salem; military experience in Civil War, enlisted as drummer boy, relatives bought his discharge, drove cattle to quartermaster depot, and worked on bridge corps at Chattanooga; married (1) Angeline M. Cook, 16 April 1870, deceased, (2) Ida Bishop, 1886 or 1887, 4 daughters; religious preference Quaker; died 3 September 1900, of heart disease in Arkansas City; buried in Maple Grove Cemetery, Wichita.

Lorenzo Dow Lewelling had come into the 1892 election as a virtual unknown, yet he led the entire slate of People's party candidates to victory. Well-educated, articulate, long acquainted with labor-management problems, and an authority on penal reform, Lewelling had joined the People's (or Populist) party and had become chairman of the Sedgwick County party organization. He presented such an impressive welcoming speech to the 1892 People's party convention in Wichita that he was nominated as their candidate for governor and was later endorsed by the Democrats. In a close general election, Lewelling won 162,507 votes, while Abram W. (Farmer) Smith, Republican, received 158,075 and the Prohibition candidate Isaac O. Pickering got 4,178.

Claiming that his administration was the first "people's party government on earth," Lewelling adhered to the party line even in his choice of gubernatorial residence: During his term, he stayed at the Dutton Hotel at 407 Kansas Avenue, much touted by the Populists because of its dollar-a-day rooms—half the cost of the Copeland, which was used by some of his predecessors. However, Lewelling's efforts to accomplish anything during his term were frustrated by the "legislative war." This name derived from the inability of the house of representatives to organize and select a speaker for most of the session because of a lack of a clear-cut majority for any party. The worst features of the legislative war were the product of Lewelling's own bungling, or at least "his Quaker aversion to the use of force." Although the state supreme court, dominated by Republicans, decided the issue in favor of Republicans, almost no legislation was passed during that session.

Legislative infighting stymied Lewelling's administration, but the legislature did adopt the Australian ballot and an eighteen-month redemption period for mortgages. Lewelling had sought a law permitting individual borrowing at 5 percent from the state's sinking fund and other state balances (to benefit those indebted, such as with mortgaged land), but the legislature did not respond. He also appointed the well-known Populist spokeswoman Mary Elizabeth Lease as superintendent of the State Board of Charities. Controversy, which became public, broke out between Lease and the governor, because Lease was unalterably opposed to Populist fusion with the Democrats—the alliance that had helped bring Lewelling's victory. He eventually fired her. Lewelling favored state action on behalf of the oppressed, thus he called out state troops to protect miners from black strikebreakers who had been brought into southeastern Kansas coal fields. Although this action might have had racial overtones, Lewelling proved that he was color-blind when on another occasion he sent state troops to Salina to protect a black man threatened with lynching.

Governor Lewelling was the spokesman for Kansas at the World

Lewelling's inaugural took place in the chamber of the Kansas House of Representatives.

Columbian Exposition in Chicago in 1893. In December of that year he gained his greatest national notoriety when he issued his controversial "tramp circular" to the metropolitan police commissioners. Lewelling condemned existing vagrancy laws and suggested better treatment for the unemployed. He stated that "thousands of men, guilty of no crime but that of seeking employment, have languished in the city prisons of Kansas or performed unrequited toil in 'rock piles' as municipal slaves, because ignorance of economic conditions has made us cruel."[61]

Lewelling's election in 1892 was the first high point for the Populist party in Kansas; the state even cast its electoral vote to the Populist presidential candidate James Weaver that year. However, Lewelling's advocacy of women's suffrage in 1894 split the Populist-Democratic alliance that had brought his victory. The Populists nominated the entire Lewelling slate in 1894, and they all went down in defeat. Lewelling lost to Republican Edmund N. Morrill, 118,329 votes to 148,697, while David Overmyer, Stalwart Democrat, got 26,709 votes, and Isaac O. Pickering, Prohibition, received 5,496. A proposed amendment to establish equal suffrage also lost in that election, 130,139 votes to 95,302. In his final action, Governor Lewelling called the legislature into special session three days before the expiration of his term so that he could present his "official version" of the legislative war.

During his youth and early manhood, Lorenzo D. Lewelling had worked at varied jobs, canal tow-path boy, carpenter, section hand on a railroad, teacher in a black school in Missouri, and newspaper publisher. Between 1868 and 1880, excluding only two years, he served as superintendent of the Iowa Women's Reform School and in other positions in the Iowa reformatory system. For two years, beginning in 1880, he edited an "anti-ring" Republican newspaper in Des Moines. After being defeated in a race for secretary of state in Iowa, he moved to Wichita, Kansas, in 1887, to open a loan business and later a commission firm concentrating on nursery stock.[62] Following his term as governor, Lewelling returned to Wichita and ran a dairy farm and creamery business, after which he became a manager of a land company and a traveling lecturer for an insurance group. He was elected on a fusion Populist-Democratic ticket to the state senate in 1896, and he served as a member of the State Railway Commission from 1897 to 1899. He also worked as a land agent for the Atchison, Topeka and Santa Fe Railroad.

REFERENCES: Carlin and Richmond, 1982; Clanton, 1969; Daniels, 1931; Garretson, 1929; Hudson, 1893; Nugent, 1963; Parrish, 1968.

EDMUND NEEDHAM MORRILL

Hiawatha (Republican), 14 January 1895–11 January 1897

Born 12 February 1834, Westbrook (Cumberland County), Maine; son of Rufus Morrill, a tanner and furrier, and Mary Webb Morrill, 1 sister and 1 brother; educated at Westbrook Academy (graduated 1855); military experience in Civil War, captain (brevetted major) in the Seventh Kansas Cavalry; married (1) Elizabeth A. Brettun, 27 November 1862, deceased, (2) Caroline Nash, 25 December 1869, 1 son and 2 daughters; religious preference Congregational; died 14 March 1909, in San Antonio, Texas; buried in Mount Hope Cemetery, Hiawatha.

Frequently mentioned in previous years as a likely gubernatorial candidate, Edmund Needham Morrill was finally nominated by the Republican state convention in 1894. Morrill, almost sixty-one years of age, was the oldest person ever elected governor of Kansas. He defeated the incumbent Lorenzo Dow Lewelling, 148,697 votes to 118,322, with two minor candidates getting 33,106. The combined total for governor in this nonpresidential election year showed a decline of almost 25,000 votes. Morrill received about 10,000 votes less than the Republican candidate two years earlier, while Lewelling's vote was down by more than four times that. Third-party candidates picked up some of the votes earlier cast for Lewelling.

In his inaugural address on 14 January 1895, Morrill issued a strong indictment against the "virus of unrest, discontent, and disloyalty" he had seen in his adopted state. Critical problems faced him as governor—a national economic depression, drouth and its contribution to destitution, and the influence of existing mortgage laws and high rates of interest for farmers. Serious concern was expressed during his administration for the health and safety of miners, purchase of seed for needy farmers, and coal for indigent persons. Morrill did not believe that he should execute laws on these issues or attempt to make laws. Because of a divided house and senate, most reform issues had difficulty getting to the governor. Like previous Populist and Republican administrations, Morrill had grave problems trying to enforce the prohibition law and the metropolitan police law, which granted significant authority in local affairs to the governor. He alienated important party leaders because he sought to allow local option for saloons. Morrill was also unsuccessful in his push for a new constitutional convention. Nevertheless, he was renominated for governor by the Republican state convention in 1896. He lost to the candidate of the combined Democratic and People's parties, John W. Leedy, in a close race, 160,530 votes to 167,041—the largest total ever cast in a Kansas election to that date. Three minor candidates—Henry L. Douthart, National; Horace Hurley, Prohibition; and A. E. Kepford, Independent—divided the remaining 3,912 votes.

Morrill's association with Kansas before taking office was longer than that of any previous governor. On 12 March 1857 Edmund Morrill arrived in Brown County, Kansas, with a colonizing group from New England. With only meager possessions, he took a claim in the northwest part of the county. He borrowed money to set up a saw mill, watched it burn down in 1860, and eventually repaid his loan for the destroyed machinery. As a farmer-stockman, he actively promoted two railroads crossing Brown County, and later he became a banker. A free stater in territorial Kansas, he was elected to two sessions of the territorial legislature. Morrill served in the Civil War; afterwards, as a Republican, he was elected clerk of the district court (1866–70) county clerk (1866–73), a state senator (1872–74 and 1876–80) and a member of the United States Congress (1883–91), where he claimed some responsibility for the generous veterans' dependent and disability act of 27 June 1890.

By the 1890s Morrill was one of the wealthiest men in Kansas, owing to his shrewd land speculation and his role as organizer of the first bank in Hiawatha, county seat of Brown County. He willingly donated to Hiawatha charities, including the Hiawatha Academy and the Morrill Free Public Library. While he was governor, he also loaned William Allen White one-third of the money he needed to acquire the *Emporia Gazette*.

During his two-year term, Morrill made his home at the Copeland Hotel at Ninth and Kansas Avenue. After his gubernatorial tenure, he went back to Hiawatha and the presidency of the Morrill and Janes Bank. He also served as president of the First National Bank of Leavenworth for seven years and as director of the Interstate National Bank of Kansas City, Kansas. He owned a loan company in Atchison and, among his considerable land holdings, an 880-acre apple orchard. Morrill, in northwestern Brown County, was named after him.

REFERENCES: Carlin and Richmond, 1982; Clanton, 1969; Nugent, 1965; White, 1946.

JOHN WHITNAH LEEDY

LeRoy (People's), 11 January 1897–9 January 1899

Born 4 March 1849, near Belleville (Richland County), Ohio; son of Samuel Keith Leedy, a farmer, and Margaret Whitnah Leedy; educated at common school; married Sarah J. Boyd, 4 November 1875, 2 daughters and 1 son; religious preference Church of the Brethren but member of no church; died 24 March 1935, Edmonton, Alberta; buried there.

Democrats and Populists in Kansas fused again in 1896, believing that separation in 1894 had cost them the election. They sought a strong candidate for governor, and State Senator John Whitnah Leedy was picked over Congressman-at-large William A. Harris—no doubt because Harris, a native of Virginia, had served in the Confederate army. Leedy's win over incumbent Edmund N. Morrill was by 167,041 votes to 160,531, with 3,912 votes split among three others. To go along with Leedy's victory, both houses of the Kansas legislature, for the first time, had a Populist majority; the supreme court was in Populist hands; and William Jennings Bryan, endorsed by Populists and Democrats, won the Kansas electoral vote for president.

Leedy lacked the reforming zeal of Lewelling, the first Populist

126

governor, but he was a better politician and more knowledgeable about the use of patronage. A stocky man who weighed almost 230 pounds, Governor Leedy was gregarious by nature, and he stationed himself in his outer office to greet visitors, while his executive secretary completed necessary paperwork in the inner office. In Leedy's administration, bank laws were altered to permit banks to deal with such rural issues as land foreclosures, new state agencies included a schoolbook commission, a state printing plant, and a state grain commission. One controversial issue was the firing of half of the faculty at the state agricultural college, causing Republicans to view it as a bastion of populism. Leedy was criticized, like his predecessors, on his enforcement of prohibition and the metropolitan police law. However, he drew favorable comment from a largely Republican press for his action at the outbreak of the Spanish-American War in 1898. When troops were requested from the state of Kansas, Leedy ordered recruitment of four regiments. The first regiment enlisted was the Twentieth Kansas Infantry, and Leedy appointed as commanding officer Frederick Funston, son of a Republican congressman.

Leedy was renominated for governor in 1898 but lost to William E. Stanley, Republican, 134,158 votes to 149,292. Former Populist United States Sen. William A. Peffer, the Prohibition candidate, got 4,092 votes; the Socialist party, a new factor in Kansas politics, nominated Caleb Lipscomb, who received 635 votes. Following the election Leedy called a special session of the outgoing legislature to enact a law to regulate railroads, creating a short-lived "Court of Visitation" that replaced the railroad commission. Leedy maintained a residence in Lawrence while governor and frequently commuted by train to Topeka; he also had a room at the Dutton Hotel, 407 Kansas Avenue, favored by Populists because its rates were half that of the Copeland. Mary Elizabeth Lease—a hard-line Populist who had had a falling-out with Populist governor Lewelling—regarded Leedy highly. She liked him and felt that he was honest, that he was a good office holder and that he had served the party well.

In the years following the war Leedy had moved from Ohio to Pierceville, Indiana, where he was employed as a clerk from 1865 to

Leedy's tombstone in Edmonton, Alberta, was paid for by the state of Kansas.

1868. He worked as a hired hand and a farmer near Carlinville, Illinois, for twelve years. In 1880 he moved to Coffey County, Kansas, near LeRoy, where he developed a profitable purebred horse-breeding farm which he lost in the depression of the 1890s. Leedy was a Republican until 1872 when he became a Democrat, and in 1890 he joined the People's party. He was elected to the state senate in 1892 as a strong supporter of Populist reforms.

For some time after he left office, Leedy maintained law offices in both Lawrence and Joplin, Missouri. He had mining interests in Galena, Kansas, and organized a Leedy Mining Company in Leavenworth. Then in late 1900 he departed for Seattle, Washington, where he was an organizer for the Ancient Order of Pyramids, a fraternal group. In 1901, he relocated to Valdez, Alaska to prospect and open a law practice. He served as city attorney and was mayor for two years. From 1904 to 1908 he held the position of referee in bankruptcy for the Third Judicial District in territorial Alaska. Then he moved to White Court, in Alberta, Canada and invested in a ranch. Accepting Canadian citizenship made him the only Kansas governor to become an expatriate. In Alberta he was a perpetual reformer and perennial candidate on either the Liberal or the United Farmers of Alberta ticket for a seat in the provincial parliament, but he never won election.

In 1936, a year after his death as a nearly indigent ward of the government of Alberta, the Kansas legislature took an unusual step and appropriated $1,000 to pay Leedy's funeral expenses and to mark his grave with a bronze plaque on a granite shaft.[63]

REFERENCES: Bicha, 1974; Carlin and Richmond, 1982; Correll, 1969; Dew, 1957; Nugent, 1963; Shepard, 1969.

WILLIAM EUGENE STANLEY

Wichita (Republican), 9 January 1899–12 January 1903

Born 28 December 1844, Knox County, Ohio; son of Almon Fleming Stanley, a physician, and Angelina Sapp Stanley, 1 sister and 1 brother; educated at Ohio Wesleyan, studied law in Kenton and Dayton; married Emma Lenora Hills, 30 May 1876, 3 sons (1 dying in infancy) and 1 daughter; religious preference Methodist; died 13 October 1910, in Wichita; buried in Highland Cemetery, Wichita.

Although offered various judicial appointments by Republican governors, William Eugene Stanley declined and stayed in Wichita until nominated for governor by the Republican state convention in 1898. He defeated incumbent governor John W. Leedy, Populist, 149,312 votes to 134,158, with two other candidates dividing less than 5,000 votes. Stanley was renominated in 1900 and won over the Democratic and People's party candidate John W. Breidenthal, 181,893 votes to 164,793. The Socialist Labor candidate G. C. Clemens and the Prohibition candidate Frank Holsinger divided 1,571 votes.

Stanley was admitted to the Ohio bar in 1868, and he moved two years later to Jefferson County, Kansas. As a Republican he served as county attorney from 1871 to 1872. Relocating to the new commu-

Governor Stanley (in dark suit next to the army officer) attending army maneuvers at Fort Riley.

nity of Wichita, he became the Sedgwick County attorney for six years, until 1880, when he won election to the state house of representatives and served from 1881 to 1883.

When Stanley became governor, there was much evidence of good economic times, with excellent business conditions, prolific livestock returns, and bountiful harvests. The governor pushed for state reorganization, and many changes were made, but his efforts to abolish "useless" offices were generally unsuccessful. Governor and Mrs. Stanley were the first to occupy the newly purchased Kansas Executive Mansion at Eighth and Buchanan. During his two terms, the number of supreme court justices was increased to seven, and railroad spokesmen consistently objected to the appointments Stanley made to fill the vacancies. Other changes in state government included the addition of the Traveling Library Commission and the manufacture of binder twine in the state penitentiary (to offer low-cost competition to the Binder Twine Trust). When Stanley strongly condemned the sheriff in Leavenworth County for permitting the lynching of a black man, the legislature passed a resolution in similar language. A short time later a new beginning was made on the issue of capital punishment. (Kansas had executed no criminal in three decades.) Prohibition lacked the urgency of former times, but Carry A. Nation confronted and lashed out at Stanley in his own office for laxity of enforcement.

Stanley did not seek a third term in 1902 because he wanted a seat in the United States Senate, which was still elected by the state legislature. After a deadlock on the first sixteen ballots, Stanley withdrew in favor of another lawyer from Wichita, Chester I. Long, who was elected. Stanley returned to his Wichita law practice. He served on the Dawes Commission to the Five Civilized Tribes from 1903 to 1904, at its headquarters in Tishomingo, Indian Territory. William Stanley was a state archery champion, while his wife, Emma, was the champion woman archer in Wichita.

REFERENCES: Argersinger, 1974; Carlin and Richmond, 1982; Dew, 1957; LaForte, 1974.

WILLIS JOSHUA BAILEY

Baileyville (Republican), 12 January 1903–9 January 1905

Born 12 October 1854, near Mount Carroll (Carroll County), Illinois; son of Monroe Bailey, a farmer, banker, and real estate promoter, and Nancy J. Melendy Bailey, 2 brothers and 1 sister; educated at Mount Carroll High School, University of Illinois (graduated 1879, honorary LL.B. 1904); married Mrs. Ida B. (Albert) Weede, 9 June 1903; religious preference Baptist; died 19 May 1932; buried in Mount Vernon Cemetery, Atchison.

In 1902 Willis Joshua Bailey, long active in Kansas Republican affairs, was nominated for governor by the Republican state convention. He won the election over Democratic candidate W. H. Craddock, also endorsed by the People's party, 159,242 votes to 117,148. Three other candidates—F. W. Emerson, Prohibition; A. S. McAllister, Socialist; and J. H. Lathrop, People's—accounted for 3.7 percent (or 10,799) of the vote.

Following his college graduation, Bailey had moved to Nemaha County, Kansas, with his father and had become a farmer-stockman. In 1880 the railroad came through their neighborhood, so Bailey and his father platted the town of Baileyville and located a bank there. As a Republican, Bailey was elected to the state house of representatives, serving from 1889 to 1891. In 1893 he was president

133

of the Republican state league, and in 1895–99 he served on the State Board of Agriculture. He was elected to the United States Congress as congressman-at-large, for the term 1899 to 1901, believing that he had an understanding with Charles Curtis in which he would become the Republican candidate from the first district in the next election. However, Curtis repudiated the agreement, ran, and won again.

Bailey became governor in an era of increasing reform, yet he had a *laissez-faire* idea of political philosophy. He did not believe in programs which intervened in people's lives. A government served best when it left the people alone. During Bailey's administration the state printer and members of the railroad commission ceased to be appointed positions and became elective. There was a severe flood in 1903, and Bailey convened a special session of the legislature to provide relief. After more than thirty years, the State Capitol was completed. For the first time, tuition was collected at state colleges and universities.

Former governor Bailey (second from left) in 1931 with former governors Capper, Allen, and Hodges (left to right).

Although Bailey was not the first Kansas governor to marry while in office—Crawford had won that caption much earlier—he was the first to bring a new bride into the Kansas Executive Mansion. Bailey hoped for a second term in 1904 but was denied that opportunity by the "boss buster," or progressive, faction of the Republican party. He believed he had been treated unfairly in being denied renomination; nevertheless, he returned to Baileyville where he resumed the presidency of its bank.

In 1907 Bailey took over the Exchange National Bank of Atchison. When the Federal Reserve System was created, he became one of the first directors of the Federal Reserve Bank of Kansas City. He served from 1914 to 1922 when he became governor of the bank, a position he held until 1932. During this period Bailey made his home in Mission Hills (Johnson County), Kansas. Bailey was considered one of the outstanding orators of Kansas and spoke on the Chautauqua circuit.

REFERENCES: Bateman, 1913; Brodhead, 1962; Carlin and Richmond, 1982; LaForte, 1974.

EDWARD WALLIS HOCH

Marion (Republican), 9 January 1905–11 January 1909

Born 17 March 1849, Danville (Boyle County), Kentucky; son of Edward C. Hoch, a baker, and Elizabeth Stout Hoch, 2 brothers and 1 sister; educated at common school and Central College in Danville; married Sarah Louisa Dickerson, 23 May 1876, 2 sons and 2 daughters; religious preference Methodist; died 1 June 1925, of lengthy illness culminating in kidney failure, in Marion; buried in Highland Cemetery, Marion.

Edward Wallis Hoch was drafted by the progressive wing of the Republican party—the "boss busters"—at the Republican state convention in 1904. This Republican faction strongly endorsed the program of Pres. Theodore Roosevelt. Hoch, nominated as a reform candidate over incumbent Willis J. Bailey, defeated Democrat David M. Dale, by 186,731 votes to 116,991, leaving Granville Lowther, Socialist, with 12,101 votes and James Kerr, Prohibition, with 6,584.

Hoch came to Kansas in 1871, settling first at Pawnee Rock but moving soon after to Marion County to a claim near Florence. In 1874 he went to Marion, where he took over the *Marion Record* as repayment of a debt. As a Republican, Hoch served two terms in the state house of representatives (1889–91 and 1893–95). In his second term, dominated by the "legislative war," he was speaker *pro tem* of the Republican-organized house.

With the active support of the progressive wing of the Republican party, many changes occurred in Kansas government during Hoch's administration. In a fight with Standard Oil Company, the state developed and built its own oil refinery at Peru to be operated by convict labor. The state supreme court found this enterprise unconstitutional because of the longtime constitutional restraint on "internal improvements." A depository law for state funds, changes in the management of state institutions and in juvenile courts, and judicial reform were all part of Hoch's first two years as governor.

After he was renominated in 1906, Hoch campaigned on a "Square Deal" for Kansas, modeled after the domestic program of Pres. Theodore Roosevelt. Hoch's platform was designed to curb railroad companies, to provide equitable assessment and taxation, and to allow direct party primary elections rather than party conventions. A popular Democrat, William Alexander Harris, was his major opponent: Hoch's margin of victory was slim—only 152,147 votes to 150,024, with the Socialist, Prohibition, and People's candidates collecting 13,208 votes. Actually, Hoch trailed the Republican ticket in 1906 because of internal factionalism in the party that brought back the old machine crowd to power. Hoch's strong prohibition stand and the impossibility of his administration's producing a vigorous economy hurt him in the election. Although most of the reform legislation he asked for in his second term was approved, Hoch did not get a direct primary law, so he convened a special session of the legislature in January 1908 to force that measure through. (This emergency session also passed a bank guaranty law, which was a kind of primitive deposit insurance.) The first party primary in Kansas was held in August 1908, and a new type of candidate emerged, more attractive to the general electorate and less responsive to party leaders.

Hoch returned to his role as publisher of the *Marion Record*. From 1913 to 1919, he served on the State Board of Administration, an agency designed to administer all public institutions except the State Capitol. Hoch was commemorated by Kansans because of the reform character of his administration and his popular oratorical style which endeared him to the Chautauqua circuit. A large auditorium at the University of Kansas was named for him, and one of his sons

THE OFFICIAL STATE SEAL AND GOVERNOR POST CARD

1905-1907

AD ASTRA PER ASPERA

Hon. EDWARD W. HOCH,
Governor of the State of Kansas

COPYRIGHTED 1905. U. S. POST CARD COMPAN
WILMINGTON, DEL.

Like many public figures of the early 20th century, former governor Hoch was a popular speaker on the Chautauqua circuit.

carried on his public-service tradition, becoming a longtime congressman and a state supreme court justice.

REFERENCES: Brodhead, 1962; Callis, 1933; LaForte, 1974; Schruben, 1968; Van Meter, 1972.

WALTER ROSCOE STUBBS

Lawrence (Republican), 11 January 1909–13 January 1913

Born 7 November 1858, near Richmond (Wayne County), Indiana; son of John T. Stubbs, a farmer, and Esther Bailey Stubbs, 12 brothers and sisters, 5 dying in infancy; educated at Hesper, Kansas, University of Kansas (preparatory department); married Stella Hostettler, 21 September 1887, 2 sons and 2 daughters; religious preference Methodist; died 25 March 1929, of heart disease, in Topeka; buried in Lawrence Cemetery.

In 1908 Walter Roscoe Stubbs, leader of the "boss busters," was nominated for governor in the first Republican party primary. He defeated Jeremiah D. Botkin, Democrat, 196,692 votes to 162,385. Third-party candidates George Francis Hibner (Socialist), Alfred L. Hope (Prohibition), and John W. Northrop (Independence League) collected a total of 15,696 votes. In 1910 Stubbs was renominated, but his margin of victory was small—although not as low as Hoch's in his second election. Stubbs defeated George H. Hodges, Democrat, by 162,181 votes to 146,014, while Socialist S. M. Stallard and Prohibition candidate William C. Cady together received 17,759 votes.

Stubbs, more than any other Republican, brought the Kansas Republican party to its progressive stance in the early twentieth century. He pushed for many reforms as governor, including a campaign expense law, commission government for towns and cities,

The telephone shown here on Governor Stubbs's crowded desk illustrates the impact of new communication devices.

normal training (teacher preparation) in high schools, and civil-service reform. He sought improvement of state administration, regulation of lobbyists, and strict enforcement of prohibition.

The Stubbs family moved from Indiana to Iowa and then to Hesper (Douglas County), Kansas in 1869. Sometime before 1880 Walter Stubbs entered business as a contractor for building railroad grades. He prospered, expanded his business, and became a bank president and an owner of much land. He was a self-made millionaire, and in keeping with his Quaker rearing, he sought to serve his neighbors through public service. He was elected as a Republican to the state house of representatives in 1902, but he had difficulty with party bosses. Frustrated by demands from party leaders, he organized his own faction—the "boss busters," who took over the Republican party in 1904. Stubbs served two more terms in the house and was chairman of the Republican central caucus and speaker of the house. He guided the Kansas primary law through the legislature.

In 1912, his last year as governor, Stubbs defeated Charles Curtis, a Republican conservative, in the party primary race for the United States Senate, only to lose in the general election to Democrat W. H. Thompson. Stubbs sought the Senate seat again in 1918 and a return to the governorship in 1922 and 1924, but he was unsuccessful on all attempts. In later years he managed his cattle ranches in Kansas, Texas, Colorado, and New Mexico. His home was Wind-Hill near the university campus in Lawrence.

REFERENCES: Blythe, 1910; Doyle, 1932; LaForte, 1974; McKee, 1967; Sageser, 1968.

GEORGE HARTSHORN HODGES

Olathe (Democrat), 13 January 1913–11 January 1915

Born 6 February 1866, Orion (Richland County), Wisconsin; son of William Wesley Hodges, a teacher, and Lydia Ann Hodges, 1 brother and 1 sister; educated at Olathe schools; married Ora May Murray, 8 March 1899, 1 son and 1 daughter; religious preference Christian Church (Disciples of Christ); died 7 October 1947, in a Kansas City, Missouri, hospital; buried in Olathe Cemetery.

The 1912 victory of George Hartshorn Hodges, the Democratic candidate for governor, was part of Woodrow Wilson's Democratic landslide taking place in elections around the country. Not only did Kansas give its electoral vote to Wilson, but five of its eight successful congressional candidates were Democrats; the Democrat running for the United States Senate won his race; and for the first time in Kansas history, both houses of the state legislature were captured by Democrats. However, Hodges actually defeated Republican Arthur Capper by a razor-thin margin—167,437 votes to 167,408. Meanwhile, George Kleihege, the Socialist candidate, received 24,767 votes. No doubt Theodore Roosevelt's decision to run for president as a Progressive, after his falling-out with Taft who sought

reelection as a Republican, had repercussions on the Kansas gubernatorial outcome, even though there was no Progressive candidate
for governor. Kansas voters in 1912 also approved by a vote of
175,246 to 159,197 an amendment to the state constitution granting
women equal suffrage.

Progressive Democrats combined with progressive Republicans to
continue the reform tradition in Kansas, and changes were made, especially in the operation and administration of state institutions.
Hodges asked for and obtained legislation for better schools,
stronger business regulation, judicial and tax reforms, and the up-
grading of state hospitals and penal institutions. The Hodges administration increased the number of women in positions of responsibility in state government from one to twenty-three. The
legislature also approved an amendment allowing recall of office
holders before their term expires, to be voted on by the electorate in
1914, and ratified the Seventeenth Amendment to the United States
Constitution, providing for direct election of United States senators. The cumbersome "blanket ballot" with its party column organization was replaced by the "office block" ballot, which made it
more difficult for a citizen to vote a straight party ticket. Hodges
proposed a small nonpartisan unicameral legislature for Kansas,
which would have set up a commission form of state government,
but his idea had little support. Hodges cooperated with Missouri
Gov. Elliott Major in a project called "Good Roads Days." On 20
and 21 August 1913, the two governors, in khaki overalls, were seen
working side by side, along with many other citizens, to improve
the roads.

The election of 1914 again pitted Hodges against Capper, with the
Progressive party fielding a state ticket headed by Henry J. Allen as
their candidate for governor. Hodges lost to Capper, 161,696 votes
to 209,543; Allen brought up a distant third with 84,060 votes; and
three minor candidates combined for about 72,000 votes.

When Hodges was only three years of age, his family moved to
Johnson County, Kansas; his father died a short time later. While
going to school, Hodges took any job offered to him—for instance,
serving as herder of the town's cows. He taught himself commercial
law and went to work in a local lumberyard when he was twenty

Billboard advertisement for Hodges's bid for reelection in 1914.

years of age. He took up traveling salesmanship for two years, then he formed a partnership with his brother. Together they operated lumberyards and hardware stores, eventually building a chain of eight stores and fourteen yards. Hodges also owned the *Johnson County Democrat*, and he held executive positions in financial institutions in Olathe. As a Democrat, he was on the Olathe City Council for four years, including one year as mayor. He served in the state senate (1905–13), where he introduced legislation that led to locally supported hard-surfaced roads. Chairman of the Democratic state convention in 1906, Hodges won the party's nomination for governor in 1910, and in that general election he suffered defeat from incumbent governor Walter Stubbs.

Following his two years as governor, Hodges returned to his lumberyard and hardware business in Olathe and did not seek elective office again. He served with the Red Cross in World War I with the courtesy title of major. He was a member of the State Textbook Commission and later of the newly created state board of regents

(1925–27). An ardent spokesman for prohibition, Hodges was well-known on the Chautauqua circuit. He was also an acknowledged champion marksman with 100 percent scores in some state target competitions.

REFERENCES: Dimmitt, 1958; LaForte, 1974; Loewen, 1967; Socolofsky, 1962.

ARTHUR CAPPER

Topeka (Republican), 11 January 1915–13 January 1919

Born 14 July 1865, Garnett (Anderson County), Kansas; son of Herbert Capper, a tin-ner and hardware dealer, and Isabella McGrew Capper; 3 sisters and 1 brother; edu-cated at Garnett High School, graduated 1884; married Florence Crawford (daughter of Samuel J. Crawford, the third governor), 1 December 1892, no children; religious preference Quaker; died 19 December 1951, of pneumonia, in Topeka; buried in Topeka Cemetery.

Without the usual background of elective positions, Arthur Capper was nominated for governor in the Republican party primary in 1912, gaining 70 percent of the vote against his one opponent. He lost in the general election to George Hodges, Democrat, by 29 votes, the closest gubernatorial contest in Kansas history. The vote cast for Hodges was 167,437; for Capper, 167,408 and for the Social-ist George W. Kleihege, 24,767. During the election of 1912, Capper had not openly supported Taft, the Republican candidate for presi-dent, against Theodore Roosevelt, the Progressive candidate. Nei-ther did he officially contest this election on grounds that ballots marked for him were illegally thrown out, since the matter would have been settled by the incoming state senate, which for the first time in Kansas history had a majority of Democrats.

In 1914 Capper and Hodges squared off again after each was nominated in his party's primary without opposition. Women were voting for governor for the first time in this election. The Progressive party fielded a ticket headed by Henry J. Allen for governor, the Socialists put up Milo M. Mitchell as their candidate, the Prohibition party nominated Silas M. Bond, and J. B. Billard, who was seeking resubmission of the prohibition issue, ran as an Independent. Capper was elected with 209,543 votes to Hodges's 161,696; Allen drew 84,060 votes, and the other three candidates split 72,908 votes. Capper was the first native-born Kansan to serve as the state's governor. He carried eighty-four counties in this election, whereas Hodges won a majority vote in nineteen and Allen captured the majority only in the two most populous counties.

About a month after he graduated from Garnett High School in 1884, Capper became a compositor of the *Topeka Capital*; he later became reporter and editor of the paper. He purchased the *North Topeka Mail* in 1893 and the *Missouri Valley Farmer* in 1900, and he held majority ownership of the *Topeka Capital* by 1901. He had good business ideas that attracted consolidations with other newspapers and Capper's wealth grew quickly as the twentieth century opened. He built an expensive mansion on Topeka Boulevard and a five-story publishing plant at Eighth and Jackson in Topeka. By 1910 Capper had a multistate farm paper syndicate, centered in Topeka, and he was turning his attention more to politics. He had served in many Republican party positions and as regent for the land grant college, but he was unsuccessful in winning appointment as state printer.

Capper began his term with the unusual situation of having the state senate in the hands of his opponents, the Democrats. World War I had begun in Europe, and the pacifist Capper endorsed every effort to maintain national neutrality. In his first inaugural address, he stated that as "the first governor chosen by the suffrage of both the men and the women of the state," he would "earnestly endeavor to be the faithful and conscientious steward . . . and to serve faithfully the whole state." The Kansas Executive Mansion was not occupied by Governor and Mrs. Capper. They lived in their own home at 1035 Topeka Boulevard.

Capper used his business experience in organizing his administration. Although his newspaper headquarters was just across the street from the state Capitol, he committed himself fully to running state government while subordinates carried out his wishes with his syndicate, Capper Publications. The law protecting investors—known as the "blue sky" law and imitated by most other states—was strengthened, and a new civil-service commission was established. Rural credit loans were made more accessible, pensions were provided for widows with dependent children, an industrial welfare commission for women was created, smaller communities were allowed to have city courts, and the fee system for compensating public officials was virtually abolished, changed to a set salary. The total cost of state government in 1916 was only about $10 million, yet Capper continually sought ways to save money. Almost 40 percent of the state budget was spent on educational institutions, about 17 percent for charitable institutions, 12 percent for penal institutions, and slightly more than 2.5 percent on soldier's homes. A greater part of government was carried out locally at that time. County taxes, for instance, brought in more than three times as much money as that spent by the state.

In 1916 Capper was unopposed for the Republican nomination. In the general election he received 61 percent of the vote over the Democratic candidate W. C. Lansdon, winning by 354,529 votes to 192,037, with 22,552 votes going to E. N. Richardson, Socialist, and 13,366 to the Prohibition candidate H. R. Ross. In his second inaugural address, Capper spoke on behalf of modernizing Kansas government. He endorsed a new constitution and proposed additional support for the common schools, free school textbooks, and support for the League of Peace. Capper later said that his duties as governor increased fourfold with United States entry into World War I in April 1917. He smothered his pacifism in favor of an all-out war effort that would end the hostilities as quickly as possible. Not a glib speaker, he still made more than three hundred patriotic speeches to Kansas audiences.

During this administration, a new state highway commission was created in response to federal pressure. Since the Kansas constitution prohibited "internal improvements," the burden of matching funds for new federal highways was passed on to counties and other

Governor Capper (far right) watching the burning of the last bonded indebtedness of the state of Kansas, 1 January 1916.

local units of government. The most restrictive Kansas prohibition law, known as the "Bone Dry" law, was enacted. Cigarettes were placed under stricter regulation, a more comprehensive workman's compensation law was passed, and state purchasing of supplies was reformed. Armistice, ending World War I, came just after the 1918 election, and in the last weeks of his tenure, Capper urged that demobilization of all troops take place quickly. Shortly before he left office, he remarked that Kansans had just "closed the most momentous year in modern history." He believed then that "we have made some progress in those four years. We have not gone far. The distance traversed seems pitiably short when we contemplate all that is yet to be accomplished; but what progress we have made is due to the alert spirit of the Kansas people; to their ready response to the call of ideals and determination to realize them; to their basically sound sense, to their strong purpose to go forward."

In 1918 Capper did not seek a third term as governor; instead he became a candidate for the United States Senate in the Republican primary against three well-known Republicans—former governor

Walter R. Stubbs, former senator Joseph L. Bristow, and former congressman Charles F. Scott. Capper carried every county but one and captured an astounding 60 percent of the Republican primary vote. Beating the incumbent, he won election to his first of five consecutive Senate terms in 1918, retiring in 1949 undefeated. By then, Capper Publications had ten journals, with a total circulation (daily, weekly, or monthly) approaching five million, and two radio stations. When Capper Publications was purchased by Stauffer Publications in the mid-1950s, Capper's estate made its most sizable bequest to the Capper Foundation for Crippled Children, which built a fine school and treatment center at Orleans and Tenth streets in Topeka. A public housing development in Washington, D.C., and a public school in Topeka also bear the Capper name. His statue, one of four under the rotunda of the State Capitol dome, commemorates his political role as governor and senator.

Governor Capper at one of his annual birthday parties for Topeka children, 14 July 1917.

REFERENCES: *Addresses and Messages*; Carlin and Richmond, 1982; Crowley, 1938; Jewell, 1947; LaForte, 1974; Socolofsky, 1958; Socolofsky, 1962; Socolofsky, 1974.

HENRY JUSTIN ALLEN

Wichita (Republican), 13 January 1919–8 January 1923

Born 11 September 1868, near Pittsfield (Warren County), Pennsylvania; son of John Allen, a farmer, and Rebecca Elizabeth Goodwin Allen, 3 brothers and 3 sisters, 3 dying in infancy; educated at district schools in Clay County, Kansas, Burlingame schools, and Baker University; married Elsie Jane Nuzman, 19 October 1893, 2 sons and 2 daughters; religious preference Methodist; died 17 January 1950, of cerebral thrombosis, in Wichita; buried in Maple Grove Cemetery, Wichita.

Henry J. Allen was the Progressive party candidate for governor in 1914, coming in third behind Capper, Republican, and Hodges, Democrat. By 1916 Allen was back in the Republican fold and was the party's candidate for governor in 1918. He was nominated in the party primary while on tour in France with William Allen White, inspecting facilities provided for the Kansas components of the American Expeditionary Force. In the 1918 campaign he did not personally spend a cent, and he learned of his election victory in a Paris newspaper. He won against W. C. Lansdon, Democrat, with 187,957 votes to 133,054; the Socialist candidate G. W. Kleihege received 12,731. Renominated in 1920, Allen won easily with 319,914 votes, to 214,940 cast for Jonathan M. Davis, Democrat, and 12,544 for Roy Stanton, Socialist.

The John Allen family moved to a homestead in Clay County,

Kansas, in 1870, when son Henry Justin was less than two years of age. John Allen lost his farm through foreclosure in 1879, after he purchased a threshing machine for which he could not pay. The family moved to Burlingame, whereupon Henry J. Allen became a barber following his graduation from high school. He enrolled at Baker University but did not graduate. Because Allen was highly recommended by the Baker University president for his speaking and writing ability, he got a job on the *Salina Republican*. In his long career in journalism, Allen's positions included reporter, war correspondent, editor, advertising manager, and owner. A succession of newspaper holdings culminating in the *Wichita Beacon* brought him great wealth. In defiance of local wisdom about the dangers of prevailing winds, he built the first ten-story office building in the state for his business in Wichita. Also, he commissioned Frank Lloyd Wright to design his Wichita home.

As a Republican, Allen was secretary for Gov. William E. Stanley from 1899 to 1901. He was chairman of the State Board of Charities until that agency was replaced by the State Board of Administration. Active in Republican party functions, Allen served as chairman of the Kansas delegation in the 1912 Republican National Convention, which walked out when their favorite, Theodore Roosevelt, failed to get the presidential nomination. Allen followed Roosevelt's lead and became a Progressive.

Allen was one of the most able speakers to serve as Kansas governor; he even made the keynote address for the Republican National Convention in 1920. He fully understood the news media, and he was colorful newspaper copy, yet his contributions to Kansas government were not long-lasting. He had a vigorous, almost combative style in dealing with the crises of his office. Each issue was a personal one to him, as his often heated correspondence shows. Postwar strikes caught his interest, and he called himself the "protector" of "the party of the third part," by which he meant the people, against the hostile parties of the first and second part—labor and management. Twice Allen convened special sessions of the Kansas legislature—the first to ratify the Eighteenth Amendment to the United States Constitution; the second, called in January 1920, to ratify the Nineteenth Amendment and to develop a Kansas Indus-

Cartoonist Albert T. Reid taking on three Kansas governors who supported the Progressive movement, W. R. Stubbs, Henry J. Allen, and Arthur Capper. Reid began his career as a cartoonist for one of Capper's newspapers. When Capper became governor, Reid bought a rival newspaper and carried out his conservative vendetta against the progressives.

trial Court that would provide compulsory arbitration of labor-management disputes. He attracted national attention because of this court, and he had a debate on the compulsory arbitration issue in New York City with Samuel Gompers, American Federation of Labor president. The Kansas Industrial Court issue was extensively litigated, and in 1925 the United States Supreme Court decided a case which resulted in the next Kansas legislature repealing the industrial court law. (Many years later, a 1938 decision of the Supreme Court would cause Allen to announce that the court had reversed itself and made the old industrial court legal.)

As governor, Allen unsuccessfully pushed for a state income tax, constitutional revision, highway improvements, and a revised workmen's compensation law. Changes were made in the bank guaranty fund, and for the first time automobile licenses were required. When he was inaugurated for a second time on 10 January 1921, Allen noted that the federal government was taxing Kansans six times more than the state was. He concluded his remarks by saying, "We have just passed through a notable political campaign, which has resulted in placing both national and state governments under the leadership of the Republican party. . . .The party of our fathers is meeting a new test everywhere. It is our duty to meet that test with devout intention—to make the high interest of government the single purpose of the organization."

Reportedly, fewer laws were passed, yet more money appropriated, in Allen's second term that in any previous legislative session. Allen voiced strong, stern opposition to the Ku Klux Klan and the Non-Partisan League, both active in postwar Kansas—although neither the Klan nor the League had as much support as Allen feared. He also denounced violence directed toward the League. Governor and Mrs. Allen lived in the Capper Mansion, rather than in the Executive Mansion.

Allen did not seek a third term but went back to the *Wichita Beacon*, still maintaining a high profile on the Kansas political scene. He served on the Near East Relief Commission in 1923 investigating disaster conditions, and he was chairman of the journalism department of "University Afloat" in 1926.

In 1929 Allen was appointed to the United States Senate by Gov. Clyde Reed to the seat vacated by the election of Charles Curtis as vice-president. Allen failed to win reelection in 1930, losing to the Democratic candidate George McGill. For a short time in 1931 he was on the staff of the Reconstruction Finance Corporation as assistant to its chairman Charles G. Dawes. Allen campaigned heavily for Alf Landon for president in 1936 and strongly supported Republican presidential candidates in 1940 and 1944. With Elsie Jane Allen, his wife, he traveled widely and wrote articles about his travels that were extensively syndicated. He was a leader of the World War II relief programs Bundles for Britain and Save the Children Federation.

REFERENCES: Carlin and Richmond, 1982; Clugston, 1940; Gagliardo, 1934; LaForte, 1974; Sageser, 1968; White, 1918; White, 1946.

JONATHAN McMILLAN DAVIS

Bronson (Democrat), 8 January 1923–12 January 1925

Born 27 April 1871, near Bronson (Bourbon County), Kansas; son of Jonathan Mc-Millan Davis, a farmer, and Eve Holeman Davis, 1 brother; educated at University of Kansas (preparatory department, 1890–92) and University of Nebraska (1892–93); married Mary Purdom, 26 September 1894, 1 son and 2 daughters; religious preference Methodist; died 27 June 1943, after several months of illness and repeated visits to a Fort Scott hospital; buried in Bronson Cemetery.

Jonathan M. Davis ran for governor in a total of six general elections. The 1922 race was his second as the Democratic candidate, and he faced the nominee of a fractured Republican party—W. Y. Morgan, Hutchinson newspaperman. Morgan had won 29 percent of the vote in a close seven-man race for the nomination, and his victory again elevated a newspaperman to be Republican candidate for governor—the same career of all their gubernatorial hopefuls since 1912. Davis won the election with 271,058 votes to Morgan's 252,602 and for Socialist M. L. Phillips's 9,138.

Davis had long been involved in Democratic party politics and had held a variety of legislative positions. He had cut short his student days at the University of Nebraska at his father's death to take over their 1,700-acre Little Osage farm in Bourbon County. His active participation in Democratic party politics included campaigning in Nebraska for William Jennings Bryan in his bid for Congress in 1892 and in his presidential race in 1896. Davis was appointed post-master of Eve—named for his mother, the first person to hold the job—in 1899, and in 1900 he was elected to the Kansas house of representatives. He did not seek reelection in 1902 but ran again in 1904 when he lost. In 1906 he won a seat in the house, was re-elected twice, and then won a four-year term in the state senate in 1912. Seeking reelection, he lost in 1916 and again in 1918, when he ran for an unexpired senate seat. In 1920 Davis was nominated for governor in the Democratic party primary and lost to the incumbent Henry J. Allen in the general election.

Jonathan Davis's two years as governor were stormy, dominated by pressure to remove Samuel J. Crumbine, popular secretary of the state board of health, who finally resigned. Davis's removal of E. H. Lindley as chancellor of the University of Kansas was upheld in court appeals, but Davis's successor provided for Lindley's reappointment. Davis gained the Democratic nomination in 1924, only to lose to Benjamin S. Paulen, Republican, 182,861 votes to 323,403. William Allen White, well-known Emporia editor, entered this race as an Independent and received 149,811 votes, while the Socialist candidate M. L. Phillips polled 3,606. After the election, Davis and his son were acquitted of charges of selling prison paroles.

Although he returned to his Little Osage farm, Davis was still in-fected by "political flu," for he sought public office in almost every election—and lost every general election race he entered. He gained the Democratic nomination for governor in 1926 and was defeated again by Paulen, 179,308 votes to 321,540 with Socialist H. Hilfrich receiving 7,046. He entered the Democratic primary for state repre-sentative in 1928, was nominated, then withdrew before the general election. He lost bids for the United States Senate in 1930, as state senator in 1932, as the party's nominee for governor in 1936, as an independent candidate for governor in 1938, as state senator in 1940, and as his party's candidate for lieutenant governor in 1942.

REFERENCES: Corley, 1962; Finger, 1964; Finger, 1967; Schruben, 1969.

BENJAMIN SANFORD PAULEN

Fredonia (Republican), 12 January 1925–14 January 1929

Born 14 July 1869, near Clinton (DeWitt County), Illinois; son of Jacob Walter Paulen, a farmer and hardware merchant, and Lucy Bell Johnson Paulen, 4 sisters and 1 brother; educated at Fredonia High School, University of Kansas, and Bryant and Stratton Business College of St. Louis; married Barbara Ellis, 14 February 1900, no children; religious preference Christian Science; died 11 July 1961, in Fredonia; buried in Fredonia Cemetery.

In 1924 Benjamin Sanford Paulen entered the Republican primary for governor against Clyde M. Reed, a future governor, and Walter R. Stubbs, a past governor, and won with 83,685 votes to Reed's 73,350 and Stubbs's 69,663. Paulen won the general election in 1924 over the incumbent Jonathan Davis, 323,403 votes to 182,861, with William Allen White, Independent, polling 149,811, and M. L. Phillips, Socialist, getting 3,606. White belatedly entered the race because he believed both Paulen and Davis were ''soft'' on the Ku Klux Klan: He dubbed them ''Tweedle-dum and Tweedle-dee'' on the Klan issue. Paulen was renominated and reelected in 1926, defeating Davis by a very similar margin, 321,540 votes to 179,308,

Governor Paulen signing the Kindergarten bill, 1927.

with the Socialist H. Hilfrich garnering 7,046 votes. Paulen's first inauguration marked the first time that a governor took his oath of office outside Topeka. Paulen was sworn into office in Fredonia, where he had been called because of the death of his father.

The Paulen family moved to Wilson County, Kansas, late in 1869, when Benjamin S. Paulen was less than six months old. After his schooling, Paulen worked in his father's hardware and general merchandise store as a partner from 1890 to 1918. He then became president of the Wilson County Bank, Fredonia, and was vice-president of the Fredonia Ice and Light Company. As a Republican, he was elected to the city council, serving from 1900 to 1904, including one year as mayor. He was in the state senate (1913–21), was appointed state oil inspector (1917–21) by Governor Capper, and was elected lieutenant governor (1923–25).

With both the Republican-controlled legislature and the dominant Republican press providing endorsement, Paulen's years as governor lacked the conflicts of earlier times. The Ku Klux Klan issue faded: It was not as significant as had been predicted. Although not considered a progressive, Paulen received the support of the progressive faction of the Republican party and led a united party by

Governor Paulen flanked by the two U.S. senators from Kansas, Charles Curtis (on the left) and Arthur Capper (on the right), in Wichita, 1 June 1925.

1926. Two years later, a Kansas Republican slogan alliterated "Peace, Prosperity, Progress, Prohibition and Paulen." Legislation during his administration included provisions for regulation of motor carriers and for a new state gasoline tax. Manufactured cigarettes had been illegal in Kansas since 1909; they were now legalized and taxed. There was consolidation of governmental agencies, creation of a new board of regents, tax support for public kindergartens, and new restraints on independents running for state offices (the anti–Bill White law, written in response to William Allen White's entry into the 1924 election) which required them to meet the same filing deadline imposed upon members of organized parties. Paulen's most difficult task was to create a state highway commission to enable Kansas to qualify for federal matching funds; he had to call a special legislative session to prepare the constitutional amendment needed.

Paulen did not seek reelection in 1928; instead, he returned to Fredonia. In 1932 he ran for the United States Senate seat but lost to the incumbent George McGill, who was the only Democrat to be reelected to the Senate from Kansas. Paulen served as president of the Kansas Bankers' Association and was appointed chairman of the State Board of Welfare in 1939. In 1957, along with other past governors, he was a member of a constitutional revision commission. In his ninety-second year, he was honored by the naming of the Ben S. Paulen Elementary School in Fredonia.

REFERENCES: Finger, 1967; McCoy, 1966; Shockley, 1986; Traylor, 1976; White, 1946.

CLYDE MARTIN REED

Parsons (Republican), 14 January 1929–12 January 1931

Born 9 October 1871, near Champaign (Champaign County), Illinois; son of Martin Van Buren Reed, a farmer, and Mary Adelaide Reed, 1 sister and 1 brother; educated at Labette County schools and normal school (teacher's certificate, 1888); married Minnie E. Hart, 1891, 4 daughters and 3 sons and 3 other children dying in infancy; religious preference Methodist; died 8 November 1949 in Parsons; buried in Oakwood Cemetery, Parsons.

Four years after his unsuccessful bid for nomination for governor in the Republican party primary, Clyde Martin Reed again announced his candidacy for governor on 4 January 1928. He relied on Alf M. Landon as the chairman of his campaign committee. Reed's two campaign issues were the large Kansas losses due to railway rate discrimination and the distress in the agricultural sector. He faced opposition in the primary from Charles Scott, D. A. N. Chase, Ferd Voiland, Frank Ryan, and John D. M. Hamilton—all well-known figures in Kansas Republican politics, many of whom were still running on the Klan issue. Reed won the nomination for governor, with Hamilton proving to be his main competitor. Reed united all

Republican candidates for statewide offices by traveling to each one's hometown and publicly conferring with him. In the general election he won with the largest popular vote—433,391—ever cast for governor. Democrat Chauncey B. Little received 219,327 votes, and Henry L. Peterson, Socialist, got 7,924. In the presidential race, Republican candidate Herbert Hoover easily won the state's electoral vote with Kansan Charles Curtis as his running mate.

Two days after the election, Reed began preparing his legislative program. He was an avowed progressive, and his reputation and enthusiasm as a "flaming millennium chaser" who would pursue every reform followed him into the governorship. Since Charles Curtis, at the request of President Coolidge, did not resign his Senate seat to take his new office as vice-president until early March, Reed became responsible for appointing his successor. From a field of thirty candidates, Reed named former governor Henry J. Allen, largely on the prompting of incoming president Herbert Hoover. Reed's administration set up the new highway commission, after voters had approved a constitutional amendment permitting the state to engage in such internal improvements. The legislature approved a new intangibles tax and an income tax amendment, but the latter was not ratified by voters until 1930.

By Kansas Day (January 29) 1930, it was obvious that Reed was in trouble with his own party. He had found it necessary to call a special session of the legislature (always an unpopular move to Kansas voters) in February 1930 to handle problems arising from the onset of the Great Depression. Republican voters had a choice in the primary between the conservative champion Frank Haucke and Reed, and Haucke won. Like many progressive Republicans, Reed and Landon sat out the general election, which no doubt contributed to the victory for Harry Woodring, the Democratic candidate.

The Martin Van Buren Reed family moved to Labette County, Kansas, in 1875. After earning his teacher's certificate, Clyde Reed taught school for only one year; the next twenty-eight years he spent as a federal employee. Reed worked for the Railway Mail Service of the Post Office Department, was head of the Wichita division for eleven years, and was superintendent of the Railway Adjustment Division from 1910 to 1917. He resigned in 1917 to take over the *Par-*

sons Sun. In 1919 he was Governor Allen's secretary, and when the Kansas Industrial Court was created in 1920, Reed was appointed to the court for the 1920–21 term. Then Allen appointed Reed to the Public Utilities Commission, where he was confirmed by a single vote in the senate, and he served from 1921 to 1924. As a Republican, he campaigned for governor in 1924, losing to Ben Paulen in the party primary.

After his two-year term as governor, Reed went back to the *Parsons Sun*. In 1938 he won election as United States senator, was reelected in 1944, and held that position at the time of his death in 1949.

REFERENCES: Cherry, 1948; McCoy, 1966; Schruben, 1963; White, 1946.

HARRY HINES WOODRING

Neodesha (Democrat), 12 January 1931–9 January 1933

Born 30 May 1887, Elk City (Montgomery County), Kansas; son of Hines Woodring, a grain dealer, and Melissa Jane Cooper Woodring, 5 older sisters; educated at Elk City schools, Independence High School, and Lebanon (Indiana) Business University; military experience in World War I, second lieutenant in army tank corps; married Helen Coolidge, 25 July 1933, 2 sons and 1 daughter, divorced March 1960; religious preference Christian Church (Disciples of Christ); died 9 September 1967, of a stroke; buried in Mount Hope Cemetery, Topeka.

Without preliminary testing in the legislature, in other elective offices, or even as a precinct committeeman of his party, Harry Hines Woodring sought the Democratic nomination for governor in 1930. First he had to win the primary race against seventy-year-old Noah Bowman, a longtime legislator, which he did—37,888 votes to 26,321—by accentuating his own youth and business (not political) experience. His Republican opponent was Frank Haucke, Council Grove farmer-rancher, who had beaten incumbent governor Clyde M. Reed, 158,113 votes to 131,988, in a fractious and bitter primary election battle. Haucke, like Woodring, was a former state commander of the American Legion and a bachelor. Forecasts of a dull

1930 Kansas gubernatorial election between two similar and color-less candidates seemed confirmed when the two young men spent ten days together in early October as delegates-at-large to the national convention of the American Legion in Boston.

But campaign conditions changed greatly because of the belated entry of the colorful and exciting Dr. John R. Brinkley, who filed as an Independent candidate. Brinkley had gained fame and prominence in the 1920s for his hospital at Milford, where he claimed to restore masculine virility; he also owned a powerful radio station, KFKB (Kansas First, Kansas Best). Since the state medical board had revoked his license to practice medicine in Kansas, Brinkley reasoned that as governor he could appoint a new board and get his license back, so he entered the race. A law passed in 1925 required independent candidates to comply with the same deadline set for major party candidates. Since Brinkley had filed too late to get his name on the ballot, he became a "write-in" candidate. Because of his wealth and communication talents, Brinkley heightened interest in this campaign and made it stand out in the minds of many Kansans. This was the first election in which radio had a significant impact on the Kansas electorate.

Neither Woodring nor Haucke took Brinkley's campaign seriously at first; there were too many obstacles for any "write-in" candidate to secure a statewide office. Woodring's strategy was to attack the Republican machine, praise the outgoing Reed administration, and present himself as the best man to provide businesslike governance. He ignored Brinkley. Haucke sought to unite a splintered party and took occasional shots at Woodring, but in a dignified manner. In the final two weeks of the campaign, it was Brinkley who was drawing the huge crowds to his rallies. His radio speeches, his emotion-packed appearances on the campaign trail, and the live shows of his radio entertainers were attracting attention. Brinkley seemed to have unlimited funds to make use of all forms of advertising, and sample polls indicated that Brinkley was the candidate voters were talking about. By then, the major party candidates were running scared.

Counting the votes in 1930 proved difficult. Usually, the totals on statewide elections in Kansas could be determined within twenty-four hours. Not until almost two weeks after the election of 4 November 1930 were the final results tabulated. Out of 621,235 total votes, Woodring won by 251 votes over Haucke, the second closest race for governor in Kansas history. The vote count gave Woodring 217,171 and Haucke 216,920. Brinkley claimed an official total of 183,278 votes, while the Socialist candidate J. B. Shields tallied 3,866. There was controversy when many ballots (perhaps as many as 60,000) were thrown out for being improperly marked—presumably losses for Brinkley since few precincts had judges representing an independent candidate. Haucke also believed he was shortchanged because of voting irregularities in precincts on the federal reservation at Fort Leavenworth in Leavenworth County. Since law permitted election outcomes to be contested only by those persons whose names were on the ballot, Brinkley could not interfere. Haucke let the totals stand.

As the youngest child and only son, Woodring's early years had been dominated by his mother and his five sisters. He grew up introverted, and while he did well in school, family finances limited his activities. After graduating from high school and briefly attending a business college, he was employed as a bookkeeper and assistant cashier of the First National Bank in Elk City, where he had lived most of his life. Then he became assistant cashier of the nearby First National Bank of Neodesha. At age thirty-one he enlisted in World War I, attended officer's candidate school, and emerged shortly before the war ended as a second lieutenant. Following the war, Woodring, no longer an introvert, was active in many local organizations: the Masons, Farm Bureau, Grange, American Legion, and his church. In 1927 he helped to organize Southeast Kansas Incorporated, an organization for promotion of commercial, industrial, and agricultural development of the region. He served as vice-president of the Kansas Bankers' Association, and in 1928 he was elected state commander of the American Legion.

Early in 1929, Woodring sold his interests in the Neodesha bank. Although his intention was to get into Kansas politics as a Democrat, his timing was fortuitous; he saved his moderate wealth by getting out of the business shortly before the collapse of banks and the beginning of the depression. Initially his sights were on a seat in Congress, but influenced by regional politics, he aimed instead for

Topeka. With this unusual background Woodring won an unexpected victory as governor.

Woodring faced many depression-imposed crises in his term. The highway commission was not subject to state civil-service rules, so Woodring appointed his campaign manager Guy T. Helvering as its director and used him to dispense patronage. Woodring sought stringent controls of state spending, along with tax relief and a variety of new government regulations. Woodring voluntarily took a 10 percent cut in his $5,000 salary and asked state employees to follow suit. Later, most state employees had to take additional salary reductions because of the depressed economy. Generally, Woodring got the legislation he favored from the Republican-controlled legislature, such as a reduction in biennial appropriations, changes in taxing, open budget hearings in all local units of government, and continuation of a road-building program.

Woodring vetoed two bills, one calling for investigation of the State Highway Commission, which had become the largest employer of state personnel and the agency with the most money. The other veto, attracting even more attention, was of a capital punishment bill that Woodring had agreed to support early in the session. Kansas had allowed capital punishment from statehood until its repeal in the early twentieth century because of nonuse for some thirty years. Woodring's veto statement that the "legislation is unsound in theory, that it has been demonstrated to be bad in practice, and that its adoption would be most unwise from every viewpoint" made use of existing sociological and historical studies.[64] Woodring proved to be an accessible governor; his office door was always open to visitors, even during the hectic days of a legislative session. He delayed most of his several hundred political appointments until after the legislature had adjourned, allowing positions that required legislative endorsement to serve until the next session, but he had applications from some six thousand job-hungry Democrats, most of whom he could not satisfy. The state's oil industry was almost without markets and threatened by big oil companies. Although he was unable to solve major oil production problems, Woodring's actions opened some markets and kept small wells producing in a proration scheme. His long fight with Cities Service Gas over prices and taxes, beginning with direct negotiation and followed by investigation by the Public Service Commission and litigation in the courts, was not completed before his term ended.

Woodring's unmarried sister, Lida, served as his official hostess in the Kansas Executive Mansion. Although he worked long hours six days a week, Woodring and his sister enjoyed having friends over for a home-cooked meal and bridge. There were social outings, but for exercise Woodring would saddle up "Governor" in the nearby stable for early morning or late night rides. He also became a fan of spectator sports and attended horse shows and the Kentucky Derby. He willingly responded to invitations to speak all over the state, which required much travel. In addition, he had many duties, official and unofficial, in connection with the Kansas Democratic party. As early as 1931 Woodring had decided that he would support Gov. Franklin D. Roosevelt of New York as the Democratic candidate for president in 1932. He was thus one of the original supporters of FDR, and throughout 1931 he continued to promote the idea, with Roosevelt announcing his candidacy in January 1932. Woodring kept the Democratic delegates from Kansas solidly behind Roosevelt in the national convention. Later, during the campaign, Roosevelt was Woodring's personal guest when he came to Topeka.

In his own reelection effort in 1932, Woodring found that the Kansas Democratic party had split into factions while the Republicans had been unified. Republicans had discovered a harmony candidate in Alf M. Landon, who had been Governor Reed's campaign manager. Woodring again faced Dr. Brinkley, who was on the ballot this time as an Independent. Voter turnout was large, since it was a presidential election year. Woodring lost with 272,944 votes to Landon's 278,581, with 3,892 votes going to H. M. Perkins, Socialist. Brinkley, in a much-better-organized campaign than two years earlier, claimed 244,607 votes and a higher proportion of the total vote than in 1930. Woodring was unable to gain reelection, something no other previous non-Republican governor had been able to achieve either.

Woodring's early support for Franklin D. Roosevelt, who won the presidency handily that year, caused him to expect a cabinet appointment. Instead he had to settle for the job of assistant secretary

Gov. Harry Woodring, with
Gov. Franklin Delano
Roosevelt, of New York, and
Rep. John ("Texas Jack")
Garner, who was Roosevelt's
first vice-president. Woodring
was an early supporter of
FDR's candidacy for presi-
dent in 1932.

of war, which he assumed on 23 April 1933. With Sec. George H.
Dern's death on 27 August 1936, Woodring became acting secretary
of war and on 27 April 1937 he was confirmed by the United States
Senate as secretary of war. He took pride that year that the army
proportion of the national budget was only 3.2 percent. But Woodring was too inflexible for Roosevelt. He could not adjust to
changes that were developing abroad. Roosevelt expected a war and
favored international rather than isolationist sentiment. At the president's request, Woodring resigned on 20 June 1940, declining at
the same time an offer to serve as governor of Puerto Rico because
he was holding out for a more important assignment. None ever
came. He had told close friends as early as 1939 that he would be returning to Kansas in 1941; he made it back a year earlier.

Woodring established his Kansas home in Topeka and resumed activity in Democratic state politics. In an address on his return, he said,

> The fact that a Kansas country boy, without previously seeking or holding public office, could be elected governor of this great commonwealth of ours, and subsequently serve in the Cabinet of the President, is further evidence that our great democracy does work. . . . It has been a great experience for me in Washington. A Kansas boy has dined with kings and queens, with princes and princesses, ambassadors and foreign diplomats, and has sat at the right hand of the President. But truly, a Kansas boy has seen Utopia from the mountaintops. But today a Kansas boy returns to heaven.[65]

In 1946 Woodring gained the party nomination for governor, receiving three times as many votes as the total for the other three candidates. However, he barely campaigned, mourning the loss of his twelve-year-old son to polio that summer. In the general election he was defeated by Frank Carlson, Republican, 254,283 votes to 309,064. He tried another comeback in 1956, but he lost in a close Democratic party primary contest for governor to George Docking, who won with 76,187 votes to 75,333 for Woodring. It was Woodring's first loss in a Democratic primary and at age sixty-nine his last political race.

REFERENCES: Carlin and Richmond, 1982; Hope, 1970; McFarland, 1975; Schruben, 1963; Schruben, 1969.

ALFRED MOSSMAN LANDON

Independence (Republican), 9 January 1933–11 January 1937

Governor of Kansas

Born 9 September 1887, West Middlesex (Lawrence County), Pennsylvania; son of John M. Landon, an Ohio oil company superintendent, and Anne Mossman Landon, 1 sister who died at age 7; educated at Marietta (Ohio) Academy and University of Kansas (graduated 1908); military experience in World War I, first lieutenant in chemical warfare service; married (1) Margaret Fleming, January 1915 (died June 1918), 1 son who died in infancy and 1 daughter, (2) Theo Cobb, January 1930, 1 daughter and 1 son; religious preference Methodist; died 12 October 1987, in Topeka; buried in Mount Hope Cemetery, Topeka.

As manager of Clyde M. Reed's unsuccessful Republican primary race against Frank Haucke in 1930, Alf M. Landon's fortunes in the Republican party fell briefly but were revived when Haucke was defeated in the general election. In 1932, with Frank Carlson as his campaign manager, Landon himself ran in the Republican primary for governor and won by accenting his role as a harmony candidate. The results were 160,345 votes for Landon, 59,326 for Lacey Simpson, and 28,456 for a belated entry, Joseph H. Brady. Landon had pounded the Republicans with his theme of harmony, and to general audiences he advocated cutting taxes and achieving material prosperity. He faced formidable opposition and was not helped by the nationwide deterioration of the Republican image. Nevertheless, Landon conducted a strenuous campaign and won in a fairly close general election race, carrying 278,581 votes to 272,944 for Woodring (Democrat), 244,607 for Brinkley (Independent) and 3,892 for H. M. Perkins (Socialist).

Alf Landon grew up in Marietta, Ohio, where his father was superintendent of an oil refinery. The family moved to the oil-boom and county-seat town of Independence, Kansas, in 1904, shortly after Alf graduated from Marietta Academy. John Landon had a fine job as manager of a gas company, and Alf attended the University of Kansas where he received a law degree in 1908. Instead of opening a law practice, Alf went to work as a bookkeeper at the Independence State Bank of Commerce, and later he moved to the First National Bank, just across the street. By 1910 Alf was investing in oil-drilling projects; in the next year he resigned from the bank to work full-time as an independent oil man, and he prospered modestly.

Landon was attracted by the actions of the progressive wing of the Republican party. His father served as one of the delegates-at-large to the Republican National Convention in 1912, endorsing Theodore Roosevelt. When Taft was renominated, both Alf and his father joined the Progressive party to get Roosevelt elected. Alf worked for the Progressive candidates in Montgomery County but also handled Republican Arthur Capper's campaign for governor in the county. In 1914 Landon became chairman of the Montgomery County Progressive party, in its unsuccessful effort to win an election. Landon's biographer says he struck a "political 'dry hole'" in 1914, but he learned from it. Slowly, Landon moved back to the progressive faction of the Republican party when in 1918 he supported Capper for United States Senate and served gubernatorial candidate Henry J. Allen as chairman in southeast Kansas and with membership on his statewide committee. With Allen's victory Landon gained a valued role as advisor of the governor, and for three months in 1922 he was Allen's executive secretary.

Landon's independent oil and gas businesses prospered in the 1920s, and he served as a director of important oil and gas associations. In 1924 Landon campaigned for Clyde Reed's nomination for governor in the Republican primary, but conservative Ben Paulen won. Paulen's silence on the Ku Klux Klan issue led to Landon's endorsement of William Allen White as an Independent candidate, but Paulen won anyway. Paulen's four years as governor proved popular with Kansas voters, but in 1928 Landon's chance to have a leading role in politics came again when he became Clyde Reed's campaign manager during a successful race for governor. Landon greatly enlarged his acquaintance throughout Kansas during that race, and even though Reed was defeated two years later, Landon had paved the way for his emergence as the Republican candidate for governor in 1932.

The mood was austere at Landon's inauguration in 1933: no parade, no invitations, a single small artillery piece in place of the seventeen-gun salute, and volunteer musicians. Neither would there be a new automobile for the governor nor new dishes for the Kansas Executive Mansion. In his inaugural address Landon said, ''We have grown to expect a lot for nothing. We expected government to strew our paths with roses. We wanted to keep on taking out, hardly realizing that we have to pay in as well. This condition 'built castles on the sand' that crumbled.'' But he was also optimistic: ''We are on the frontier of a new world. . . . We have come a long way since governments were chiefly of a patriarchal nature over agricultural states.'' Landon recognized that change was inevitable, but he was cautious: ''We all wish for improvement, but we of Kansas must not direct our legislative theory to-day on this supposition alone.''

Landon's four years as governor represented a mildly progressive, businesslike administration, unencumbered by commitments to pressure groups. Depression still gripped the state and nation, and Landon sought lower taxes and fees (for instance, a minimum vehicle registration fee of sixty cents instead of eight dollars), a reorganized state administration, and relief for farmers and the unemployed. State employee salaries were further reduced. He also asked for an agency that became the Legislative Council, paid for initially by a foundation grant, in an effort to free the state from nongovernmental tax experts. An income tax rate was set which lifted some tax burden from property. State limits were imposed on bank withdrawals and savings and trust companies just before the federal bank holiday in early March 1933. Landon also participated in the devel-

Governor Landon reading to his three-year-old daughter, Nancy Josephine. In 1978, Nancy Landon Kassebaum of Kansas became the first woman not a widow of a senator to be elected to the United States Senate. She was reelected in 1984.

opment of the National Recovery Administration's Oil Code that went into effect in July 1933. Unemployment and drouth were severe problems in 1933. Landon had only about two hundred jobs to fill but he interviewed as many as two hundred to three hundred applicants a day in an effort to provide hope for the unemployed. By 1934 Kansas was using more federal programs, and a bipartisan Kansas Emergency Relief Commission was replaced by other agencies. State funds for relief purposes were minimal, and reliance on federal moneys became necessary. Landon sought to combine job relief, agricultural relief, and conservation in one agency. In his first term, the Republicans had a bare majority in each house of the state legislature, so cooperation with the Democratic minority was evident. Two years later the Republicans gained much more control of the Kansas legislature.

Demanding a significant amount of Landon's time during his first term was the Finney bond scandal. He promptly called in state troops to guard the statehouse. He also convened a special session of the legislature. The attorney general and state auditor were impeached but acquitted, while the state treasurer, who resigned, and Warren and Ronald Finney were all convicted of fraud and given long sentences in the penitentiary. Also dealt with in that special session were unemployment relief laws, whether beer could be sold in Kansas, and a prohibition repeal referendum. The beer bill was narrowly defeated, and the prohibition issue was passed on to the voters in 1934 where prohibition was retained by a substantial majority.

Landon was a candidate for reelection in 1934. John R. Brinkley, in a third try for the governorship, ran in the Republican primary against Landon, who defeated him 233,956 votes to 58,938. Landon then won in the general election by a sizable margin over Topeka Mayor Omar B. Ketchum, Democrat, 422,030 votes to 359,877, with George M. Whiteside, Socialist, receiving 6,744 votes. In his second inaugural address, Landon commented on unemployment and public debt:

> Every right-thinking person prays that the need for relief to the unemployed may speedily pass away, but until it does pass it is entirely fair, in a complex, social and economic situation such as ours, that government exert all its powers to prevent suffering. We should, however, attempt to attain as nearly as possible a pay-as-you-go basis. We will then pay for our own mistakes, which is right and fair. We should not expect our children to pay for them. Certainly an increasing public debt will lessen the ability of our succeeding generations to meet their emergencies as they may arise.

By 1935, as Landon's second term got under way, the intensity of the drouth led an Associated Press reporter to identify parts of Kansas and four other states as the Dust Bowl. Landon worked primarily for a law that would require uniform accounting and auditing in local government; perhaps this financial reform was his chief victory. The cash basis law was also put in operation, providing essential ser-

HE HAS A POOR
SPEAKING
VOICE

HE LACKS
THE
PERSONAL
CHARM
OF HIS
OPPONENT

HE IS FROM
A TYPICAL
PRAIRIE
STATE"

SLURS
AGAINST
LANDON

W.C.MORRIS

Echoes Out of the Past

"They Said the Same Thing About Lincoln"

This supportive W. C. Morris cartoon appeared in 1936, when Alf Landon was the Republican candidate for president.

vices at a greatly reduced cost with the result that per capita expenses of state government dropped during his years in office. (The cumulative effect of this law has left Kansas with the smallest debt of any state in the country.) With few other Republican governors in office after 1934, Landon was a logical contender for the presidency in 1936.

In 1936 Landon, in a campaign initiated by the press and bolstered by support from Republican rank-and-file, was nominated on the first ballot of the Republican National Convention as a presidential candidate. Landon became a full-time contender following the national convention, and Kansas affairs were handled by his assistants. However, Pres. Franklin D. Roosevelt, running for a second term, turned out to be almost unbeatable in 1936, and Landon lost the presidential election. The popular vote was 27,478,945 for FDR, 16,674,665 for Landon. Landon received only the eight electoral votes of Vermont and Maine. Maine had always voted earlier than

Alf Landon, about 1950, visiting with George Gallup of the Gallup Poll, former senator Arthur Capper, and Henry S. Blake, chief executive officer of Capper Publications.

other states, so the old saying, "As Maine goes, so goes the nation," was altered to "As Maine goes, so goes Vermont!" The Republican numbers in Congress were drastically reduced, and Landon's executive secretary Will G. West lost the race for Kansas governor.

After his defeat in the presidential race, Landon established his home in Topeka and did not again seek or accept public office. His business, following his four years as governor, was primarily independent oil development and ownership of radio stations. He attended the Republican National Conventions of 1940, 1944, and 1948 as delegate-at-large, and he was a member of the Kansas commission on constitutional revision in 1957. He sought to avoid interference in Republican primary races, but his preference for certain candidates sometimes showed. He became the Grand Old Man of the Grand Old Party. His ninety-fifth birthday was celebrated by a visit from Pres. Ronald Reagan, who gave the address in the long-running Landon Lecture Series at Kansas State University; Reagan also visited Landon at his Topeka home shortly before his one-hundredth birthday. Landon's name in Topeka was commemorated by the Landon Middle School, closed in 1986, and the Landon Arena of the Topeka

Expocentre. The Alf M. Landon State Office Building at Ninth and Jackson streets, formerly housing offices of the Santa Fe railroad, was refitted as a major state facility. Landon died one month and three days after his one-hundredth birthday. His body lay in state for a day under the rotunda of the State Capitol before his funeral.

REFERENCES: Bader, 1982; Carlin and Richmond, 1982; McCoy, 1966; Schruben, 1963; Schruben, 1969.

WALTER AUGUSTUS HUXMAN

Hutchinson (Democrat), 11 January 1937–9 January 1939.

Born 16 February 1887, near Pretty Prairie (Reno County), Kansas; son of Augustus Huxman, a farmer and preacher of the Church of the New Jerusalem (Swedenborgian), and Mary Graber Huxman, 2 sisters and 2 brothers; educated at Reno County district schools, Emporia State University, and University of Kansas (graduated 1915); married Eula M. Biggs, 21 January 1915, 1 daughter; religious preference Christian Church (Disciples of Christ); died 26 June 1972, of an apparent heart attack, in Topeka; buried in Memorial Park Cemetery, Topeka.

In 1936 the Democratic state convention met in Hutchinson. Walter A. Huxman was chairman and keynoter, and he attracted such favorable attention that he was drafted as candidate for governor. He defeated Will G. West, Republican, who had been secretary for both Gov. Clyde Reed and Gov. Alf M. Landon. The tally was Huxman, 433,319 votes; West, 411,446; and Socialist candidate George M. Whiteside, 3,318.

Huxman had graduated from college with a law degree and had then taught school for a year. He opened a law practice in Hutchinson in 1915. He was assistant county attorney for four years, then city attorney for Hutchinson for two years. In a Republican county, he had little hope of winning elective office. He ran for a position

Governor Huxman (far right) at the Mother-In-Law Celebration, Amarillo, Texas, 9 March 1938.

on the Kansas Supreme Court in 1928 and lost. He campaigned for Woodring in his successful race for governor in 1930 and was appointed to the Kansas Tax Commission (1931–33), where he won an important case against the M. K. & T., popularly known as the Katy Railroad.

As a Democratic governor, Huxman proved generally more successful in dealing with a Republican legislature than either Davis or Woodring. He recommended a 1 percent sales tax, but the legislature raised it to 2 percent. A major public issue was the use of aluminum one mill and zinc two mill sales-tax tokens, known popularly as "Huxies" or "money for the governor," which were put into service to make small tax payments. Most of the new tax receipts went to social welfare and to school aid. Beer, with no more than 3.2 percent alcoholic content, was defined by the legislature as nonintoxicating and therefore legal under prohibition laws. Huxman failed to get legislative support on federal irrigation, conservation, and flood control projects.

Huxman won Democratic renomination in 1938. While he ran ahead of other Democratic candidates in the general election, he lost to Republican Payne Ratner, 341,271 votes to 393,989, with three other candidates, including former governor Jonathan M. Davis (running as an Independent), getting a total of 21,438 votes. When his term ended, he returned to his Hutchinson law practice. A short time later President Roosevelt appointed him as judge of the Tenth United States District Court in Topeka, a position he held until his retirement in 1962.

REFERENCES: McCoy, 1966; McFarland, 1975; Schruben, 1969; Swank, 1968.

PAYNE HARRY RATNER

Parsons (Republican), 9 January 1939–11 January 1943

Born 3 October 1896, Casey (Clark County), Illinois; son of Harry Ratner, a Wichita merchant, and Julia Ratner, 1 sister; educated at Blackwell (Oklahoma) High School and Washington University Law School in St. Louis (graduated 1920); military experience in World War I, ensign in navy; married Cliffe Dodd, 21 August 1920, 2 sons and 1 daughter; religious preference Christian Church (Disciples of Christ); died 27 December 1974; buried in mausoleum of Wichita Park Cemetery.

Payne Harry Ratner was the last governor to be elected from southeastern Kansas—the end of a twenty-year phenomenon in which governors Davis, Paulen, Reed, Woodring, Landon, and Ratner all hailed from four southeastern counties. (In all of Kansas history, only one other governor—Lyman Humphrey—fit this classification.)

Ratner, considered a liberal and a Landon man, won the Republican nomination for governor in 1938 over a field of five in the party primary and faced incumbent Walter Huxman in the general election. Ratner was the target of ethnic slurs in this campaign because his father was Jewish, although Ratner was a Christian and an elder in the Christian Church in Parsons. Ratner won with 393,989 votes to 341,271 for Huxman. Three other candidates polled 21,438 votes.

After his graduation from law school, Payne Ratner established his

183

law practice in Sibley, Iowa. A few months later, in 1920, he moved to Parsons, Kansas. As a Republican he was elected Labette County attorney, serving from 1923 to 1927. He was twice elected to the state senate, serving 1929–33 and 1937–39.

In 1940 Ratner was renominated and faced William H. Burke as his Democratic opponent. In spite of Wendell Willkie's ability to put Kansas back in the Republican column for a presidential candidate, the governor's race came down to the wire. The outcome was the third closest governor's race in Kansas history, with the margin of only 430 votes in favor of Ratner coming after the absentee votes were counted. The vote was Ratner, 425,928, and Burke, 425,498. The Socialist and Prohibition candidates totaled 6,863 votes. There is no indication of irregularity in the tally for governor in 1940, but the law was changed so that hereafter absentee ballots were not segregated but were counted at the same time as other ballots.

In his first inaugural address in 1939, Ratner contrasted the desire for security and the search for opportunity, opting for opportunity. He stated that "it is just as fundamental that government help to insure opportunity to all as it is to insure security. But in providing this opportunity there is a basic difference in the method. Opportunity is only a fertile field. The individual must plant his crop and harvest it, if he is to profit from it. Government cannot till the soil, harvest the crop and put it on his table. But government should protect the individual from unfair rivalry when he seeks to harvest his crop grown in the field of opportunity." He also pointed out that "self-reliance is the keynote of Kansas character. Kansas has in her blood and history, the vision, the capacity for solving her own problems, for living her own life, for overcoming her own difficulties. In this day these qualities are particularly needed. Kansas can point the way in their application."

During Ratner's administrations about forty state fee-collecting and taxing agencies were combined into a single department of revenue and taxation. Sales-tax tokens were eliminated in favor of a bracket system of tax payment, with the smallest tax being one cent, but most retail sales including food continued to be taxed. Departments in the state administration were reorganized, and new consumer protection agencies were created. World War II began

When the Kansas Society of New York City gave a dinner in November 1942 honoring Dr. Samuel J. Crumbine (secretary of the Kansas State Board of Health, 1904–1923), the guests included Osa Johnson, noted Kansas explorer-writer, and Gov. Payne Ratner.

during Ratner's second term, causing difficulties in operating state government. Rated most important and long-lasting from his administration were repeal of the recovery clause for welfare recipients, the beginning of a pension plan for teachers, and a new merit system for state employees.

Ratner did not seek a third term or any further elective office. He moved to Wichita where he opened a successful law office. In 1962 Ratner was accused of unethical professional conduct, but he was fully exonerated.

REFERENCES: Finger, 1967; McCoy, 1966; Postal and Koppman, 1954; Socolofsky, 1962.

ANDREW FRANK SCHOEPPEL

Ness City (Republican), 11 January 1943–13 January 1947

Born 23 November 1894, near Claflin (Barton County), Kansas; son of George J. Schoeppel, a grain dealer and farmer, and Anna Phillip Schoeppel, 1 brother and 4 sisters; educated at Ness County schools, Ransom High School, University of Kansas (1916–18), and University of Nebraska (1921–23, graduated); military experience in World War I, naval reserve aviation corps; married Marie Thomsen, 2 June 1924, no children; religious preference Methodist; died 21 January 1962, of abdominal cancer, at Bethesda (Maryland) Naval Hospital; buried in Old Mission Cemetery, Wichita.

As a virtual unknown in state politics, Andrew Frank Schoeppel resigned in 1942 as chairman of the Kansas Corporation Commission to enter the Republican party primary for governor against three established Republican leaders, including former governor Clyde M. Reed, the Lieutenant Governor Carl Friend, and longtime state senator Paul Wunsch. Schoeppel's first campaign advertisements showed voters how to pronounce his name. He stumped extensively and won the primary by about 7,000 votes. In the general election he received a majority in all but two counties, with a vote of 287,895 to 212,071 against Democrat William H. Burke, who had been defeated by Ratner two years earlier by only a few hundred votes. Perennial Socialist and Prohibition candidates drew support from 7,963 voters. Schoeppel was elected to a second term in 1944, when he was opposed by Robert S. Lemon. The governor carried all 105 counties in Kansas with 463,110 votes to Lemon's 231,410, with 10,077 going to two other candidates. Schoeppel was the second "western Kansan" to become governor.

While attending the University of Nebraska where he graduated with a law degree, Andrew Schoeppel played football, making "honorable mention" on one of Walter Camp's first All-American football teams. Schoeppel set up his law practice in Ness City and served in local government as county attorney, city attorney, city councilman, mayor, and member of the school board. He was a well-known sports official in western Kansas, and in 1929 he filled in as the coach of the Fort Hays State football team when the head coach was on leave for a year. As a Republican, he was drafted against his wishes as a candidate for state representative from Ness County. He lost by a very few votes, even though he had not campaigned at all; Schoeppel vowed that he would never let that happen again. In 1939 Governor Ratner appointed Schoeppel chairman of the Kansas Corporation Commission, and he got his first exposure to statewide politics.

The issues surrounding World War II dominated attention during Schoeppel's first term and he stressed economy of state operations. Unlike previous governors, Schoeppel provided no leadership for the overwhelmingly Republican legislature, and it broke into factions, each of which supported favorite programs. Schoeppel's administration was interpreted as friendly to business and punitive to organized labor. The war was nearing its conclusion when Schoeppel cautioned Kansans in his second inaugural speech on 8 January 1945:

Following the war will come many other problems. The readjustment to peacetime pursuits will likewise be difficult. Our returning service men and women must be welcomed home, not only with parades and public receptions, but with genuine opportunities and a real place in our economic, social and political life. Our great war plants must be converted in the greatest possible degree to the manufacture of the goods and com-

Gov. Andrew Schoeppel shows off his athletic prowess just before the game between the Kansas City Blues and the Minneapolis Millers, 17 April 1946.

modities of peace. . . . But in achieving all of these objectives, we must not lose sight of the cause for which we fight. Tyranny and oppression are our enemies. Our purpose is to keep men free. The tyranny of foreign dictators is not the only enemy of freedom. We also must not enslave ourselves by making our own governmental processes so complicated and complex that freedom of choice, freedom of action and freedom of opportunity are no longer possible.

Prohibition was again an issue when it was discovered that more than four hundred wholesale and retail federal liquor stamps were sold to Kansans. Alf Landon became an opponent of Schoeppel's political ambitions, believing that Schoeppel was not supporting prohibition laws as vigorously as he could. Capital punishment also stirred controversy, even though Kansas had had no legal executions for more than seventy years. The legislature in 1935 had reimposed capital punishment for certain major crimes, but there had been no executions. The issue resurfaced in Schoeppel's term. He placed no bar to the execution of a habitual criminal who was convicted of murder. The warden resigned rather than take charge of the execution, so Schoeppel appointed a new warden and the penalty was carried out. As one of his last actions as governor, Schoeppel recommended parole for Ronald Finney, who had served a longer prison term for embezzlement than anyone else in Kansas.

Schoeppel did not seek a third term, retiring instead to Wichita where he went into law practice. In 1948 he campaigned for the United States Senate seat being vacated by Arthur Capper, and he won and was reelected in 1954 and 1960. In 1952 he waived his Kansas allegiance to support Sen. Robert Taft for president over Dwight D. Eisenhower. Schoeppel died in office in 1962.

REFERENCES: Boles, 1967; Hopkins, 1943; Owens, 1943.

FRANK CARLSON

Concordia (Republican), 13 January 1947–28 November 1950

Born 23 January 1893, near Concordia (Cloud County), Kansas; son of Charles Eric Carlson, a farmer, and Anna Johnson Carlson; educated at local schools, Concordia Normal and Business College, and short courses at Kansas State University (1910–12); military experience in World War I, private in army; married Alice Fredrickson, 26 August 1919, 1 daughter and 1 foster son; religious preference Baptist; died 30 May 1987, in Concordia; buried in Pleasant Hill Cemetery, Concordia.

Frank Carlson was well qualified by prior service in the state legislature and in Congress when he won the Republican primary for governor in 1946. Carlson spent the next two-and-one-half months campaigning in his low-key style through all Kansas counties. His Democratic opponent was former governor Harry Woodring, who made repeal of prohibition his major issue, while Carlson was silent on prohibition. Carlson defeated Woodring 309,064 votes to 254,283, with 14,347 votes going to the Socialist and Prohibition candidates. In 1948 Carlson was reelected over Democrat Randolph Carpenter, 433,396 votes to 307,485, with 19,526 votes collected by the Socialist and Prohibition candidates.

Following service in World War I, Carlson went back to his Cloud County farm. As a Republican, he served two terms in the state house of representatives, from 1929 to 1933, and as Landon's state campaign manager in his 1932 bid for governor, resulting in his appointment as chairman of the Republican state committee (1932–34). In 1934 Carlson won the first of six consecutive terms in Congress by defeating an incumbent congresswoman, Kathryn O'Laughlin McCarthy.

When Carlson became governor in 1947, World War II was over, but it was still uppermost in people's minds. In his first inaugural address, he said, "It is too obvious that all over the nation a strange and inverted prosperity prevails. It is almost spurious in its economic effect, because it is born of destruction. We created, we produced and we labored to destroy. In the desperation of war we achieved a productive capacity of farm and factory once thought impossible. Can we now beat our terrible tanks into tilling tractors so that in peace the struggles for living and security may be lightened, and so that we shall know neither poverty nor war any more?"

During wartime the state treasury had accumulated a sizable balance, and Carlson's initial proposal to the legislature was a comprehensive outline for action in many areas. The administration recommended a new highway program, broad developments in education at all levels, and state aid to returning veterans. Later a twenty-year highway building program, reorganization of social welfare programs, transformation of the state's mental hospitals, and a broad plan for rural medical services were implemented. Carlson would later count the state's new enterprise in the treatment of mental illness as his major contribution. Carlson also supported but did not obtain a severance tax and a small loan act. The legislature approved an amendment repealing prohibition which voters endorsed in the election of 1948. For his second inaugural address on 10 January 1949, Carlson indicated that he shared with all Kansans "a deep pride in the glories of the past and in our rich and sturdy traditions. But I want you to know that there is something new under the Kansas sun in the form of a truly inspiring spirit of progress. I see it everywhere. Wherever the machinery of government is creaky or rusty, there is a universal demand that it be overhauled and geared to a new concept of service—a concept which envisions true service to our people for the things they want and deserve."

When Sen. Clyde Reed died in 1949, Carlson appointed a Kansas City businessman, Harry Darby, to take over Reed's seat. In 1950

Frank Carlson (second from right), who had just resigned from the governorship, watching his lieutenant governor, Frank Hagaman, being sworn in as governor, 28 November 1946.

Carlson campaigned for the United States Senate and won. After the election Darby resigned to enable Carlson to gain seniority in the Senate. So Carlson resigned as governor on 28 November 1950; Lieutenant Governor Frank Hagaman moved into the governor's office and appointed Carlson to the Senate for the remainder of Darby's term.

Throughout his political career Carlson was a humble and unassuming man. He had a saying: "There are no self-made men. It is your friends who make you what you are." Carlson was reelected to the Senate in 1956 and 1962 and then retired voluntarily in 1969. He was the only Kansas governor to serve in both houses of Congress; he had competed in thirteen primary election races and thirteen general election races without a loss. He also played a leading role in recruiting Dwight D. Eisenhower as a Republican candidate for president in 1952. An active Baptist, Carlson was a cofounder of the annual President's Prayer Breakfast, later known as the National Prayer Breakfast. He received many honors from his native state, including designation as "favorite son" candidate in the 1968 Republican National Convention. In his home town of Concordia, he was recognized by the Frank Carlson Library; in addition, there is a Frank Carlson Lecture Series at Wichita State University, and the federal court building in Topeka is named for him.

REFERENCES: Hope, 1970; Linn, 1961.

FRANK LESLIE HAGAMAN

Fairway (Republican), 28 November 1950–8 January 1951

Born 1 June 1894, Bushnell (McDonough County), Illinois; son of Frank Hagaman, a clerk, and Martha Hagaman; educated at Rosedale High School, University of Kansas, and George Washington University Law School in Washington, D.C. (graduated 1921); military experience in World War I, private with the 117th Kansas Ammunition Train, severely wounded; married Elizabeth Blair Sutton, 1920, no children; religious preference Episcopal; died 23 June 1966, in Kansas City; buried in Fairmount Cemetery, Denver, Colorado.

Frank Hagaman became governor on 28 November 1950 when Carlson resigned to accept appointment to the United States Senate. He had already lost his bid for the Republican nomination for governor in the 1950 party primary. His administration was short, and he primarily served a caretaker role overseeing final preparations for the state budget. The legislature was not in session during the less than two months that Hagaman was governor.

After graduating from law school in 1921, Frank Hagaman set up his first law office in Wyandotte County, where he also served as assistant county assessor. He moved to Fairway in Johnson County

Governor Hagaman in his office.

and relocated his law practice. As a Republican, he served in the state house of representatives from 1935 to 1945 and in the senate for the next four years. He was elected lieutenant governor in 1948, primarily responsible for presiding over the senate and over the Kansas Legislative Council. After his brief stint as governor of Kansas, he returned to his law practice in Fairway.

REFERENCES: Linn, 1961.

EDWARD F. ARN

Wichita (Republican), 8 January 1951–10 January 1955

Born 19 May 1906, Kansas City (Wyandotte County), Kansas; son of Edward F. Arn, a coal, feed, and building materials salesman, and Grace Bell Edwards Arn; educated at Kansas City and Muncie schools, Kansas City Junior College (1925–27), University of Kansas, and Kansas City School of Law (graduated 1931); military experience in World War II, lieutenant and security officer in navy; married (1) Marcella Ruth Tillmans, 28 October 1933 (died 6 June 1966), 2 daughters, (2) Catherine Philippi Ross, 8 June 1967; religious preference Congregational.

Edward F. Arn resigned as judge in the state supreme court in 1950 to campaign for governor in the Republican party primary, which he won over Frank Hagaman and Willard Mayberry. Arn's Democratic opponent that year was Kenneth T. Anderson, and Arn defeated him with 333,001 votes to 275,494; 10,815 votes went to two minor candidates. In 1952 Arn was reelected over Charles Rooney, Democrat, 491,338 to 363,482, with 17,319 votes going to the Prohibition and Socialist candidates. Republican Dwight D. Eisenhower easily won the Kansas electoral vote for president that year. Arn was the first governor of Kansas born in the twentieth century; all later governors were also born in the twentieth century.

Arn's father died when Ed was four months old. An only child, he grew up in Kansas City and Muncie with his mother. He attended college, graduated from law school, and was admitted to the Missouri bar in 1930 and the Kansas bar in 1931. From 1933 to 1936 Arn was an investigator for the State Highway Commission. He relocated to Wichita and maintained a law practice there from 1936 to 1947. An active Republican since his freshman year in college when he served as chairman of the Wyandotte County Republicans, Arn was precinct committeeman for six years, chairman of the congressional district young Republican group, and manager of both Ratner's and Schoeppel's gubernatorial campaigns. Arn, sporting the big white hat that was his trademark, could be seen in almost any political gathering. He was elected attorney general in 1946 and reelected in 1948. In 1949 he resigned as attorney general to accept appointment to the state supreme court.

A major change in state government during the Arn administration was the development of the State Department of Administration which assumed broad powers in coordinating budgets, accounting, and purchasing within all levels of state government. The severe flood of 1951, the biggest in the state's history, taxed the state's resources and was followed by a serious drouth. Arn acknowledged these natural disasters in his second inaugural address on 12 January 1953 but observed with pride:

Over many past years, we as a state have been making exceptional progress in such fields as education and science, of human welfare and needs of agricultural and industrial development. We are gaining new goals in public health service, we are steadily improving our highways according to an efficient and long-range plan. We are building up our institutional plants and rendering a broader mission of mercy to unfortunates. All of these achievements we have managed to accomplish with the means at hand, and without plunging our state into debt.

In 1954 the United States Supreme Court unanimously opposed segregation in public education, declaring it unconstitutional in the case of *Brown v. Board of Education of Topeka*, involving Kansas and four

Gov. Edward Arn visiting the General Motors assembly line in Kansas City, Kansas.

other states. Because Kansas law provided for permissive segregation in the public schools (certain classes of cities could opt for segregation), the state, through the office of the Attorney General, carried this case to the highest court in the land. Governor Arn's office was not involved in this appeal.

Illegal lobbying by the state's Republican national committeeman caused a minor scandal during Arn's administration. The committeeman, who was trying to sell a building to the state, lost his party job. The national economy, in general, boomed, and the state shared in the bounty. Expenses greatly increased for state government, but revenues from sales-tax receipts and other sources more than made up the difference.

Arn did not seek a third term, and he returned to Wichita to his law practice. In 1962 he sought the party's nomination to the United States Senate but lost to James B. Pearson. The chief justice of the state supreme court appointed him as chairman of the Judicial Study Advisory Committee in 1973.

REFERENCES: Bright, 1956; Richmond, 1988.

FREDERICK LEE HALL

Dodge City (Republican), 10 January 1955–3 January 1957

Born 24 July 1916, Dodge City (Ford County), Kansas; son of Frederick Lee Hall, a railroad engineer, and Etta Lucille Brewer Hall, 1 sister; educated at Dodge City High School and University of Southern California (graduated 1938; LL.B. 1941); married Leadell Schneider, 25 April 1942, 1 son; religious preference Methodist; died 18 March 1970, at Shawnee; buried in Maple Grove Cemetery, Dodge City.

At age thirty-nine, Fred Hall became the youngest Kansas governor elected since 1873. He stated in his inaugural address, "I describe myself neither as a 'do-gooder' nor a 'do-nothing.' For lack of a better term I describe myself as a 'do-something.' Perhaps I am what the President has termed a 'progressive moderate.'" He further defined his role as head of the Republican party, and "put in power by the people," with "the solemn obligation of service to the people—but to administer the affairs of government with efficiency and integrity." As a party "outsider" who was willing to exercise the full prerogatives of his office, Hall became the center of intraparty feuding. Although he had a large Republican majority in the legislature, his appropriation requests were still cut. Controversy erupted when he fired the director of the State Purchasing Agency, then quickly changed the membership of the appeal board before the director could present his case. The "right-to-work" bill, plac-

Gov. Fred Hall showing his opposition to the "right-to-work" bill.

ing additional restraint on labor unions, also attracted controversy. Hall, coming from a family where union membership was expected, vetoed the bill in favor of a more moderate labor management bill, and the legislature sustained his veto.

When Hall decided to run for a second term, his campaign manager, who served as state Republican chairman, severed ties with him, and Hall went down in defeat in 1956, in a divisive Republican primary, to a Topeka attorney, Warren W. Shaw. Hall resigned as governor on 3 January 1957 after a friendly supreme court justice resigned from the court. Lieutenant Governor John McCuish became governor and appointed Hall to the vacant court position. This legal but questionable "triple-jump" embroiled Hall in further controversy. In 1958 he resigned from the court to run again for governor in the Republican primary. However, no Kansas governor, once leaving office, has ever regained the governorship, and Hall was no exception to that tradition.

Fred Hall had had outstanding success as a debater in high school, and he won a scholarship to the University of Southern California where he was on the International Debate Team in 1938. Following graduation from law school, he became an attorney for Douglas Aircraft in Long Beach from 1941 to 1942. Unable to pass the armed forces physical examination for service in World War II, he went to Washington to serve as assistant director of the Combined Production and Resources Board for the Combined Chiefs of Staff for two years. He returned to Kansas in 1944 and worked for a law firm in Topeka. Then in 1946 he moved back to Dodge City and set up his own law office. As a Republican, he was elected Ford County attorney in 1947 but was defeated for reelection in 1949.

On the last day of filing for statewide offices in 1950, Hall entered the Republican primary for lieutenant governor in contest with eight other candidates, all of whom lived in the more populous eastern half of the state. Ambitious, independent, and aggressive, Hall won nomination and the election. Described by Republican party leaders as a troublemaker and a young man in too big a hurry, Hall was nevertheless renominated and elected in 1952 and thus established himself as a likely candidate for governor in 1954. He won the nomination in 1954 and defeated George Docking, Democrat, 329,868 votes to 286,218 (with 6,547 votes polled by two minor party candidates) in a campaign in which television made its first big impact on Kansas voters.

After his defeat in 1958, when he sought the governorship for the third time, Hall became an executive with Aerojet-General in Sacramento, California. In 1960 he opened a law practice in Beverly Hills, and in 1962 he became president of the California Republican assembly. For a while he was executive president of a proposed California world's fair. He ran for the Republican nomination to the United States Senate but lost to George Murphy who was elected. After suffering a stroke, Hall returned to Dodge City and established a law practice in the late 1960s. He moved to Wichita in October 1968 and to Shawnee a year later.

REFERENCES: Ehrlich, 1963; Hall, 1956; Karson, 1955.

JOHN BERRIDGE McCUISH

Newton (Republican), 3 January–14 January 1957

John M Cuish (signature)

Born 22 June 1906, Leadville (Lake County), Colorado; son of John Berridge Mc-Cuish, Presbyterian minister, and Anna Hulbert McCuish, 2 sisters; educated at Newton (Kansas) schools, Kemper Military School (Boonville, Missouri), and Washburn University (graduated 1925); military experience in World War II, private in army; married Cora Hedrick, 10 September 1925, no children; religious preference Presbyterian; died 12 March 1962, of a stroke, in Newton; buried in Greenwood Cemetery, Newton.

Elected lieutenant governor in 1954, John McCuish became governor when Fred Hall resigned on 3 January 1957. His eleven-day term was the shortest of any Kansas governor, and no major events occurred. The political support he had enjoyed earlier was dissipated through his participation in Fred Hall's infamous "triple jump" over which he had no control, so McCuish retired from active politics.

Following graduation from college, John McCuish had become advertising salesman for the *Newton Kansan* (1927–28) and later owner of the *Hillsboro Star* (1929–30). He then acquired the *Harvey County News* in Newton, which he operated from 1930 to 1958. He served as chairman of the Kansas Commission on Revenue and Taxation from 1939 to 1943. An active Republican, McCuish was chair-

Governor McCuish inspecting the troops following his inauguration, 3 January 1957. The Santa Fe Office Building in the background later became the Alf M. Landon State Office Building.

man of the Harvey County Republican committee from 1930 to 1957, a delegate to the national convention in 1936 and 1948, treasurer of the state Republican committee in 1948, and director of the Kansas "Eisenhower for President" campaign in 1952.

Outside of Kansas, McCuish had participated in such activities as a short postwar assignment with the Red Cross in Germany and a three-month post in Japan for the Defense Department in 1950. His brief role as Kansas governor was disastrous for him. It even affected his business; returning to his newspaper in Newton, he ended up selling it in 1958. McCuish then became an independent oil producer; four years later, at age fifty-five, he died.

REFERENCES: Ehrlich, 1963.

GEORGE DOCKING

Lawrence (Democrat), 14 January 1957–9 January 1961

George Docking

Born 23 February 1904, Clay Center (Clay County), Kansas; son of William Docking, a banker, and Alameda Donley Docking, 1 sister; educated at schools in Lawrence, Western Military Academy (Alton, Illinois), and University of Kansas (graduated 1925); married Mary Virginia Blackwell, 24 January 1925, 2 sons; religious preference Presbyterian; died 20 January 1964, of emphysema, in Kansas City, Kansas; buried in Highland Park Cemetery, Kansas City.

Gaining renomination in 1956, George Docking won a narrow primary election victory over Harry Woodring, former governor, 76,544 votes to 75,548. He was able to lead a unified Democratic party against a Republican party shattered by a bitter primary fight, and he defeated Republican Warren W. Shaw by a vote of 479,701 to 364,340, with Harry O. Lytle, Prohibition candidate, taking 20,894 votes. Docking's victory was a personal one, as Kansas gave a heavy majority to Eisenhower that year and Republicans won all statewide races except the governor's. Docking was reelected in 1958, the first time in Kansas history that a second term was awarded to a non-Republican. His major opponent was Clyde M. Reed, Jr., son of a former governor, and the vote was 415,506 to 313,036, with 7,397 going to Prohibition candidate Warren C. Martin.

After graduation from the University of Kansas, George Docking was a bond salesman—first in Kansas City, Missouri, from 1925 to 1926, and then in Topeka, until 1928. He was cashier for the Kansas Reserve State Bank in Topeka for three years. Then he moved to the First National Bank in Lawrence, eventually becoming president. Docking organized and was the primary owner of the Lawrence gas company. During these years, he became a champion amateur tennis player and a master of the game of bridge. Docking first sought elective office as a member of the Lawrence school board, but he was unsuccessful. Inactive politically, he moved away from Republican loyalties when Franklin D. Roosevelt first accepted nomination for the presidency. It was not until twenty years later, in 1952, that Docking declared himself a Democrat; he became a fundraiser in the "Adlai Stevenson for President" campaign. In 1954 George Docking won the Democratic nomination for governor against William C. Salome, 54,351 votes to 41,479, then lost to Fred Hall in the general election, 286,218 votes to 329,868.

Docking was the first Democratic governor since Huxman, and he was no doubt elected because he somehow combined conservatism on fiscal policy with social liberalism. To exemplify his fiscal restraint, he refused to live in Cedar Crest, given to the state as an executive mansion. In contrast with his "secretive and inaccessible" predecessor, Docking had daily press conferences so that he was highly visible to the public. In his second inaugural address, Docking said, "We have made great efforts in the past two years to open informational doors to all of our citizens so that they may know what is happening at all times in their government. We call it 'government in a goldfish bowl.' It is our duty as officials to furnish you as much information as possible. It is your duty to know your government so that you may vote in the best interests of all of our people. We hope that the next two years will open the doors of information on all the departments and branches of state government."

Generally, Docking was even more conservative than his Republican opposition, and he used this to his political advantage. For instance, a special session of the legislature called by the governor to raise more revenue passed an increase in sales tax. It was vetoed by Docking but passed over his veto, so Docking blamed his opposi-

Pres. Dwight D. Eisenhower being greeted by Gov. George Docking.

tion for increases in taxes. He continually questioned expenditures at all levels of state government and published the names of the state's highest-paid employees. Nevertheless, state spending increased greatly during his four years as governor.

In 1960 Docking sought a third term. The only Kansas governor to try that before was St. John in 1882; neither of them succeeded. Docking's Republican opponent was Attorney General John Anderson, Jr., who won with 511,534 votes to Docking's 402,261, with J. J. Steele, Prohibition, receiving 8,727. Docking had been an early supporter of John F. Kennedy's effort to gain the Democratic nomination for president. With Kennedy's election in 1960, Docking was appointed director of the Export-Import Bank, necessitating his move to Washington, D.C.

REFERENCES: Hajda, 1976; Harder and Rampey, 1972; Roe, 1981.

JOHN ANDERSON, JR.

Olathe (Republican), 9 January 1961–11 January 1965

John Anderson Jr.

Born 8 May 1917, near Olathe (Johnson County), Kansas; son of John Anderson, Sr., a farmer, and Ora Bookout Anderson, 2 brothers; educated at Olathe High School, Kansas State University, and University of Kansas (graduated 1943; LL.B. 1944); married Arlene A. Auchard, 16 March 1943, 2 sons and 2 daughters; religious preference Methodist.

In 1960 John Anderson gained the Republican nomination for governor and defeated incumbent governor George Docking who was seeking a third term. The vote for Anderson was 511,534 to Docking's 402,261 and 8,727 for the Prohibition candidate. Anderson was reelected in 1962 with 341,257 votes to 291,285 for Dale E. Saffels, Democrat, and 6,248 for Prohibition candidate Vearl A. Bacon.

After completing his law degree John Anderson spent two years (1944–46) on the staff of federal judge and former governor Walter A. Huxman. He then returned to his own law office in Olathe. He was elected to three terms as Johnson County attorney as a Republi-

John Anderson was governor during the Kansas Centennial Celebration. Here he is being given a Kansas Centennial Model "G" Colt Revolver, gold plated with walnut stock, by Charles Kidwell, Wichita, representative of the Colt Arms Company. H. W. Brawley, deputy postmaster general, looks on.

can serving from 1947 to 1953. Elected to the state senate in 1952, his term was cut short on 1 March 1956 when he was appointed to an unexpired term as attorney general. He was reelected in 1956 and 1958.

Anderson was the first to occupy Cedar Crest as the executive mansion. Education changes were a priority in Anderson's administration: Public schools were reorganized into about three hundred unified districts in place of thousands of diverse districts legislated through the years; a state technical institute was established at Salina; a large number of vocational-technical schools were organized; and the University of Wichita came into the state system as Wichita State University. Other new legislation included reorganization of a state psychiatric and medical facility, highway construction, public employee retirement benefits, and legislation for fair employment practices.

Anderson did not seek a third term in 1964 but retired to his law practice in Overland Park. In 1965 he was appointed attorney for both the Kansas Turnpike Authority and the State Board of Healing Arts. He was also executive director of the Citizens' Conference on State Legislature (1965–72), with headquarters in Kansas City, Missouri. Several times he was nominated for an opening in the federal judicial system, but he was never appointed. In 1972 he campaigned for the Republican nomination for governor, but legislator Morris Kay defeated him. He continued in later years with his law practice in Johnson County and kept a ranch near Olathe, where he farmed and bred Shetland ponies and Hereford cattle.

REFERENCES: Harder and Rampey, 1972.

WILLIAM HENRY AVERY

Wakefield (Republican), 11 January 1965–9 January 1967

Born 11 August 1911, near Wakefield (Clay County), Kansas; son of Herman W. Avery, a farmer-rancher, and Hattie W. Coffman Avery, 1 sister and 1 brother; educated at Wakefield High School and University of Kansas (graduated 1934); married Hazel Bowles, 16 June 1940, 2 sons and 2 daughters; religious preference Methodist.

In 1964 William Avery won the Republican party primary as a candidate for governor. He defeated his Democratic opponent, Harry G. Wiles, by 432,667 votes to 400,264, while the Prohibition and Conservative candidates collected 17,483 votes. Avery entered the governorship in an era of rapid change, inflation, and expanding government. His decade of service in Congress, where budgets mounted into the hundreds of billions of dollars, made him unafraid to ask for increased revenues to improve state services. However, his push for more taxes to improve schools and his suggestion to use withholding on income taxes were effective but unpopular. International attention during the mid-1960s was focused on the Vietnam War; at home civil rights demonstrations erupted. Avery was widely supported as he remained calm about violent protest in

Governor Avery with Luann Nelson, the Kansas Angus Queen, and Renee Was-
senberg, Baileyville, and the Grand Champion Steer at the 1966 Kansas National
Junior Livestock Show.

the state. Avery was renominated in 1966, but he lost the general
election race to Robert Docking, Democrat, by a vote of 304,325 to
380,030, with 4,742 going to the Prohibition candidate and 3,858
to the Conservative candidate.

William Avery returned to his home in Wakefield after college to
raise crops and livestock on the family farm. He was on the local
school board and served as a Republican in the state house of representatives from 1951 to 1955. In 1954 he gained the Republican nomination from a field of five for the United States House of Representatives; his anti–big dam platform opposed the Tuttle Creek project
under construction on the Blue River. Although he defeated the in-

cumbent congressman, who also opposed the dam, Avery was unable to halt completion of the Tuttle Creek dam. However, he continued to be reelected and served five terms in Congress (1955–65).

After his term as governor, Avery moved to Wichita, since most of his farm and ranch near Wakefield was now under Milford Reservoir. He was associated with Garvey Enterprises (1967–68) and Clinton Oil Company (1969–71); then he became president of the Real Oil Company. In 1968 he sought the Republican nomination for the United States Senate but lost to Cong. Robert Dole. He was a member of a fact-finding tour of Africa for the Agency for International Development, followed by service as a congressional liaison for the assistant secretary of the Department of Interior. In 1977 he returned to Wakefield to resume a role in the Farmers and Merchants Bank.

REFERENCES: Collins, 1978.

ROBERT BLACKWELL DOCKING

Arkansas City (Democrat), 9 January 1967–6 January 1975

Robert Docking
Governor of Kansas

Born 9 October 1925, Kansas City (Jackson County), Missouri; son of George Docking, a banker, and Mary Virginia Blackwell Docking, 1 brother; educated at Lawrence schools, Western Military Academy (Alton, Illinois, 1939–41), University of Kansas (1942–43, 1946–48, graduated), Graduate School of Banking, University of Wisconsin; military experience in World War II, corporal in army air corps, 1943–46, first lieutenant in USAF reserve, 1946–51; married Meredith Marina Gear, 15 June 1950, 2 sons; religious preference Presbyterian; died 8 October 1983, at his home in Arkansas City, of emphysema and complications; buried in Highland Park Cemetery, Kansas City, Kansas.

Robert Docking gained the Democratic nomination for governor in 1966 and won the general election over incumbent William Avery, 380,030 votes to 304,325, with about 8,600 votes going to two other candidates. He followed his father, George Docking, as governor by six years.

Like his father, Robert Docking expressed a consistently conservative viewpoint on fiscal policy while espousing liberal views on social issues. He criticized his predecessor for traveling outside the state, yet Docking became the most traveled governor in Kansas his-

215

tory and still retained local popularity. He could support liberal Democratic national leaders without losing his conservative base of operations at home. Moreover, state expenditures rose rapidly during his administration in spite of his avowed fiscal conservatism. His ability to sense where tax dollars came from and to know voting strength of specific taxpayer blocs enabled him to retain the governorship through four terms in a period of rapid inflation and governmental expansion.

Following his university studies, Robert Docking had worked as a credit analyst for the William Volker Company in Kansas City. He became vice-president of the First National Bank in Lawrence in 1950 and, as a sideline, organized Docking Development, an oil drilling company. In 1956 he moved to Arkansas City to take over the presidency of the Union State Bank. While still in Lawrence he was chairman of the Douglas County Democratic committee from 1954 to 1956; following his move to Arkansas City, he was treasurer of the fifth district Democratic committee, and vice-president of the Kansas Democratic Veterans in 1957. He was the Kansas Junior Chamber of Commerce "Young Man of the Year" in 1966. In Arkansas City he served on the city commission from 1963 to 1966 and was mayor for one year.

In his second race for governor in 1968, Docking defeated Rick Harmon, Republican, 447,269 votes to 410,673, with the Prohibition candidate drawing 4,528 votes. In 1970, he was opposed by Attorney General Kent Frizzell, Republican, and he won an unprecedented third term as governor. The vote was 404,611 to 333,227, with 7,352 votes garnered by two other candidates. In 1972 Docking gained his fourth term by overwhelming Morris Kay, Republican, 571,256 votes to 341,440, while the Prohibition candidate received 8,856.

In 1972 the legislature drafted a constitutional amendment that revised the Executive Article in the Kansas Constitution—the first change in the article since the constitution was approved in 1859. The voters approved the amendment in the 1972 general election. It provided for a four-year term for statewide offices, with the governor and lieutenant governor running as a team, and limited their tenure to two successive terms. It also authorized the governor to

Gov. Robert Docking at the commissioning ceremony of the U.S.S. Wichita, *June 1969.*

reorganize certain parts of the administrative structure of government by executive order. A series of constitutional amendments in 1972 and 1974 abolished the state auditor's office and removed the state treasurer and state printer from the list of constitutional offices.

The Robert Docking period in Kansas history was generally one of growth in the economy and expansion of governmental services. Although he tried, he was unable to get a turnpike for southeast Kansas. But, like the preceding administration of William Avery, Docking was also faced with eruptions associated with the war in Vietnam. He would later remark that his most agonizing period as governor was when he had to send state troops to Lawrence and Kansas City to curb violence accompanying civil rights demonstrations.

Docking did not seek reelection in 1974 but returned to Arkansas

Just before a Landon Lecture at Kansas State University, 1970: (left to right) Pat Nixon, James A. McCain, Pres. Richard Nixon, Theo Landon, former governor Alf Landon, Gov. Robert Docking, Meredith Docking.

City and his position as president of the Union State Bank. Three years after his death, the state office building at 915 Harrison was renamed the Robert B. Docking State Office Building. Docking's son Tom served as lieutenant governor during John Carlin's second term (1983–87) and was the Democratic candidate for governor in 1986.

REFERENCES: Drury, 1980; Flentje, 1979; Harder and Rampey, 1972.

ROBERT FREDERICK BENNETT

Prairie Village (Republican), 13 January 1975–8 January 1979

Born 23 May 1927, Kansas City (Jackson County), Missouri; adopted son of Otto Francis Bennett, a farmer, and Dorothy Bass Dodds Bennett; educated at Shawnee Mission High School and University of Kansas (graduated 1950; LL.B. 1952); military experience in World War II and Korean War; private first class in Marine Corps; married (1) Mildred Joan Gregory, 10 June 1949, 1 son and 3 daughters, divorced, (2) Oliva A. D. Fisher, 16 July 1971; religious preference Presbyterian.

Robert Bennett won the Republican nomination for governor in 1974 by 530 votes with about one-third of the total in a four-way race. This election marked the first time that the candidates for governor and lieutenant governor ran as a team and for a four-year term. Bennett and his running mate Shelby Smith faced a Democratic ticket of Attorney General Vern Miller and State Senator Jack Steineger. Bennett won a narrow victory—387,792 votes to 384,115—with the Prohibition candidate polling 11,968 votes, much more than the difference. Attorney General Miller's strong antidrug campaign and the lengths to which he went may have made the difference in this election: He was ridiculed for hopping out of a car trunk in one raid. An issue of undetermined impact on the election was Bennett's beard, and there was much comment about whether he should keep it. Bennett was the first Kansas governor elected in the twentieth century with whiskers—the reverse of nineteenth-century style, when only one governor, Lyman Humphrey, was clean shaven and all others wore a beard or at least a moustache. Bennett was also the first governor to come directly from state legislative service since Payne H. Ratner in 1937, and he had more experience in public office than any Kansas governor except for Edmund Morrill, who was elected in 1894.

Robert Bennett served as a clerk for Sen. James A. Reed of Missouri after graduating from law school. He was admitted to the Kansas and Missouri bars and to practice in the federal courts. He founded the law firm of Bennett, Lytle, Wetzler and Winn in Prairie Village. As a member of the Prairie Village city council (1955–57) and mayor (1957–65), he gained his first experience with elective offices. His baptism into state politics occurred when he won a Republican primary race for the state senate by 54 votes out of 8,300 votes cast. He was elected to the Kansas senate for three terms, serving from 1965 through the end of 1974, during which time he chaired various committees and was president of the senate (1973–74).

Bennett's long service in state affairs made him an astute student of Kansas government, and his handling of the governor's office has been labeled "civics book" politics. (Oddly enough, this may also have been the basis of his political weakness, since it reinforced a perception that he was distant.) A conglomeration of executive offices, some previously elective, was replaced by cabinet-level departments.[66] The power of Kansas' chief executive to appoint and remove officers had been increased, but there were still many state officials whose appointment was not in the hands of the governor. Bennett slowly filled vacancies and positions. Throughout his four years as governor, Bennett sought to provide balance among his state appointments on the basis of race, sex, and geography. He appointed the first woman to the state supreme court and the first black to the court of appeals. He sought also to infuse new blood into state boards and commissions by not reappointing persons who had served two consecutive terms.

State government had grown to immense proportions by the time

*Governor Bennett seated in front of his cabinet, a new feature in Kansas govern-
ment: (left to right) W. Keith Weltmer, secretary of administration; Edward G.
Bruske, secretary of economic development; F. Kent Kalb, secretary of revenue; Jim
J. Marquez, secretary of corrections; James A. McCain, secretary of human resources; O. D. Turner, secretary of transportation; Dwight F. Metzler, secretary of
health and environment; Shelby Smith, lieutenant governor; Robert C. Harder,
secretary of social and rehabilitation services; and James F. McCormack, acting
secretary of aging.*

Bennett became governor. Bennett stressed economy, and early in
his administration a hiring freeze was imposed on state agencies.
However, the state of Kansas was also administering approximately
170 federal assistance programs of different magnitudes which involved about one-sixth of the state government's work force. Local
units of government, at the same time, also dealt directly with various federal agencies. Bennett's frustrations in dealing with the fed-

eral government were evident; one commentator stated that "he sought to manage that which was unmanageable."[67]

Financing education and highway improvement continued to be important issues in Bennett's administration and board of regents's funding requests generally fared better than those coming from other agencies. Branch offices for the governor's staff were created in Wichita and in western Kansas to stress Bennett's concern for all sections of the state. His efforts to abolish the port of entry system and to make the meat inspection program more restrictive met with defeat in the legislature. Likewise, in 1978, Bennett's support for reinstatement of a death penalty and construction of a medium security prison failed to pass, even though he turned to longtime friends in the legislature for backing. Similarly, his attempt to take highway improvements out of the political sphere may have cost him allies when he sought a return to the governor's office.

Unlike most twentieth-century Kansas governors, Bennett had no speechwriters on his staff. He preferred writing his own speeches or speaking extemporaneously. He viewed his annual legislative message as his most important single act each year, and his formal messages to the Kansas legislature numbered well over one hundred. His subject matter for public speeches dealt with taxing and spending, cultural heritage, the value of political parties, and the role of individuals. Although not elected with a mandate from rural farm interests, Bennett, half-way through his term, became a symbolic advocate of Kansas agriculture. He spoke heatedly against the national farm policy, and he lent his support to state tax relief for farmers. He also served as a symbolic spokesman for Kansas energy producers in an effort to influence federal policy, during a period when energy issues regularly besieged all levels of government. Occasionally in his role as governor, Bennett would intentionally confront an audience, based on his concept of the governorship, in an effort to rise above special-issue politics and competing factions. He was aware that his vision of a broadly united Kansas, lacking in political factionalism, carried with it some immediate costs to his own political future.

Bennett led the Kansas delegation to the Republican National Convention in Kansas City in 1976. In the fall elections that year, midway through his term, Republicans lost control of the house of representatives to the Democrats, while the senate remained Republican by a single seat. In 1978 Bennett ran for a second term as governor. More conservative in fiscal philosophy as governor than as state senator, Bennett had repeatedly expressed concern about legislative irresponsibility on spending. It was thus appropriate that his principal opponent should be John Carlin, Democratic speaker of the house of representatives. Bennett's running mate in 1978 was Larry Montgomery of Dover, while Carlin was paired with Paul Dugan of Wichita. Straw polls indicated that Bennett was ahead until Carlin interjected the last-minute issue of "rising utility rates," to which Bennett made no response. Bennett lost with 348,403 votes to 364,738 for Carlin, but the Republicans regained control of the state house of representatives. A comparison of the 1974 and 1978 election returns shows that Bennett lost most heavily in the counties containing regents institutions.

Bennett returned to his law practice in Prairie Village. In 1986 popular rumor put Bennett in the governor's race again, but he never filed as a candidate.

REFERENCES: Flentje, 1979.

JOHN WILLIAM CARLIN

Smolan (Democrat), 8 January 1979–12 January 1987

Born 3 August 1940, Salina (Saline County), Kansas; son of Jack W. Carlin, a dairy-man, and Hazel L. Johnson Carlin, 1 sister; educated at Lindsborg High School and Kansas State University (graduated 1962); married (1) Ramona Lenore Hawkinson, 28 January 1962, 1 son and 1 daughter, divorced November 1980, (2) Karen Bigsby Hurley, 29 May 1981, divorced June 1985, (3) Diana Prentice, 17 March 1987; religious preference Lutheran.

Nominated for governor in the Democratic party primary of 1978, John Carlin defeated incumbent Robert Bennett with a vote of 364,738 to 348,403. The American and Prohibition party candidates received 23,651 votes, or about 3 percent of the total. After initial ceremonies in Topeka, Carlin's formal inauguration took place in Wichita. Since the Democrats had lost control of the house of representatives, he faced a legislature where the majority of both houses was Republican. Carlin brought eight years of experience in the legislature into the governor's office, and he continued the pattern of fiscal conservatism established by his Democratic predecessors, the Dockings. And as in their administrations, the overall costs of government rose with the inflationary pressures of the time. At

John Carlin at his inaugural ceremony, held in the Topeka auditorium 8 January 1979, with outgoing governor Robert Bennett behind him.

age thirty-eight, Carlin was the youngest executive in many years; although four Kansas governors before him were younger. He also became one of the state's most traveled governors, leading delegations at various times during his eight years to the Orient and to Europe.

A decrease in tax revenues in mid-1982 caused Carlin to reduce budgets set by the legislature. A proposed severance tax to boost state coffers was a big issue in the campaign of 1982. The Republicans fielded five candidates for governor in their party primary; in a hard-fought battle, Sam Hardage of Wichita was nominated as their candidate. Tom Docking, son of Robert and grandson of George, joined Carlin as his running mate. They encountered opposition in the Democratic primary but still won overwhelmingly. In the general election, Hardage won more counties, but Carlin won a majority of the vote in nine of the ten largest counties which had over half of the state's population. The tally was Carlin 405,772, Hardage 339,356, with the American, Libertarian, and Prohibition candidates collecting 16,135. One of Carlin's last executive orders renamed two state office buildings located adjacent to the State Capitol square—one for Alf M. Landon and the other for Robert B.

Docking. Never before had state buildings been named for individuals, except for those on university campuses or operated by the Department of Social and Rehabilitation Services.

An active dairyman, John Carlin was an accredited judge of the Holstein Association and was appointed to the board of directors of the Kansas Holstein Association in 1970. He also served as director of the First National Bank and Trust Company in Salina. As a Democrat, Carlin was elected to the Kansas house of representatives in 1970 and reelected three times, serving from 1971 to 1979 in such positions as assistant minority leader, minority leader, and speaker. As speaker of the house, he was also a member of the State Finance Council and the Legislative Coordinating Council.

State issues handled by the practical, no-gimmicks Governor Carlin included passage of a severance tax, development of legislation to handle problems in correctional institutions, in environmental issues, in the relationship of utilities to the state, in transportation, and in a start on a broad-based program of economic development. A major issue implemented during this period was reappraisal of property for tax purposes. Carlin served as president of the nation's governors' association, 1985–1986.

At the end of his second term, Carlin did not seek reelection; the amended constitution limited a governor to two consecutive terms. He accepted appointment to a privately funded position as professor of public administration at Wichita State University, while retaining his residence in Topeka. He has served in various visible committees in state government, causing comment that he might again be a candidate for governor or some other statewide office.

JOHN MICHAEL HAYDEN

Atwood (Republican), 12 January 1987–

Born 15 March 1944, Colby (Thomas County), Kansas; son of Irven Wesley Hayden, a farmer, and Ruth Kelly Hayden, 3 brothers and 2 sisters; educated at Atwood High School, Kansas State University (graduated 1966), and Fort Hays State University (Master's degree 1974); military experience in Vietnam, 1967–70, first lieutenant in army; married Patti Ann Rooney, 26 August 1968, 2 daughters; religious preference Methodist.

As early as 1980, Kansas newspapers were predicting a Republican scenario that cast Mike Hayden as a candidate for governor. It was 1986 before Hayden was nominated in the Republican party primary, and that was a tight, seven-way race involving millionaire businessmen Gene Bicknell from Pittsburg and Larry Jones from Wichita, Secretary of State Jack Brier, Bill McDonald of Meriden, Barbara Pomeroy of Whitewater, and Richard Peckham, Andover. Hayden won the primary with 99,534 votes and a plurality of about 15,000 votes. In spite of the strength of his fellow Republicans, he carried 92 of the 105 counties. His Democratic opponent in the general election was Lieutenant Governor Tom Docking, son and grandson of previous Democratic governors, who won nomination handily in a two-way race. Hayden was victorious in the general election with 437,420 votes to 401,226 for Docking.[68] There was also a Republican majority in each house of the state legislature.

Following his service in Vietnam, Hayden had attended Fort Hays State University to add a master's degree in biology to his undergraduate degree in wildlife conservation. He was a grantee in 1972 of the National Science Foundation. He was executive manager of the Rawlins County Promotional Council from 1973 to 1977, after which he became an independent insurance agent with an agency in Atwood. An active member of many veterans' and fraternal groups, Hayden was president of the U.S. Highway 36 Association. His first political experience came in 1972, when he was elected to the state house of representatives from a northwest Kansas district that included his home county, Rawlins, and neighboring counties Cheyenne, Decatur, Sheridan, and portions of Norton. He was reelected for a total of seven terms. He served on the governor's Kansas Advisory Council on Ecology (1973–75), and accepted appointment to the governor's Advisory Commission on Developmental Disabilities in 1976. In the house of representatives, he was chairman of the Republican caucus, chairman of the Ways and Means Committee, and speaker of the house where he used his influence on budget making.

Promptly after the gubernatorial election, Hayden and outgoing governor Carlin confronted a shortage of $60 million in state income that had been appropriated by the previous legislature. With no possibility of deficit financing for Kansas state government, the two agreed to an immediate cut in the state budget of 3.8 percent.

As governor, Hayden was able to get legislative approval for most of the significant issues on which he had expressed an opinion in the campaign. He had frequently promised that as governor he would return the "windfall" tax that the state of Kansas would gain as a result of federal income tax reform. However, as governor he worked through two legislative sessions to use much of that money on state projects in education and highways. Reinstatement of capital punishment had been a big issue for Hayden during his campaign, and he labeled his inability to win legislative approval for such a law as his biggest disappointment of his first year in office.

The forty-first Kansas governor, Mike Hayden.

Also frustrating for him was failure to get legislative endorsement in a special session convened in 1987 for a massive highway improvement program, although major changes in highway construction projects were made later. In a more encouraging vein, the state revenues were increasing. Four times in the previous five years, the state had borrowed money from other funds to pay the costs of basic state governmental operations, a practice known as "deficit borrowing." At the end of Hayden's second year as governor, such borrowing was no longer necessary.

Republicans retained control of the legislature at a reduced margin following the election in 1988. With the state treasury balance considerably higher than in earlier years, Hayden renewed his approval for returning the one-year "windfall" tax that was a product of changes in the federal income tax. The governor seemed to be unable to control his own party in the legislature, but in the closing days of his third legislative session, he obtained virtually everything he had sought in earlier years, except a capital punishment law. Education was addressed and a major highway program was approved, along with funding for a new prison and for a state water plan. Hayden explained that partisanship, this time, was reduced. "In '87 we tried a frontal assault, calling a special session with very special recommendations. That failed. This time we changed tactics. The frontal attack drew opposition. These tactics worked."[69] Some newspaper columnists called it the most productive legislative session ever.

NOTES

1. The urgency for another slave state was prompted by the admission of California as a free state in 1850, resulting in sixteen free states as opposed to fifteen slave states. Since each state had two United States senators, there was a slight majority favoring free states. For more than thirty years, strong supporters of the institution of slavery had followed a strategic policy of maintaining a balance in the Senate to protect slavery.

2. Kenneth N. Owens, "Pattern and Structure in Western Territorial Politics," in *The American Territorial System*, ed. John Porter Bloom (Athens: Ohio University Press, 1973), p. 163.

3. Ibid., p. 166.

4. James P. Shenton, "Introduction," in Robert Sobel and John Raimo, eds., *Biographical Directory of the Governors of the United States, 1789–1978* (Westport, Conn.: Meckler Books, 1978), 1:xv. Three women have been elected governor since Sobel and Raimo's publication—in Kentucky, Vermont, and Nebraska—while another woman became the eighteenth governor of Arizona with the conviction of the sitting governor in an impeachment trial. An extension of this book, edited by John Raimo, included governors between 1978 and 1985.

5. James W. Drury, *The Government of Kansas* (Lawrence: University Press of Kansas, 1970), p. 95; (1980), 117; *Kansas Facts*, (Topeka, Kans.: State Printer, 1987).

6. Shenton, "Introduction," p. xv.

7. Ibid., p. xiii.

8. Two percent, based on the election of 1986, would require almost 17,000 valid signatures.

9. Marvin A. Harder, *Electoral Politics in Kansas: A Historical Perspective* (Topeka, Kans.: Capitol Complex Center, 1981), pp. 53–54.

10. Also useful in this study were James E. Titus, "Kansas Governors: A Resume of Political Leadership," *Western Political Quarterly* 17, no. 2 (June 1964): 356–70, and *American Governors and Gubernatorial Elections, 1775–1978*, comp. Roy R. Glashan (Westport, Conn.: Meckler Books, 1979).

11. T. H. Gladstone, *The Englishman in Kansas* (New York: Miller, 1857), p. 14.

12. *Kansas Historical Collections* 3 (1881–84): 223.

13. William E. Connelley, *Kansas Territorial Governors* (Topeka, Kans.: Crane & Co., 1900), 19.

14. James A. Rawley, *Race and Politics: "Bleeding Kansas" and the Coming of the Civil War* (Philadelphia, Pa.: J. B. Lippincott, 1969), pp. 86–87; Charles Robinson, *The Kansas Conflict* (New York: Harper, 1898), p. 97.

15. Gen. Benjamin Stringfellow and Dr. John Stringfellow were brothers, and frequently the action of one was attributed to the other. John was speaker

of the territorial house of representatives, while Benjamin, former attorney general of Missouri, had not yet come to Kansas when this altercation took place.

16. James R. McClure, "Taking the Census in 1855," *Kansas Historical Collections* 8 (1903–4): 227, 307n.

17. Alice Nichols, *Bleeding Kansas* (New York: Oxford University Press, 1954), p. 34. The Territorial Capital Museum, within the borders of the Fort Riley Reservation, belongs to the state and is operated by the Kansas State Historical Society.

18. "Address of Gov. Charles Robinson," *Kansas Historical Collections* 1 and 2 (1875–81): 119.

19. Gladstone, *Englishman in Kansas*, pp. 14–15.

20. Samuel A. Johnson, *The Battle Cry of Freedom: The New England Emigrant Aid Company in the Kansas Crusade* (Lawrence: University of Kansas Publications, 1954), p. 203.

21. William E. Connelley, *Kansas Territorial Governors* (Topeka, Kans.: Crane, 1900), p. 91.

22. A. T. Andreas, *History of the State of Kansas* (Chicago: A. T. Andreas, 1883), 1:720.

23. Gladstone, *Englishman in Kansas*, p. 15.

24. Nichols, *Bleeding Kansas*, p. 54.

25. Ibid., p. 139.

26. Connelley, *Kansas Territorial Governors*, p. 62.

27. Frank W. Blackmar, *Kansas: A Cyclopedia of State History*, 2 vols. (Chicago: Standard Publishing, 1912), 1:720.

28. John H. Gihon, *Geary and Kansas: Governor Geary's Administration in Kansas with a Complete History of the Territory until July 1857* (Philadelphia, Pa.: Charles C. Rhodes, 1857), p. 216.

29. Ibid., pp. 309–327.

30. Johnson, *Battle Cry*, pp. 233–234.

31. Gihon, *Geary and Kansas*, pp. 293–299.

32. Elbert B. Smith, *The Presidency of James Buchanan* (Lawrence: Regents Press of Kansas, 1975), pp. 33–34.

33. For many years, this bust has been exhibited in the first floor hallway of the Kansas State Historical Society's Memorial Building.

34. James P. Shenton, *Robert John Walker: A Politician from Jackson to Lincoln* (New York: Columbia University Press, 1961), p. 142.

35. Gihon, *Geary and Kansas*, pp. 328–48.

36. Smith, *Presidency of Buchanan*, p. 31.

37. C. E. Cory, "Slavery in Kansas," *Kansas Historical Collections* 7 (1901–2): 233–34.

38. George C. Barns, *Denver, the Man: The Life, Letters and Public Papers of the Lawyer, Soldier and Statesman* (Wilmington, Ohio: n.p., 1949), p. 199.

39. *Kansas Historical Collections* 5 (1891–96): 161.

40. Frank W. Blackmar, *Kansas: A Cyclopedia of State History* (Chicago: Standard Publishing, 1912), 2:258.

41. *Kansas Historical Collections*, 5 (1891–96): 162.

42. Actually, Lincoln's candidacy in 1860 was in opposition to the extension of slavery into the territories. Lincoln did not then believe that slavery in existing states could be curtailed by congressional action. Blackmar, *Cyclopedia*, 1:166; G. M. Beebe, *Governor's Annual Message*, 10 January 1861.

43. Both Blackmar, in his 1902 biography of Robinson, and Wilson, in his 1975 biography of Robinson, provide a vote total for Robinson of 7,908 and 5,395 for Medary. My smaller total for Robinson comes from official Kansas voting sources.

44. Frank W. Blackmar, *The Life of Charles Robinson: The First State Governor of Kansas* (Topeka, Kans.: Crane & Co., 1902), p. 425.

45. A "secretary-bookcase, custom made for Gov. Thomas Carney in the 1860s," is now in Cedar Crest, the Kansas executive mansion, as the "first acquisition for the residence" by the Friends of Cedar Crest Association.

46. Nyle H. Miller and Joseph Snell, *Why the West Was Wild* (Topeka: Kansas State Historical Society, 1963), pp. 11–12.

47. Crawford was a colonel and later a brevet brigadier general.

48. Mark A. Plummer, in *Frontier Governor: Samuel J. Crawford of Kansas* (Lawrence: University of Kansas Press, 1971), p. 42, cites Daniel W. Wilder, *Annals of Kansas* (Topeka, Kans.: State Printer, 1886), p. 384, and uses election figures of 13,387 votes to 8,448. Crawford's total included 2,181 votes from soldiers.

49. None of the first eight lieutenant governors served longer than two years.

50. Ross did not retain his seat as United States senator from Kansas because most Kansans in 1868 favored conviction in the impeachment trial of Pres. Andrew Johnson.

51. Robert Held, *The Crawford-Green Winchester Model 1866 Presentation Rifle*, a fifteen-page pamphlet (1976?) subsequently to appear in *The Arms and Armour Treasury*.

52. There were probably even more Indians killed by military units and Kansas settlers in the same two years than in all other years.

53. Custer was given a brevet rank of major general during the Civil War, but in the smaller postwar army, he possessed a regular rank of lieutenant colonel.

54. This was Crawford's only daughter, Florence, who in 1893 married Arthur Capper, the twentieth governor of Kansas. The town of Florence was named for her.

55. Crawford's biographer says his "handling of the Indian situation in Kansas was the most successful aspect of his administration" (Plummer, *Frontier*

Governor, p. 134), possibly because there were few Indian raids after the Crawford years.

56. In early America, there was a tradition that a community named for a prominent, living person would receive a gift, such as a bell, from its patron.

57. One of Otis's granddaughters was Amelia Earhart.

58. One wag said of John Ingalls, "Up was he stuck and in the upness of his stuckitude, he fell."

59. State Senator York had a leading role in bringing bribery charges against United States Sen. Samuel C. Pomeroy in 1873. Pomeroy was not reelected; the state legislature instead elected John James Ingalls. York's brother, Dr. William H. York, was one of the murder victims of the "Bloody Benders," a family operating a small business in their home in Labette County along a well-used trail. People in the area slowly became aware that travelers who used the trail were disappearing. When a neighbor discovered the Benders had left the site, an investigation showed graves of many victims in the Bender orchard.

60. Salter was the father-in-law of Susanna Madora Salter, who was elected the mayor of Argonia, Kansas, in 1887, the first woman to serve as mayor.

61. *Kansas Historical Collections* 7 (1901-2): 125-26.

62. Other members of the Lewelling family, in Iowa and in Oregon, had engaged in the nursery business.

63. Although the engraving lists Leedy as the "thirteenth governor of Kansas," he was actually the fourteenth governor, if one counts Nehemiah Green, who became governor in 1868 when the third governor, Samuel J. Crawford, resigned to lead the Nineteenth Kansas Cavalry against the Indians. The concurrent resolution, providing for this expenditure, stated that Leedy died on 28 March 1935, several days after his real date of death.

64. Keith L. McFarland, *Harry H. Woodring: A Political Biography of FDR's Controversial Secretary of War* (Lawrence: Regents Press of Kansas, 1975), p. 44.

65. Ibid., p. 66.

66. H. Edward Flentje, ed. and comp., *Selected Papers of Governor Robert F. Bennett: A Study in Good Government and "Civics Book" Politics* (Wichita, Kans.: Center for Urban Studies, 1979), p. 2. A study made in 1965 rated governors of all fifty states on their power to appoint and remove executives in state government. Kansas was in the bottom third, suggesting that the Kansas governor possessed less power than most state governors.

67. Flentje, *Selected Papers*, p. 301.

68. Thelma Helyar, ed., *Kansas Statistical Abstract, 1986-87* (Lawrence, Kans.: Institute for Public Policy and Business Research, 1986).

69. Manhattan *Mercury*, 7 May 1989.

BIBLIOGRAPHY

Addresses and Messages of Arthur Capper, Twenty-Second Governor of Kansas. Topeka, Kans.: Capper Printing Co., n.d. (Capper actually was the twentieth governor.)

"Address of Gov. Charles Robinson." *Kansas Historical Collections* 1 and 2 (1875–81); 115–30.

Andreas, A. T. *History of the State of Kansas.* Chicago: A. T. Andreas, 1883.

Argersinger, Peter H. "Road to a Republican Waterloo: Farmers' Alliance and the Election of 1890 in Kansas." *Kansas Historical Quarterly* 33 (1967): 443–69.

___. *Populism and Politics: William Alfred Peffer and the People's Party.* Lexington: University Press of Kentucky, 1974.

Bader, Robert Smith. *The Great Kansas Bond Scandal.* Lawrence: University Press of Kansas, 1982.

___. *Prohibition in Kansas: A History.* Lawrence: University Press of Kansas, 1986.

Barns, George C. *Denver, the Man: The Life, Letters and Public Papers of the Lawyer, Soldier and Statesman.* Wilmington, Ohio: n.p., 1949.

Bateman, Newton. *Historical Encyclopedia of Illinois and History of Carroll County.* Chicago: Munsell, 1913.

Baughman, Robert W. *Kansas Post Offices.* Topeka: Kansas State Historical Society, 1961.

Beebe, G. M. *Governor's Annual Message.* 10 January 1861.

Bicha, Karel D. "John W. Leedy: Continental Commoner." *Alberta Historical Review* 22 (1974): 13–23.

Blackmar, Frank W. *Kansas: A Cyclopedia of State History.* 2 vols. Chicago: Standard Publishing, 1912.

___. *The Life of Charles Robinson: The First State Governor of Kansas.* Topeka, Kans.: Crane & Co., 1902.

Blythe, Samuel G. "The Red-headed Quaker, Being an Account of Some of the Activities of Walter Roscoe Stubbs." *Saturday Evening Post,* 19 November 1910, pp. 3–4, 48.

Boles, David C. "Andrew Frank Schoeppel, Governor of Kansas, 1943–1947." Master's thesis, Kansas State University, 1967.

Bright, John D., ed. *Kansas: The First Century.* 2 vols. New York: Lewis Publishing, 1956.

Brodhead, Michael J. "The Early Career of E. W. Hoch, 1870–1904." Master's thesis, University of Kansas, 1962.

Brown, George W. *Reminiscences of Gov. R. J. Walker; with the True Story of the Rescue of Kansas from Slavery.* Rockford, Ill.: Brown Printing, 1902.

Bumgardner, Edward. "Autographs of the Governors of Kansas." N.p., 1951.

Callis, George H. "A History of the Progressive Party in Kansas." Master's thesis, Pittsburg State University, 1933.

Carlin, Karen, and Robert W. Richmond, eds. *Kansas First Families at Home: Residences, Residents, and Recipes.* N.p.: Friends of Cedar Crest, 1982.

Castel, Albert. *A Frontier State at War: Kansas, 1861–1865.* Ithaca, N.Y.: Cornell University Press, 1958.

Cherry, Roger Beaumont. "A Study of Clyde Martin Reed in the United States Senate." Master's thesis, Pittsburg State University, 1948.

Clanton, O. Gene. *Kansas Populism: Ideas and Men.* Lawrence: University of Kansas Press, 1969.

Clark, Carrol D., and Roy L. Roberts. *People of Kansas: A Demographic and Sociological Study.* Topeka: Kansas State Planning Board, 1936.

Clugston, William G. "A Mid-American D'Artagnan: Henry Justin Allen." *Rascals in Democracy.* New York: Richard R. Smith, 1940.

Collins, D. Cheryl. "History of Wakefield, Kansas." Master's thesis, Kansas State University, 1978.

Connelley, William E. *Kansas and Kansans.* 5 vols. Chicago: Lewis Publishing, 1918.

———. *Kansas Territorial Governors.* Topeka, Kans.: Crane & Co., 1900.

Corley, Roger M. "Jonathan M. Davis: Farmer in the State House." Master's thesis, Kansas State University, 1962.

Correll, Charles M. "Revolution and Counter-revolution." *Kansas Quarterly* 1 (1969): 89–103.

Cory, C. E. "Slavery in Kansas." *Kansas Historical Collections* 7 (1901–2): 229–42.

Crawford, Samuel J. *Kansas in the Sixties.* Chicago: A. C. McClurg, 1911.

Crowley, Byron M. "The Public Career of Arthur Capper prior to His Senatorial Service." Master's thesis, Pittsburg State University, 1938.

Daniels, Dawn. "Lorenzo D. Lewelling—A Leader of the Kansas Populists." Master's thesis, Northwestern University, 1931.

Davis, Kenneth S. *Kansas: A Bicentennial History.* New York: W. W. Norton & Co., 1976.

Dew, Lee A. "The Populist Fusion Movement as an Instrument of Political Reform, 1890–1900." Master's thesis, Pittsburg State University, 1957.

Dimmitt, Albert M. "The Progressive Party in Kansas, 1911–1917." Master's thesis, University of Kansas, 1958.

Doyle, Alberta. "The Progressive Movement in the Republican Party in Kansas, 1902–1912." Master's thesis, University of Kansas, 1932.

Drury, James W. *The Government of Kansas.* Lawrence: Regents Press of Kansas, 1980.

Ehrlich, Larry G. "A Study of the Public Speaking Ability of Frederick Lee Hall II in the 1956 Kansas Republican Primary Election." Master's thesis, University of Kansas, 1963.

Finger, John R. "Jonathan M. Davis, 1925–1942: A Kansas Democrat's Political Demise." Master's thesis, University of Kansas, 1964.

———. "The Post-Gubernatorial Career of Jonathan M. Davis." *Kansas Historical Quarterly* 33 (1967): 156–71.

Flentje, H. Edward, ed. *Kansas Policy Changes: Report of the Special Commission on a Public Agenda for Kansas.* Lawrence: University Press of Kansas, 1986.

Flentje, H. Edward, ed. and comp. *Selected Papers of Governor Robert F. Bennett: A Study in Good Government and "Civics Book" Politics.* Wichita, Kans.: Center for Urban Studies, 1979.

Frederickson, Edna T. "John P. St. John, the Father of Constitutional Prohibition." Doctoral diss., University of Kansas, 1930.

Gaeddart, G. Raymond. *The Birth of Kansas.* Lawrence: University of Kansas Publications, 1940.

Gagliardo, Domenico. "The Gompers-Allen Debate on the Kansas Industrial Court." *Kansas Historical Quarterly* 3 (1934): 385–95.

Garretson, O. A. "The Lewelling Family." *Iowa Journal of History and Politics* 37 (1929): 548–63.

Gihon, John H. *Geary and Kansas, Governor Geary's Administration in Kansas with a Complete History of the Territory until July 1857.* Philadelphia, Pa.: Charles C. Rhodes, 1857.

Gladstone, T. H. *The Englishman in Kansas.* New York: Miller, 1857.

Glashan, Roy R., comp. *American Governors and Gubernatorial Elections, 1775–1978.* Westport, Conn.: Meckler Books, 1979.

"Governor Andrew H. Reeder." *Kansas Historical Collections* 1 and 2 (1875–81): 145–56.

Hajda, Joseph. "Choosing the 1960 Democratic Presidential Candidate: The Case of the Unbossed Delegation." *Kansas Quarterly* 13 (1976): 71–87.

Hall, Frederick Lee. "What the Farmer Really Wants." *American Magazine,* April 1956, pp. 28–29.

Harder, Marvin. *Electoral Politics in Kansas: A Historical Perspective.* Topeka, Kans.: Capitol Complex Center, 1981.

Harder, Marvin, and Carolyn Rampey. *The Kansas Legislature: Procedures, Personalities and Problems.* Lawrence: University of Kansas Press, 1972.

Hein, Clarence J., and Charles A. Sullivant, comps. *Kansas Votes: Gubernatorial Elections, 1859–1956.* Lawrence, Kans.: Governmental Research Center, 1958.

Held, Robert. *The Crawford-Green Winchester Model 1866 Presentation Rifle.* Pamphlet in the files of the Kansas Museum of History, Topeka.

Helyar, Thelma, ed. *Kansas Statistical Abstract, 1986–87.* Lawrence, Kans.: Institute for Public Policy and Business Research, 1986.

Hope, Clifford R., Sr. "Kansas in the 1930s." *Kansas Historical Quarterly* 36 (1970): 1–12.

Hopkins, Richard. "Governor of Kansas." *The Delta,* March 1943, p. 174.

Hudson, J. K. *Letters to Governor Lewelling*. Topeka, Kans.: Topeka Capital Co., 1893.

Humphrey, James. *Administration of George W. Glick*. Topeka: Kansas State Historical Society, 1906.

Jewell, Jesse P. "The Senatorial Career of Arthur Capper." Master's thesis, Pittsburg State University, 1947.

Johnson, Samuel A. *The Battle Cry of Freedom: The New England Emigrant Aid Company in the Kansas Crusade*. Lawrence: University of Kansas Publications, 1954.

Kansas Facts. Topeka, Kans.: State Printer, 1987.

Karson, Marc. "William Allen White's Kind of Republican." *New Republic*, 18 April 1955, p. 7.

Knauer, Delbert Deane. "The Senatorial Career of James Madison Harvey, 1874–1877." Master's thesis, University of Kansas, 1953.

LaForte, Robert S. *Leaders of Reform: Progressive Republicans in Kansas, 1900–1916*. Lawrence: University Press of Kansas, 1974.

Liebengood, Dorothy. "Labor Problems in the Second Year of Governor Martin's Administration." *Kansas Historical Quarterly* 5 (1936).

Linn, Shirley H. "The Political Career of U.S. Senator Frank Carlson: A Description of His Constituents' Support." Master's thesis, University of Kansas, 1961.

Loewen, W. Merle. "George H. Hodges: State Senator and Governor of Kansas, 1905–1914." Master's thesis, Emporia State University, 1967.

Lujan, Herman D., comp. *Kansas Votes: National and General Elections, 1956–1964*. Lawrence, Kans.: Governmental Research Center, 1965.

McClure, James R. "Taking the Census in 1855." *Kansas Historical Collections* 8 (1903–4): 227–50.

McCoy, Donald R. *Landon of Kansas*. Lincoln: University of Nebraska Press, 1966.

McFarland, Keith L. *Harry H. Woodring: A Political Biography of FDR's Controversial Secretary of War*. Lawrence: Regents Press of Kansas, 1975.

McIlvain, Zelma E. "Governor Glick and Prohibition, 1883–1884." Master's thesis, University of Kansas, 1931.

McKee, Judith. "Comparative Legislative Programs of Governor Stubbs of Kansas and Governor Hadley of Missouri." Master's thesis, Kansas State University, 1967.

McMullin, Thomas A., and David Walker, eds. *Biographical Directory of American Territorial Governors*. Westport, Conn.: Meckler Books, 1984.

Malin, James C. *A Concern about Humanity: Notes on Reform, 1872–1912, at the National and Kansas Levels of Thought*. Lawrence, Kans.: n.p., 1964.

———. "Was Governor John A. Martin a Prohibitionist?" *Kansas Historical Quarterly* 1 (1931): 63–73.

Mechem, Kirke L., ed. *Annals of Kansas, 1886–1925.* 2 vols. Topeka: Kansas State Historical Society, 1954–56.

Miller, Nyle H., and Joseph Snell. *Why the West Was Wild.* Topeka: Kansas State Historical Society, 1963.

Moore, H. Miles. "The Nineteenth Kansas Cavalry." *Kansas Historical Collections* 6 (1897–1900): 35–52.

Nichols, Alice. *Bleeding Kansas.* New York: Oxford University Press, 1954.

Nugent, Walter T. K. "How the Populists Lost in 1894." *Kansas Historical Quarterly* 31 (1965): 245–55.

___. *The Tolerant Populists: Kansas Populism and Nativism.* Chicago: University of Chicago Press, 1963.

Owens, Jennie Small, "Kansas Folks Worth Knowing." *Kansas Teacher* (February 1943): 26–29.

Owens, Kenneth N. "Pattern and Structure in Western Territorial Politics." In *The American Territorial System,* ed. John Porter Bloom. Athens: Ohio University Press, 1973.

Parrish, William E. "The Great Kansas Legislative Imbroglio of 1893." *Journal of the West* 7 (1968): 471–90.

Pickett, Calder. *Ed Howe: Country Town Philosopher.* Lawrence: University of Kansas Press, 1968.

Plummer, Mark A. *Frontier Governor: Samuel J. Crawford of Kansas.* Lawrence: University of Kansas Press, 1971.

___. "Governor Crawford's Appointment of Edmund G. Ross to the United States Senate." *Kansas Historical Quarterly* 28 (1962): 145–53.

Postal, Bernard, and Lionel Koppman. *A Jewish Tourist's Guide to the U.S.* Philadelphia, Pa.: Jacob R. Schiff Library of Jewish Contributions to American Democracy, 1954.

Rawley, James A. *Race and Politics: "Bleeding Kansas" and the Coming of the Civil War.* Philadelphia, Pa.: J. B. Lippincott, 1969.

Richmond, Robert W. *Kansas: Land of Contrasts.* St. Charles, Mo.: Forum Press, 1988.

Riley County Genealogical Society. *Pioneers of the Bluestem Prairie.* Marceline, Mo.: Walsworth, 1976.

Robinson, Charles. *The Kansas Conflict.* New York: Harper, 1898.

Roe, Jon. "Kansas, A Rugged Land, A Rugged People." *Wichita Eagle-Beacon* 25 January 1981.

Sageser, A. Bower. *Joseph L. Bristow: Kansas Progressive.* Lawrence: University Press of Kansas, 1968.

Schruben, Francis W. *Harry H. Woodring Speaks: Kansas Politics during the Early Depression.* Los Angeles: [Los Angeles Trade-Technical College], 1963.

___. *Kansas in Turmoil, 1930–1936.* Columbia: University of Missouri Press, 1969.

___. "The Kansas Refinery Law of 1905." *Kansas Historical Quarterly* 34 (1968): 299–324.

Shenton, James P. *Robert John Walker: A Politician from Jackson to Lincoln.* New York: Columbia University Press, 1961.

Shepard, John C. "The State Senatorial and Gubernatorial Career of John W. Leedy, 1892–1899." Master's thesis, University of Kansas, 1969.

Shockley, Dennis M. "George McGill, New Deal Senator from Kansas." Doctoral diss., Kansas State University, 1986.

Smith, Elbert B. *The Presidency of James Buchanan.* Lawrence: Regents Press of Kansas, 1975.

Snell, Joseph W. "Kansas and the 1876 United States Centennial." *Kansas Historical Quarterly* 40 (1974): 337–48.

Sobel, Robert, and John Raimo, eds. *Biographical Directory of the Governors of the United States, 1789–1978.* 4 vols. Westport, Conn.: Meckler Books, 1978.

Socolofsky, Homer E. "The Agricultural Heritage." In *The Rise of the Wheat State*, ed. George Ham and Robin Higham. Manhattan, Kans.: Sunflower University Press, 1987, pp. 19–28.

___. *Arthur Capper: Publisher, Politician, Philanthropist.* Lawrence: University of Kansas Press, 1962.

___. "Arthur Capper, Vote-Getter Par Excellence." *Journal of the West* 13 (1974): 26–39.

___. "The Evolution of a Home Grown Product: Capper Publications." *Kansas Historical Quarterly* 24 (1958): 151–67.

___. "Kansas in 1876." *Kansas Historical Quarterly* 43 (1977): 1–43.

Swank, Jim L. "Walter A. Huxman's Gubernatorial Administration: A Partial Investigation of the Executive-Legislative Relations." Master's thesis, Emporia State University, 1968.

Titus, James E. "Kansas Governors: A Resume of Political Leadership." *Western Political Quarterly* 17, no. 2 (June 1964): 356–70.

Traylor, Jack W. "William Allen White's 1924 Gubernatorial Campaign." *Kansas Historical Quarterly* 42 (1976): 180–91.

Tripp, Martin F. "Reaction to the Birth of the Labor Party in Kansas." Master's thesis, University of Kansas, 1968.

U.S. Congress. *Statue of George Washington Glick: Erected in Statuary Hall of the United States Capitol by the State of Kansas.* 63d Cong., 2d. Sess. Washington, D.C.: Government Printing Office, 1915.

Van Meter, Sondra. *Marion County, Kansas: Past and Present.* Hillsboro, Kans.: M. B. Publishing House, 1972.

Walker, Edith. "Labor Problems during the First Year of Governor Martin's Administration." *Kansas Historical Quarterly* 5 (1936): 33–53.

White, William Allen. *The Autobiography of William Allen White.* New York: Macmillan, 1946.

___. *The Martial Adventures of Henry and Me.* New York: Macmillan, 1918.

Wilder, Daniel W. *Annals of Kansas*. Topeka, Kans.: State Printer, 1886.

Williams, Burton J. *Senator John James Ingalls: Kansas' Iridescent Republican*. Lawrence: University Press of Kansas, 1972.

Wilson, Don W. *Governor Charles Robinson of Kansas*. Lawrence: University Press of Kansas, 1975.

Zornow, William F. *Kansas: A History of the Jayhawk State*. Norman: University of Oklahoma Press, 1957.

INDEX

Aberdeen, Mississippi, 71
Adams County, Illinois, 96
Ad valorem tariff duty, 60
Alabama, 71
Alaska, 29, 63, 128
Albany Law University, 75
Albemarle County, Virginia, 3, 40
Alberta, Canada, 29, 129
Alexandria, part of the District of Columbia, later in Virginia, 3, 55
Alf M. Landon State Office Building, 179, 205, 226
Allegheny College, 99
Allen, Elsie Jane Nuzman, 152, 155
Allen, Henry Justin, 10, 11, 14, 17, 20, 25, 28, 29, 134, 143, 147, 152–55, 157, 163, 164, 173
Allen, John, 152, 153
Allen, Rebecca Elizabeth Goodwin, 152
Amarillo, Texas, 181
Amendments: Thirteenth, 54, 91; Fourteenth, 54, 91; Fifteenth, 54, 97; Seventeenth, 143; Eighteenth, 153; Nineteenth, 153
American Expeditionary Force, 152
American Federation of Labor, 154
American Legion, 165, 166, 167
American Libertarian party, 225
American party, 19, 224
Amherst Academy, 81
Anderson, Arlene A. Auchard, 209
Anderson, John, Jr., 11, 19, 25, 26, 28, 208, 209–11
Anderson, John, Sr., 209
Anderson, Kenneth T., 18, 196
Anderson, Ora Bookout, 209
Anderson County, Kansas, 39, 48, 63, 89, 90
Andover, Kansas, 227
Anthony, Anna Odell, 102
Anthony, Benjamin, 102
Anthony, Daniel R., 102
Anthony, George Tobey, x, 10, 16, 22, 24, 28, 29, 93, 102–4, 105
Anthony, Rosa A. Lyon, 102
Anthony, Susan B., 102
Anthony (Harper County), Kansas, 104
Anti–Bill White law, 160
Anti-Semitism, 183

Arapaho County, Kansas Territory, later Colorado, 68
Arizona, 97, 231 n4
Arkansas, 90
Arkansas City, Kansas, 25, 119, 215, 216, 217
Arn, Catherine Philippi Ross, 196
Arn, Edward F., 11, 18, 19, 22, 23, 25, 26, 29, 196–99
Arn, Edward F., Sr., 196
Arn, Grace Bell Edwards, 196
Arn, Marcella Ruth Tillmans, 196
Atchison, David, 36
Atchison, Kansas, 24, 30, 42, 109, 113, 115, 125, 133, 135
Atchison County, Kansas, 26, 110
Athletic skills, 12, 13, 132, 145
Atlanta, Georgia, 52
Atwood, Kansas, 25, 227
Australian ballot, 120
Avery, Hattie W. Coffman, 212
Avery, Hazel Bowles, 212
Avery, Herman W., 212
Avery, William Henry, 11, 19, 25, 29, 30, 212–14, 215

Background of state governors, 24–25
Bacon, Vearl A., 19, 209
Bailey, Ida B. Albert Weede, 133
Bailey, Monroe, 133
Bailey, Nancy J. Melendy, 133
Bailey, Willis Joshua, 10, 17, 23, 25, 28, 29, 30, 133–135, 136
Baileyville, Kansas, 25, 30, 133, 135
Baker University, 152
Baldwin City, Kansas, 94
Baptist Church, 2, 22, 55, 57, 113, 133, 190, 192
Batavia (Clermont County), Ohio, 73
Baxter Springs, Kansas, 93
Bedford (Lawrence County), Indiana, 10, 89
Beebe, Cornelia Bennett, 75
Beebe, George Monroe, 3–7, 75–78
Beebe, Gilbert, 75
Beebe, Mary Louise Markey, 75
Beebe, Phebe Ann Cunningham, 75
Beets, Barry, 19
Belleville (Richland County), Ohio, 10, 126
Beloof, Ida A., 18

243

Belvidere, Kansas, 112
Bennett, Dorothy Bass Dodds, 219
Bennett, Mildred Joan Gregory, 219
Bennett, Olivia A. D. Fisher, 219
Bennett, Otto Francis, 219
Bennett, Robert Frederick, xi, 8, 11, 14, 19, 23, 25, 219–23, 224, 225
Berkshire, Ohio, 86
Berkshire Medical School, 81
Bethesda, Maryland, 186
Beverly Hills, California, 202
Bicknell, Gene, 227
Billard, J. B., 17, 147
Birthplaces of state governors, 24–25
Bismarck Grove, 67
Black, Jerome, 62
Blackwell, Oklahoma, 183
Blaine, James G., 108
Blake, Henry S., 178
"Bleeding Kansas," 7, 8, 22, 43, 50, 85
"Blue Sky" law, 41, 148
Blue Valley, Kansas, 95
"Bogus laws," 41
Bolivia, 101
Bond, Silas M., 17, 147
"Bone Dry" law, 149
"Border ruffians," 35, 44
"Boss busters," 135, 136, 139, 140
Botkin, Jeremiah D., 16, 17, 117, 139
Bowman, Noah, 165
Brady, Joseph H., 172
Branscombe, C. H., 16, 113
Brawley, H. W., 210
Brazil, 101
Breidenthal, John W., 17
Brewerton, George Douglas, 45
Brier, Jack, 227
Brinkley, Dr. John R., 14, 15, 18, 21, 166, 173, 176
Bristow, Joseph L., 149
Bronson (Bourbon County), Kansas, 10, 25, 156
Brookfield (Franklin County), Indiana, 10, 105
Brown, John, 45, 70
Brown County, Kansas, 124, 125
Brownsville (Fayette County), Pennsylvania, 10, 113
Brown v. Board of Education of Topeka (1954), 197
Bruske, Edward G., 221
Bryan, William Jennings, 108, 157
Bryant and Stratton Business College, 158

Buchanan, James, 1, 52, 59, 60, 61, 62, 65, 66, 67, 70, 72
Bumgardner, Edward, xi
Burke, William H., 15, 18, 184, 186
Burlingame, Kansas, 152
Bushnell (McDonough County), Illinois, 11, 194

Cabinet, governor's, 220, 221
Cady, William C., 17, 139
Caldwell, Alexander, 93
Calhoun, John, 49
Calhoun, John C., 60
California, 2, 30, 34, 61, 65, 66, 68, 81, 106
Cameron, Simon, 53
Camp, Walter, 13, 187
Campaign techniques, 20–21, 166
Capital punishment, 131, 168, 189, 222, 228, 230
Capitol, state, 134, 148, 150, 179
Capper, Arthur, x, 9, 10, 15, 17, 20, 23, 25, 26, 28, 29, 134, 142, 143, 146–51, 152, 154, 159, 173, 178, 189
Capper, Florence, 146, 233 n54
Capper, Herbert, 146
Capper, Isabella McGrew, 146
Capper Foundation for Crippled Children, 150
Capper Mansion, 155
Capper Publications, 148, 150, 178
Carlin, Diana Prentice, 224
Carlin, Hazel L. Johnson, 224
Carlin, Jack W., 224
Carlin, John William, 11, 14, 19, 23, 25, 27, 218, 223, 224–26
Carlin, Karen Bigsby Hurley, 224
Carlin, Ramona Lenore Hawkinson, 224
Carlinville, Illinois, 128
Carlson, Alice Fredrickson, 190
Carlson, Anna Johnson, 190
Carlson, Charles Eric, 190
Carlson, Frank, x, 11, 12, 18, 22, 25, 27, 29, 172, 190–93, 194
Carney, James, 86
Carney, Rebecca Ann Canaday, 86
Carney, Sarah, 86
Carney, Thomas, 9, 10, 16, 24, 28, 86–88, 233 n45
Carpenter, Randolph, 18
Casey (Clark County), Illinois, 11, 183
"Cash basis" law, 176
Cass, Lewis, 44, 70
Catholic Church, 2, 43

Cedar Crest, 207, 210
Central College of Danville, Kentucky, 136
Central College of Ohio, 109
Central Illinois Democrat (Peoria, Illinois), 75
Champaign (Champaign County), Illinois, 10, 162
Chase, D. A. N., 162
Chase, Salmon P., 63
Chattanooga, Tennessee, 119
Chautauqua circuit, 20, 135, 137, 145
Cherokee Neutral Tract, 91
Cherry Creek, Colorado (then Kansas Territory), 68–69
Cheyenne County, Kansas, 228
Chile, 101
Christian Church (Disciples of Christ), 22, 142, 165, 181
Christian Science Church, 22, 105, 158
Church membership of governors, 24–25
Church of the Brethren (Dunkard), 22, 126
Church of the New Jerusalem, 180
Cincinnati, Ohio, 44, 65, 74, 86
Cincinnati College, 89
Cities Service Gas Company, 168
Civil rights demonstrations, 212, 217
Civil War: Confederate army, 22, 126; general, 8, 22, 49, 52, 57, 62, 82, 83, 86; Union army, 22, 52, 68, 83, 89, 94, 96, 102, 105, 109, 113, 116, 119, 123
Claflin (Baron County), Kansas, 11, 186
Claremore, Indian Territory, 40
Clay Center (Clay County), Kansas, 11, 95, 152, 206
Clemons, G. C., 17, 130
Cleveland, Grover, 77, 84, 108
Clinton (DeWitt County), Illinois, 10, 158
Cloud County, Kansas, 27, 190
Clymer, Hiester, 53
Coffey County, Kansas, 128
Coffeyville, Kansas, 40, 42
Coffeyville Journal (Coffeyville, Kansas), 42
Colby (Thomas County), Kansas, 11
Colorado, 9, 141
Columbian University, 55, 56
Columbus, Ohio, 72, 73, 74
Commissioner of Indian Affairs, 66
Compromise of 1850, 61, 231 n53
Concordia (Cloud County), Kansas, 11, 25, 190, 191
Congregational Church, 22, 83, 105, 116, 123, 196
Connelley, William Elsey, x

Conservative party, 19, 212, 213
Constitutional revision, 100, 154, 216–17
Continental Monthly (New York City), 62
Cook, J. B., 17
Cooke, P. St. George, 41
Coolidge, Calvin, 163
Copeland Hotel, 110, 117, 120, 127
Corwin, Thomas, 44
Cost of electioneering, 21
Council Grove, Kansas, 165
Craddock, W. H., 17, 133
Crawford, Carson E., 19
Crawford, Florence. *See* Capper, Florence
Crawford, Isabel Marshall Chase, 89
Crawford, Jane Morrow, 89
Crawford, Samuel Johnson, x, 10, 12, 16, 22, 23, 24, 29, 89–93, 146, 233 n55
Crawford, William, 89
Crawford County, Kansas, 90
Crawfordville, Kansas, 90
Crisis (Columbus, Ohio), 74
Crumbine, Samuel J., 157, 185
Culver, J. P., 16
Curtis, Charles, 111, 134, 140–41, 163
Cusey, James C., 16, 100
Custer, George Armstrong, 92, 233 n53
Czechoslovakia, 9

Daily Bulletin (Leavenworth, Kansas), 103
Daily Champion (Atchison, Kansas), 114
Dale, David, 17, 136
Dallas, George Mifflin, 60
Daniel, Peter V., 34
Danville (Boyle County), Kentucky, 10, 136
Darby, Harry, 191
Davis, Eva Holeman, 156
Davis, Jefferson, 54, 71
Davis, Jonathan McMillan, x, 10, 17, 18, 25, 28, 29, 152, 156–57, 158, 182, 183
Davis, Jonathan McMillan, Sr., 156
Davis, Mary Purdom, 156
Davis County, Kansas, 42, 54
Dawes, Charles G., 155
Dawes Commission to the Five Civilized Tribes, 132
Dawson, John L., 37
Dayton, Ohio, 130
Decatur County, Kansas, 228
"Deficit borrowing," 229
Democratic and Resubmission party, 16, 19, 117

Democratic National Convention: 1844, 60, 73; 1856, 73; 1860, 76; 1868, 110; 1876, 68, 78; 1880, 68, 78; 1884, 68, 110; 1892, 78; 1932, 169
Democratic-Populist party, 164
Denver, James William, x, 1–7, 65–69, 70
Denver, Jane Campbell, 65
Denver, Louise C. Rombach, 65
Denver, Patrick, 65
Denver, Colorado, 69, 194
Dern, George H., 170
Des Moines, Iowa, 122
Divorce, 23
Docking, Alameda Donley, 206
Docking, George, 9, 11, 13, 19, 25, 26, 28, 29, 171, 202, 206–8, 209, 215, 224
Docking, Mary Virginia Blackwell, 206, 215, 218
Docking, Meredith Marina Gear, 215
Docking, Robert B., 8, 11, 14, 19, 23, 25, 28, 213, 215–18, 224
Docking, Thomas, 19, 218, 225, 227
Docking, William, 206
Dodge City (Ford County), Kansas, 11, 25, 30, 87, 200, 202
Dodge City Times (Dodge City, Kansas), 87
Dole, Robert, 214
Doniphan County, Kansas, 75, 101
Douglas, Stephen A., 59
Douthart, Henry L., 17, 124
Dover, Kansas, 223
Dred Scott decision, 52
Drouth, 76, 82, 100, 175, 176, 197
Duel, 5, 62, 66
Dugan, Paul, 223
Dust Bowl, 176
Dutton Hotel, 120, 127

Earhart, Amelia, 234 n57
Eastman's Business College, Poughkeepsie, New York, 119
Easton (Northampton County), Pennsylvania, 3, 33, 38
Edmonton, Alberta, 126
Education, 134, 140, 148, 160, 181, 210, 212, 220, 228, 230
Educational attainments of governors, 6, 24–25
Eisenhower, Dwight D., 189, 193, 196, 205, 206, 208
Elder, Peter P., 16, 117
Election data, 16–19

Elk City (Montgomery County), Kansas, 11
Elwood, Kansas, 101
Emancipation Proclamation, 63
Emerson, F. W., 17, 133
Emigrant Aid Company, 82
Emporia, Kansas, 29, 87, 93, 103
Emporia Gazette (Emporia, Kansas), 125
Emporia State University, 180
England, 9
Episcopal Church, 22, 89, 194
Eve, Kansas, 157
Exodusters, 106

Fairway (Johnson County), Kansas, 25, 194, 195
Farmers Alliance party, 84, 117
Farm issues, 116, 120, 148, 153, 174
Farmwell, Virginia, 57
Fathers of governors, 24–25
Federal appointments, 6, 24–25, 41, 44, 50, 60, 63, 73, 84, 97, 101, 110, 128, 132, 135, 155, 163, 170, 181, 202, 208, 213, 220
Federal Reserve System, 135
Finney, Ronald, 176, 189
Finney, Warren, 176
Finney bond scandal, 175
Fisher, Rolland E., 19
Fitchburg News (Fitchberg, Massachusetts), 82
Flenniken, Robert P., 35
Flood: of 1903, 134; of 1951, 197
Florence, Kansas, 136
Florida, 58
Ford County, Kansas, 27
Forney, John W., 33
Fort Hays State University, 187, 227, 228
Fort Kearney, Nebraska, 96
Fort Leavenworth, Kansas, 34, 37, 50, 68, 167
Fort Riley, Kansas, 36, 41, 97, 232 n17
Fort Scott, Kansas, 156
France, 152
Frank Carlson Federal Court Building, Topeka, Kansas, 193
Frank Carlson Lecture Series, Wichita (Kansas) State University, 193
Frank Carlson Library, Concordia, Kansas, 193
Franklin College, 43
Franklin County, Kansas, 90
Fredonia, Kansas, 25, 158, 161
Freedom's Champion (Atchison, Kansas), 114

Free-Soil party, 38, 45
Free-State party, 56, 82
Free stater, 124
Free states, 4, 36, 37, 41, 49, 67
Fremont, John Charles, 5, 38
Friend, Carl, 186
Frizzell, Kent, 19, 216
Funston, Frederick, 127
Fusion ticket, 120, 122, 126, 130

Galena, Kansas, 128
Gallup, George, 178
Garfield, James A., 101
Garner, John Nance, 170
Garnett (Anderson County), Kansas, 10, 24, 89, 146, 147
Geary, John White, x, 2–7, 41, 46, 49–54
Geary, Margaret Ann Logan, 49
Geary, Margaret White, 49
Geary, Mary C. Henderson, 49
Geary, Richard, 49
Geary City (Doniphan County), Kansas, 54
Geary County, Kansas, 42, 54
Geary Street, San Francisco, 54
Georgetown, Washington, D. C., 73
George Washington University Law School, Washington, D. C., 194
Gihon, Dr. John H., 51
Gilham, Harry, 17
Glasgow, Missouri, 46, 49
Glick, Elizabeth Ryder, 109
Glick, Frederick, 110
Glick, George Washington, x, 10, 13, 16, 24, 26, 28, 29, 84, 97, 107, 109–11, 112, 113
Glick, Isaac, 109
Glick, Mary Vickers Sanders, 109
Glick, Kansas, 112
Gompers, Samuel, 154
Goodin, John R., 16, 105
Graber, Harry, 18
Graham County, Kansas, 39
Grand Army of the Republic, 114
Grant, Ulysses S., 106
Grantville, Kansas, 70
Grasshopper plague, 100
Grassy Point (Hardin County), Ohio, 10, 94
Great Depression, 163, 167
Greeley (Anderson County), Kansas, 63
Green, Ida K. Leffingwell, 94
Green, Mary A. Fisher, 94

Green, Mary Sturdevant, 94
Green, Nehemiah, 9, 10, 22, 23, 24, 29, 90, 91, 94–95, 234 n56
Green, Shepard, 94
Green (Clay County), Kansas, 95
Greenback-Labor party, 17, 19, 107, 109
Greenback party, 17, 19
Greencastle (Fairfield County), Ohio, 10, 109
Guaranty law, 137, 154

Hadley Academy, 81
Hagaman, Elizabeth Blair Sutton, 194
Hagaman, Frank, 194
Hagaman, Frank Leslie, 11, 22, 23, 25, 192, 194–95, 196
Hagaman, Martha, 194
Hall, Frederick Lee, x, 11, 19, 20, 21, 25, 26, 27, 28, 30, 200–203, 204
Hall, Frederick Lee, Sr., 200
Hall, Leadell Schneider, 200
Hall, Lucille Brewer, 200
Hamilton, John D. M., 162
Hardage, Sam, 19, 225
Harder, Marvin, 21
Harder, Robert C., 221
Hardwick (Worcester County), Massachusetts, 10, 81
Harman, Rick, 19, 216
Harper's Weekly, 105
Harris, William Alexander, 17, 22, 104, 126, 137
Harrisburg, Pennsylvania, 49
Harvey, Charlotte Richardson Cutter, 96
Harvey, James Madison, x, 8, 10, 16, 22, 24, 29, 96–98, 109
Harvey, Mary Walker, 96
Harvey, Thomas, 96
Harvey County, Kansas, 27, 97
Harvey County News (Newton, Kansas), 204
Haskell Indian Institute, 84
Haucke, Frank, 15, 18, 163, 165, 166, 167, 172
Hawaii, 106
Hayden, Irven Wesley, 227
Hayden, John Michael, 9, 11, 19, 23, 25, 27, 28, 227–30
Hayden, Patti Ann Rooney, 227
Hayden, Ruth Kelly, 227
Hayes, Rutherford B., 101, 106, 109
Helvering, Guy T., 168
Hesper, Kansas, 139, 140

Hester, C. Floyd, 18
Hiawatha (Brown County), Kansas, 123, 125
Hiawatha Academy, 125
Hibner, George Francis, 17, 139
Highways and roads, 143, 148, 154, 160, 163, 168, 191, 197, 210, 217, 222, 228, 229, 230
Hilfrich, H., 18, 157, 159
Hillsboro Star (Hillsboro, Kansas), 204
Hoch, Edward C., 136
Hoch, Edward Wallis, x, 8, 10, 17, 25, 136–38, 139
Hoch, Elizabeth Stout, 136
Hoch, Louisa Dickerson, 136
Hodges, George Hartshorn, x, 10, 12, 15, 17, 25, 28, 134, 139, 142–45, 146, 152
Hodges, Lydia Ann, 142
Hodges, Ora May Murray, 142
Hodges, William Wesley, 142
Holsinger, Frank, 17, 130
Hoover, Herbert, 163
Hope, Alfred L., 17, 139
Hudson, M. E., 16, 102
Humphrey, Amanda Leonard, 116
Humphrey, Elizabeth A. Everhart, 116
Humphrey, Lyman Underwood, 10, 16, 22, 24, 26, 116–18, 183
Humphrey, Lyman Underwood, Sr., 116
Hurley, Horace, 17, 124
Hutchinson, Kansas, 25, 156, 180, 181
"Huxies," 181
Huxman, Augustus, 180
Huxman, Eula M. Biggs, 180
Huxman, Mary Graber, 180
Huxman, Walter Augustus, x, 11, 18, 25, 27, 29, 30, 180–82, 183, 207, 209

Illinois, 4, 8, 11, 38, 96, 106
Impeachment, 23, 83, 90, 100, 101
Independence, Kansas, 24, 25, 116, 117, 118, 165, 172, 173
Independence, Missouri, 106
Independence League party, 139
Independent, 14, 16, 19, 124, 157, 158, 169, 173, 182
Independent Greenback party, 84, 93
Independent Reform (or National) party, 19, 84, 102
Indiana, 4, 8, 11, 35, 96, 106, 140
Indians, 91–92, 100, 106
Ingalls, John James, 117, 234 n58, n59
"Internal improvements," 137, 148, 163

Iowa, 4, 8, 11, 34, 96, 140
Iowa Women's Reform School, 122

Jackson, Andrew, 60
Jefferson College, 49
Jefferson County, Kansas, 71, 130
Johnson, Andrew, 90, 101
Johnson, Osa, 185
Johnson County, Kansas, 27, 28, 106, 135, 143, 209, 211
Johnson County Democrat (Olathe, Kansas), 144
Jones, Larry, 227
Jones, Samuel J., 44–45
Joplin, Missouri, 128
Judicial Advisory Committee, 198
Junction City, Kansas, 96

Kalb, F. Kent, 221
Kansa Indian lands, 37
Kansas City (Wyandotte County), Kansas, 11, 84, 125, 194, 196, 197, 206, 215, 217
Kansas City (Jackson county), Missouri, 11, 134, 142, 207, 215, 216, 219
Kansas City Junior College, 196
Kansas City School of Law, 196
Kansas Emergency Relief Commission, 175
Kansas Executive Mansion, 23, 131, 134–35, 147, 155, 169, 174
Kansas Farmer (Leavenworth and Topeka), 103
Kansas Magazine, 114
Kansas military units: Eighteenth Cavalry Regiment, 91; Eighth Infantry Regiment, 113; Frontier Battalion, 91; National Guard, 114; Nineteenth Cavalry Regiment, 92; 117th Kansas Ammunition Train, 194; Second Colored Regiment, 90; Second Infantry Regiment, 90, 109; Seventh Cavalry Regiment, 123; Twentieth Infantry Regiment, 127
Kansas-Nebraska Act, 5, 33, 34, 44, 51, 52, 56, 82
Kansas River, 35
Kansas State: agent, 93; Board of Administration, 137, 153; Board of Agriculture, 97, 103, 110, 134; Board of Centennial Managers, 103, 110; Board of Charities, 120, 153; Board of Healing Arts, 210–11; Board of Health, 114, 157, 185; Board of Regents, 160; Bureau of Labor Statistics, 114; Commission on Constitutional Revision, 178; Commission on Revenue

and Taxation, 204; Corporation Commission; 186, 187; Court of Visitation, 127; Department of Administration, 197; Department of Revenue and Taxation, 184; Department of Social and Rehabilitation Services, 226; Finance Council, 226; Highway Commission, 148, 160, 168, 197; Industrial Court, 26, 153–54, 164; Legislative Coordinating Council, 226; Legislative Council, 174, 195; Livestock Sanitary Commission, 110; oil refinery, 137; Public Service Commission, 169; Public Utilities Commission, 164; Purchasing Agency, 200; Railway Commission, 122; Tax Commission, 181; Technical Institute, 210; Textbook Commission, 144; Traveling Library Commission, 131; Turnpike Authority, 210–11

Kansas State University (formerly Kansas State Agricultural College), 26, 95, 190, 207, 224, 227

Kansas territory, 2, 70, 75

Kassebaum, Nancy Landon, 175

Kay, Morris, 19, 211, 216

Keefer, Horace, 17

Kemper Military School, Boonville, Missouri, 204

Kennedy, John F., 208

Kenton, Ohio, 130

Kentucky, 4, 8, 14, 50, 231 n4

Kepford, A. E., 17, 124

Kerr, James, 17, 136

Ketchum, Omar B., 18, 176

Kickapoo, Kansas, 41

Kindergarten bill, 159–60

Kiowa County, Kansas, 39, 112

Kleihege, George, 17, 142, 146, 152

Knox College, 119

Knox County, Ohio, 10

Korean War, 23, 219

Ku Klux Klan, 155, 158, 159, 162, 173

Labette County, Kansas, 162, 184

Labor issues, 103, 114, 120, 149, 153–54, 200–201

Landon, Alfred Mossman, x, 11, 15, 18, 22, 23, 25, 26, 29, 30, 155, 162, 169, 172–79, 180, 183, 190, 218

Landon, Anne Mossman, 172

Landon, John M., 172, 173

Landon, Margaret Fleming, 172

Landon, Nancy Josephine. *See* Kassebaum, Nancy Landon

Landon, Theo Cobb, 172, 218

Landon Arena, Topeka Expocentre, 179

Landon Lecture Series, Kansas State University, 178, 218

Landon Middle School, Topeka, 178–79

Lane, James H., 37, 57, 87, 90

Lansdon, W. C., 17, 147, 152

Lathrop, J. H., 17, 133

Laughlin, W. R., 16, 97

"Law and Order party." *See* Proslavery party

Lawrence, Kansas, 13, 24, 25, 29, 45, 48, 50, 67, 72, 81, 84, 87, 127, 128, 139, 206, 207, 215, 216, 217

Leadville (Lake County), Colorado, 11, 204

Lease, Mary Elizabeth, 120, 127

Leavenworth, Kansas, 24, 67, 86, 87, 88, 99, 102, 103, 125, 128, 167

Leavenworth County, Kansas, 26, 104, 131

Lecompton, Kansas, 3, 45, 46, 48, 50, 72, 83

Lecompton constitution, 50, 55, 56, 62, 66, 67

Leedy, John Whitnah, x, 10, 11, 17, 22, 24, 29, 124, 126–29, 130, 234 n63

Leedy, Margaret Whitnah, 126

Leedy, Samuel Keith, 126

Leedy, Sarah J. Boyd, 126

"Legislative war," 120, 133

Lemon, Robert S., 18

LeRoy, Kansas, 24, 126, 128

Lewelling, Angeline M. Cook, 119

Lewelling, Cyrena Wilson, 119

Lewelling, Ida Bishop, 119

Lewelling, Lorenzo Dow, x, 10, 13, 16, 22, 23, 24, 26, 29, 119–22, 123, 234 n62

Lewelling, William, 119

Lexington Academy, Virginia, 40

Liberal Republican party, 17, 19, 93, 99

Libertarian party, 19, 225

Lincoln, Abraham, 38, 41, 74, 233 n42

Lindley, E. H., 157

Lindsborg, Kansas, 224

Linn County, Kansas, 58

Lipscomb, Caleb, 17, 127

Little, Chauncey B., 18, 163

Livermore, Harry E., 19

Long, Chester I., 132

Lowther, Granville, 17, 136

Lutheran Church, 22, 109, 224

Lynchburg, Virginia, 40
Lynchburg Republican (Lynchburg, Virginia), 40
Lytle, Harry O., 19, 206

McAllister, A. S., 17, 133
McCain, James A., 218, 221
McCarthy, Kathryn O'Laughlin, 191
McClure, James R., 35
McCormack, James F., 221
McCuish, Anna Hulburt, 204
McCuish, Cora Hedrick, 204
McCuish, John Berridge, 11, 23, 25, 27, 201, 204–5
McCuish, John Berridge, Sr., 204
McDonald, Bill, 227
McDowell, J. L., 16, 90
McGill, George, 155, 160
McGrew, James, 90
Maderia family, 73. *See also* Medary *entries*
Maine, 123, 178
Major, Elliott, 143
Manhattan, Kansas, 24, 87, 94, 95
Marion, Kansas, 25, 136
Marion Record (Marion, Kansas), 136, 137
Marquez, Jim J., 221
Marriage, 23
Marshall, W. K., 16, 100
Martin, Evan Challis, 115
Martin, Ida Challis, 113
Martin, James, 113
Martin, Jane Montgomery Crawford, 113
Martin, John, 16, 102, 116
Martin, John Alexander, 10, 16, 22, 24, 28, 103, 105, 109, 113–15
Martin, John Alexander, Jr., 115
Martin, Warren C., 19, 206
Massachusetts, 15, 81, 82
Massachusetts Emigrant Aid Company, 82
Massilon, Ohio, 116
Mayberry, Willard, 196
Mayfield (Fulton County), New York, 10, 102
Meadville (Crawford County), Pennsylvania, 10, 99
Medary, Eliza Scott, 72
Medary, Jacob, 72
Madary, Samuel, 1, 3–7, 16, 70, 72–74, 76, 82
Memphis, Tennessee, 56
Meriden, Kansas, 227
Methodist Church, 22, 94, 95, 99, 130, 136, 139, 152, 156, 162, 172, 200, 227

Metropolitan police issue, 117, 127
Metzler, Dwight F., 221
Mexican War, 2, 22, 44, 49, 50, 61, 65, 73, 109
Mexico, 29, 44, 106
Miami County, Kansas, 58
Michigan, 101
Middletown Academy, 75
Milford Reservoir, 213–14
Miller, Vern, 19, 219
Mine Creek, Battle of, 90
Minneola, 37
Minnesota, 7, 73
Mission Hills, Kansas, 30, 135
Mississippi, 60
Missouri, 4, 8, 11, 34, 65
Missouri Compromise of 1820, 33, 34
Missouri Valley Farmer (Topeka, Kansas), 147
Mitchell, D. P., 16, 105
Mitchell, Milo M., 17, 147
Mobile, Alabama, 71
Montgomery, James, 70
Montgomery, Larry, 223
Montgomery Alabama, 71
Montgomery County, Kansas, 42, 173
Montgomery County, Maryland, 73
Montgomery Square (Montgomery County), Pennsylvania, 3, 72
Monticello, New York, 77
Moonlight, Thomas, 16, 113
Moore, Ely, 33
Morgan, W. Y., 17, 156
Morrill, Caroline Nash, 123
Morrill, Edmund Needham, 8–10, 12, 16, 17, 22, 23, 24, 122, 123–25, 126, 220
Morrill, Elizabeth A. Brettun, 123
Morrill, Mary Webb, 123
Morrill, Rufus, 123
Morrill, Kansas, 125
Morrill and Janes Bank, Hiawatha, 125
Morrill Free Public Library, Hiawatha, 125
Mothers of governors, 9
Mount Carroll (Carroll County), Illinois, 10, 133
Mount Gilead (Anderson County), Kansas, 63
Mount Olivet (Belmont County), Ohio, 3, 43
Mount Pleasant (Westmoreland County), Pennsylvania, 3, 49
Mount Union College, 116
Muncie, Kansas, 196, 197

Murphy, George, 202
Museum Hall, Topeka, 83
Myers, Kenneth L., 19

Nantucket Island, Massachusetts, 93
Natchez, Mississippi, 60
Nation, Carry A., 132
National Guard. *See under* Kansas military
    units
National Intelligencer (Washington, D. C.),
    56
National Labor Greenback party, 83
National party, 17, 19, 107, 124
National Prayer Breakfast, 193
National Union party, 16, 19
Nebraska, 157, 231 n4
Nebraska territory, 34
Nelson, Luann, 213
Nemeha County, Kansas, 133
Neodesha, Kansas, 25, 165, 167
Ness City, Kansas, 25, 186
Ness County, Kansas, 27, 186
Nevada, 97
New Baltimore (Stark County), Ohio, 10,
    116
Newburgh (Orange County), New York,
    3, 70
New England, 4, 8, 11, 124
New Hampshire, 1
New Mexico, 97, 141
Newton, Kansas, 25, 204
Newton Kansan (Newton, Kansas), 204
New Vernon (Westchester County), New
    York, 3, 75
New York (city), 56, 87
New York (state), 2, 4, 8, 11, 108, 169
Nice, N. W., 18
Niehaus, Charles Henry (sculptor), 111–12
Nixon, Pat, 218
Nixon, Richard, 218
Non-Partisan League, 155
Norristown Academy, 72
Norristown Herald (Norristown, Pennsylva-
    nia), 73
North Carolina, 56
Northrop, John W., 139
North Topeka Mail, 147
Northumberland (Northumberland
    County), Pennsylvania, 3, 59
Norton County, Kansas, 228

Ocala, Florida, 58
Occupations of governors, 24–25

Occupations of governors' fathers, 24–25
Ohio, 2, 4, 8, 11, 43, 44, 72, 73, 127, 172
Ohio River Valley, 8
Ohio Statesman (Columbus, Ohio), 73
Ohio Sun (Bethel, Ohio), 73
Ohio University, 43
Ohio Wesleyan College, 130
Oklahoma, 97, 117
Olathe (Johnson County), Kansas, 11, 24,
    25, 105, 106, 142, 144, 209
"One-man, one-vote" rule, 27
Oregon, 7, 61
Orion (Richland County), Wisconsin, 10,
    142
Orleans County, New York, 103
Osage Indian lands, 91
Osawatomie, Kansas, 87
Osborn, Carpenter, 99
Osborn, Elizabeth Morton, 99
Osborn, Julia Delahy, 99
Osborn, Thomas Andrew, 10, 16, 24, 26,
    29, 99–101
Otis, Alfred G., 110
Ottawa, Kansas, 29, 104
Ottawa County, Kansas, 58
Ottawa Republican (Ottawa, Kansas), 104
Overland Park, Kansas, 210
Overmyer, David, 122

Packer, Asa, 33, 53
Palmyra (Baldwin City), Kansas, 94
Panic: of 1873, 99, 103; of 1893, 128
Parker (Montgomery County), Kansas, 42
Parrott, Marcus, 38, 57
Parsons, Kansas, 25, 162, 183, 184
Parsons Sun (Parsons, Kansas), 164
Paulen, Barbara Ellis, 158
Paulen, Benjamin Sanford, 10, 18, 23, 25,
    26, 157, 158–61, 173, 174, 183
Paulen, Jacob Walter, 158
Paulen, Lucy Bell Johnson, 158
Paulson, J., 16, 102
Pawnee, Kansas territory, 36
Pawnee Rock, Kansas, 136
Pearson, James B., 198
Peckham, Richard, 227
Peffer, William A., 17, 117, 127
Pennsylvania, 1, 2, 4, 5, 8, 11, 33, 35, 50,
    52, 54, 101
People's Alliance party, 14, 16, 19, 117
People's party. *See* Populist party
Perkins, Bishop W., 117
Perkins, H. M., 18, 169, 173

Perquisites of governors, 12
Peru, 101
Peterson, Henry L., 18, 163
Phillips, H. L., 16, 109, 113
Phillips, M. L., 17, 18, 156, 157, 158
Pickering, Isaac O., 16, 120
Pierce, Franklin, 1, 33, 36, 37, 40, 43, 46,
    49, 61
Pierceville, Indiana, 127
Pike's Peak gold strike, 96
Pittsburg, Kansas, 227
Pittsburgh, Pennsylvania, 59
Pittsfield (Warren County), Pennsylvania,
    10, 152
Platte City, Missouri, 66
Plumb, Preston B., 101, 117
Polar Star, 34
Polk, James, 44, 50, 60, 73
Pomeroy, Barbara, 227
Pomeroy, Samuel C., 51, 57
Pontiac, Michigan, 101
"Popular Sovereignty," 34, 51
Population, U. S., foreign-born, 4, 11
Populist party, 13, 14, 16, 17, 19, 24, 119,
    121, 126, 128, 130, 133, 137
Pottawatomie City (Anderson County),
    Kansas, 63
Pottawatomie County, Kansas, 104
Pottawatomie Massacre, 45–46
Prairie Village, Kansas, 25, 219, 220, 223
Presbyterian Church, 2, 22, 65, 204, 206,
    215, 219
Presidential candidates, 29, 108, 155, 177–
    178
Pretty Prairie (Reno County), Kansas, 11,
    180
Price, Sterling, 47, 87, 90, 97
Progressive party, 14, 17, 19, 142, 146, 147,
    152, 153, 173
Prohibition issue, 107, 117, 140, 145, 149,
    176, 181, 189, 190, 191
Prohibition party, 15, 16, 17, 18, 19, 108,
    113, 117, 124, 127, 133, 136, 137, 139, 147,
    148, 184, 187, 190, 196, 201, 208, 209,
    212, 213, 219, 224, 225
Proslave partisans, 45, 51, 70
Proslavery party, 40, 45, 61
Puerto Rico, 170

Quakers (Society of Friends), 22, 102, 119,
    120, 140, 146
Quantrill's raid, 87
Quindaro State Normal School, 84

Radio, 21, 166
Ransom, Kansas, 186
Ratner, Cliffe Dodd, 183
Ratner, Harry, 183
Ratner, Julia, 183
Ratner, Payne Harry, 9, 11, 15, 18, 22, 25,
    30, 181–82, 183–85, 197, 220
Rawlins County, Kansas, 27, 228
Reagan, Ronald, 178
Reconstruction Finance Corporation, 155
Reed, Clyde Martin, x, 10, 18, 25, 26, 28,
    29, 155, 158, 162–64, 165, 172, 173, 174,
    180, 183, 186, 191
Reed, Clyde Martin, Jr., 19, 206
Reed, James A., 220
Reed, Martin Van Buren, 162, 163
Reed, Mary Adelaide, 162
Reed, Minnie E. Hart, 162
Reeder, Absalom, 33
Reeder, Amelia Hutter, 33
Reeder, Andrew Horatio, 1–7, 33–39, 40,
    44, 45
Reeder, Christina Smith, 33
Reeder post offices in Anderson, Kiowa,
    and Graham counties, 39
Reid, Albert T., 154
Reno County, Kansas, 27, 180
Republican (Ottawa, Kansas), 104
Republican Advocate (Richmond, Virginia),
    41
Republican National Convention: 1860, 5,
    31, 114; 1868, 114; 1872, 114; 1880, 114;
    1884, 114; 1888, 101; 1912, 153, 173; 1920,
    153; 1936, 205; 1940, 178; 1944, 178;
    1948, 178, 205; 1968, 193; 1976, 222
Republican Union party, 90
Republican Watchman (Monticello, New
    York), 77
Rhode Island, 14
Richardson, A. M., 16, 117
Richardson, E. N., 17, 148
Richmond (Wayne County), Indiana, 10,
    139
Richmond, Virginia, 41
"Right-to-work" legislation, 200, 201
Riley County, Kansas, 96
Robert B. Docking State Office Building,
    Topeka, 218, 226
Robinson, Charles, x, 8–10, 16, 22, 23, 24,
    28, 29, 51, 57, 74, 81–85, 109, 117
Robinson, Huldah Woodward, 81
Robinson, Jonathan, 81
Robinson, Sarah Adams, 81

Robinson, Sarah Tappan Doolittle, 81
Robinson, Kansas, 84
Rooney, Charles, 19, 196
Roosevelt, Franklin D., 169, 170, 177, 207
Roosevelt, Theodore, 136, 137, 142, 146,
    153, 173
Rosedale, Kansas, 194
Ross, Edmund G., 16, 90, 106, 233 n50
Ross, H. R., 17, 148
Russia, 9, 63
Ryan, Frank, 162

Sacramento, California, 66, 81, 202
Saffels, Dale E., 19, 209
St. John, John Pierce, x, 10, 16, 20, 22, 23,
    24, 28, 29, 103, 105–8, 109, 208
St. John, Mary Jane Brewer, 105
St. John, Samuel, 105
St. John, Sophia Snell, 105
St. John, Susan J. Parker, 105
St. John, Kansas, 108
St. Joseph, Missouri, 77
St. Louis, Missouri, 46
Salaries of governors, 1, 12
Salem (Henry County), Iowa, 10, 119
Salina (Saline County), Kansas, 11, 224,
    226
Salina Republican (Salina, Kansas), 153
Saline County, Kansas, 27
Salome, William C., 207
Salter, Melville J., 118, 234 n60
Salt Sulphur Springs (Monroe County),
    Virginia (later West Virginia), 10, 96
San Antonio, Texas, 123
San Francisco, California, 50, 54
Schoeppel, Andrew Frank, x, 9, 11, 12, 18,
    22, 23, 25, 27, 29, 30, 186–89, 197
Schoeppel, Anna Phillip, 186
Schoeppel, George J., 186
Schoeppel, Marie Thomsen, 186
Scott, Charles F., 149, 162
Scott, Winfield, 50, 66
Seattle, Washington, 29, 128
Sedgwick County, Kansas, 27, 28, 119, 131
Shannon, Elizabeth Ellis, 43
Shannon, George, 43
Shannon, Jane Milligan, 43
Shannon, Sarah Osbun, 43
Shannon, Wilson, 1–7, 37, 41, 43–48
Shannon (Anderson County), Kansas, 48
Sharp, Isaac, 16, 97
Shaw, Warren W., 19, 201, 206
Shawnee, Kansas, 30, 200, 202

Shawnee County, Kansas, 27, 28, 101
Shawnee Mission, Kansas, 35, 37, 219
Shelby County, Missouri, 118
Shelton, Frank W., Jr., 19
Sheridan County, Kansas, 228
Shields, J. B., 18, 167
Sibley, Iowa, 184
Simpson, Lacey, 172
Slave states, 4, 24, 36, 40, 41, 59, 67
Smith, Abram F., 16, 120
Smith, Shelby, 219, 221
Smolan, Kansas, 25, 224
Socialist-Labor party, 130
Socialist party, 15, 17, 18, 19, 127, 133, 139,
    142, 146, 148, 156, 158, 159, 163, 167, 169,
    172, 176, 180, 184, 187, 190, 196
Society of Friends. *See* Quakers
Southeast Kansas, 71, 183
South Kansas Tribune (Independence, Kan-
    sas), 118
Spanish-American War, 22, 127
Speaking ability of governors, 120
Square Deal, 136
Squatter association, 82
Squatter Sovereign (Atchison, Kansas), 114
Stafford County, Kansas, 108
Stallard, S. M., 17, 139
Stalwart Democrat party, 16, 19, 122
Standard Oil Company, 137
Stanley, Almon Fleming, 130
Stanley, Angeline Sapp, 130
Stanley, Emma Lenora Hills, 130
Stanley, William Eugene, 10, 12, 17, 24,
    29, 127, 130–32, 153
Stanton, Frederick Perry, 2–7, 55–58, 62,
    63, 65, 70, 232 n33
Stanton, Harriet Perry, 55
Stanton, Jane Harriet Sommers Lamphier,
    55
Stanton, Richard, 55
Stanton, Roy, 17, 152
Stanton, Florida, 55, 58
Stanton (Miami County), Kansas, 58
State legislature, special sessions of, 134,
    137, 153, 163, 176, 207, 229
Stauffer Publications, 150
Steele, J. J., 19, 208
Steineger, Jack, 219
Stevenson, Adlai, 207
Stone, Horatio (sculptor), 58
Strike: of 1877, 103; of 1886, 114; after
    World War I, 153
Stringfellow, Benjamin, 231 n15

Stringfellow, Dr. John, 35, 231 n15
Stubbs, Esther Bailey, 139
Stubbs, John T., 139
Stubbs, Stella Hostettler, 139
Stubbs, Walter Roscoe, x, 9, 10, 17, 25, 28, 29, 139–41, 144, 149, 154, 158

Taft, Robert, 189
Taft, William Howard, 142, 146, 173
Tamplin, W. W., 18
Taney, Roger B., 52
Taxes: sales, 181, 184, 198; severance, 191, 225; "windfall," 228, 229
Tecumseh, Kansas, 45
Tefft House, 83, 96, 105
Television, 21, 202
Temperance party, 16, 19, 100, 102
Tennessee, 2, 7, 55
Tenth United States District Court, Topeka, 181
Texas, 60, 141
Thacher, Solon O., 90
Thayer, Eli, 82
Third and fourth terms, 107, 208, 216
Thompson, W. H., 141
Tipton (Delaware County), Ohio, 10, 86
Topeka, Kansas, 25, 29, 30, 37, 48, 83, 86, 89, 93, 101, 102, 127, 139, 146, 165, 168, 171, 178, 181, 207, 224, 225
Topeka Capital (Topeka, Kansas), 141
Topeka constitution, 38, 82
"Tramp circular," 121
Transylvania University, 43
Traveling Man party, 16, 19
Troy (Doniphan County), Kansas, 75
Turner, O. D., 221
Tuttle Creek dam controversy, 213
Tyler, John, 44

Uncapher, Marshall, 19
Unemployment, 174, 175, 176
Union Labor party, 16, 19, 116
Union party, 16, 19, 84
United States: land office, 41, 118; Senate, 60, 93, 97, 101, 117, 123, 132, 140–41, 143, 149–50, 155, 157, 160, 164, 189, 198
U.S.S. Wichita, 217
Universalist, 81
University: of Illinois, 133; of Kansas, 84, 137, 139, 156, 157, 158, 172, 173, 180, 186, 194, 196, 206, 207, 209, 212, 215, 219; of Michigan, 116; of Nebraska, 12, 156,

186–87; of Pennsylvania, 59; of Southern California, 200, 202; of Wichita, 210; of Wisconsin, 215
Utah, 49, 97

Valdez, Alaska, 128–29
Van Buren, Martin, 60
Vance, Joseph, 44
Vermont, 51, 178, 231 n4
Vietnam War, 22, 23, 227, 228
Vinton, Kansas, 24, 96, 97
Virginia, 2, 11, 40, 41, 44, 97
Virginia City, Nevada, 77
Voiland, Ferd, 162

Wagstaff, W. R., 16, 87
"Wakarusa War," 45
Wakefield, John A., 35
Wakefield (Clay County), Kansas, 11, 25, 30, 212, 213–14
Walker, Duncan, 60
Walker, Jonathan Hoge, 59
Walker, Lucretia Duncan, 59
Walker, Mary B. Bache, 59
Walker, Robert John, x, 3–7, 55, 56, 57–58, 59–64
Walker, Thaddeus H., 16, 99
Walker (Anderson County), Kansas, 63
Walker tariff, 60
Walsh, DeWitt, 71
Walsh, Elizabeth DeWitt, 70
Walsh, Ellen Beckman, 70
Walsh, Hugh Sleight, 2–7, 70–71
Ward, James H., 19
Washburn University, 204
Washington, D. C., 2, 29, 30, 34, 35, 40, 52, 55, 56, 57–58, 61, 66, 68, 208
Washington University Law School, St. Louis, 181
Wassenberg, Renee, 213
Weaver, James, 121
Weltmer, W. Keith, 221
West, Will G., 18, 178, 180
Westbrook (Cumberland County), Maine, 123
Western Kansas, 27, 187
Western Military Academy, Alton, Illinois, 206, 215
West Middlesex (Lawrence County), Pennsylvania, 11, 172
Weston, Missouri, 35
West Virginia, 96
Whig party, 56, 97

White, David C., 18, 19
White, William Allen, 14, 18, 125, 152, 157, 158, 160, 173
White Court, Alberta, 129
Whiteside, George M., 18, 176, 180
Whitewater, Kansas, 227
Whitfield, John W., 35, 38, 45
Whittier College, 119
Wichita, Kansas, 24, 25, 30, 119, 122, 130, 131, 132, 152, 153, 183, 185, 189, 198, 202, 210, 213–14, 223, 224, 225, 227
Wichita Beacon (Wichita, Kansas), 155
Wichita State University, 193, 210, 226
Wiles, Harry G., 19, 212
Willits, John F., 14, 16, 117
Willkie, Wendell, 184
Wilmington, Ohio, 65
Wilson, Woodrow, 142
Wilson County, Kansas, 159
Wilson's Creek, Battle of (1861), 90
Winchester (Frederick County), Virginia, 3, 65
Wisconsin, 8
Women's suffrage, 91, 107, 121, 143

Woodring, Harry Hines, x, 11, 15, 22, 23, 25, 26, 28, 29, 30, 57, 163, 165–71, 173, 181, 183, 190, 206
Woodring, Helen Coolidge, 165
Woodring, Hines, 165
Woodring, Lida, 169
Woodring, Melissa Jane Cooper, 165
Woodson, America Fuqua Christian Palmer, 40
Woodson, Daniel, 2–7, 36, 40–42, 44, 46, 49, 55
Woodson County, Kansas, 42
Workingman party, 16, 19
World War: I, 22, 144, 147–49, 152, 165, 167, 172, 183, 186, 190; II, 22–23, 155, 185, 187, 191, 196, 204, 215, 219
Worrall, Henry, 107
Wright, Frank Lloyd, 153
Wunsch, Paul, 186
Wyandotte constitution, 72, 73, 74, 114
Wyandotte County, Kansas, 28, 194

Xenia (Greene County), Ohio, 66

York, Alexander M., 118, 234 n59